pr 19/6/08

About this book

This is a provocative account of the ways in which Muslim identities have come to play an increasingly political role in recent years. Theoretically innovative, it shows how Islamic movements – despite the wide variety of their manifestations – are best understood as a continuation of political and cultural decolonization.

The fear and anxiety aroused by the so-called Islamic threat is not a myth, nor is it simply a consequence of terrorism or fundamentalism. The emergence of Islamism signals the end of the uncontested notion that 'West is best'. As the author demonstrates, Islamism means having to rethink Western identity and its place in the world, having to come to terms with the idea that the West is just another civilization among many.

This study draws upon the full breadth of post-structuralist thought as a means of better understanding Islamism. As such, it is necessary reading for all those who are interested in the Muslim world – in both its state and diasporic forms – as well as academics concerned with questions of 'race' and place in a poststructuralist context.

About the author

S. Sayyid has taught at the Universities of East London, Manchester and Salford. Currently he is a research fellow at the University of Leeds.

University of Chester Library
Tel: 01925 534284

A FUNDAMENTAL FEAR
Eurocentrism and the emergence of Islamism

S. Sayyid

Zed Books Ltd
LONDON • NEW YORK

To my parents

A Fundamental Fear: Eurocentrism and the emergence of Islamism was first published by Zed Books Ltd, 7 Cynthia Street, London N1 9JF, UK, and Room 400, 175 Fifth Avenue, New York, NY 10010, USA, in 1997.

Second edition 2003.

Cover designed by Andrew Corbett.
Set in Monotype Baskerville and Univers by Ewan Smith.
Printed and bound in Malta by Gutenberg Press Ltd

Distributed in the USA exclusively by Palgrave, a division of St Martin's Press, LLC, 175 Fifth Avenue, New York, NY 10010, USA

A catalogue record for this book is available from the British Library

Library of Congress Cataloging-in-Publication Data: available

ISBN 1 84277 196 5 cased
ISBN 1 84277 197 3 limp

Contents

Acknowledgements

I would like to thank Lilian Zac for holding on to the base and keeping the beat, Mohammed Reza Tajik for making no apologies for the fundamentals, Barnor Hesse for pitching perpetual possibilities on the phone, Laura Turney for her keyboards and Lusakan-style kung fu, Louise Murray for exorcizing gremlins and remaining enthusiastic, Lamya Kanoo, Warren Chin and Hana Kanoo for their off-stage prompting and impromptu playing, Katherine Tyler for *en passant* reflections and theological discussions, Pandeli Glavanis for reading the script and hologramming the scene, the crew at CGEM for doing the things they do, the Charterhouse dining club for whispering in the wings, but still acting out their parts, the House Muzak society for Sumerian disco(urse)s and Socratic parodies, the keepers of the faith for being steadfast even when stranded in fragmenting ethnoscapes.

In addition, a word or two of appreciation must go out to David Sanders for his support, Albert Weale for his advice, Barry Clarke and Paul Gilroy for their comments. Of course the usual disclaimers apply.

Earlier versions of some of the themes presented here appeared as 'Sign O' Times: Kaffirs and Infidels Fighting the Ninth Crusade' in Ernesto Laclau (ed.) (1994) *The Making of Political Identities*, London: Verso.

Preface to the Second Edition: Islamism and the Postcolonial Condition

When *A Fundamental Fear* was first published in 1997, it set out to account for the contemporary assertion of a Muslim identity and to ask the question – why has the name of Islam been used as a banner for political protest and mobilization? This phenomenon has been variously described as (very problematically) 'Islamic fundamentalism', or (rather vaguely) 'political Islam'. I prefer the term 'Islamism'. Prior to the attacks on the mainland of the United States on September 11 2001, it had been thought that Islamism had burnt itself out.[1] It seemed that Islamist movements had stalled and, with the exception of Afghanistan and Iran, no other Muslim country had 'fallen' to the Islamists. Islamist movements seemed to be running into a cul-de-sac of violence and counter-violence that was alienating ordinary Muslims without being strong enough to remove the repressive regimes of the Islamicate world (that is, the totality of communities historically transformed by the 'venture of Islam').

Anyone who studies Islamism over a long enough period will recognize the cyclical nature of commentary on Islamism. Islamism's demise is often prophesied and as often deferred. One of the reasons for this is the confusion about the exact nature of this phenomenon. Islamism inhabits a zone at the very limit of dominant contemporary discourses. Investigative models based on a de-contextualized reading of Western historical developments have found it difficult to analyse Islamism, which has at best a rather ambiguous relationship with historical accounts. As analysts such as Marshal G. Hodgson, Anour Malek and most decisively Edward Said have pointed out, the study of the Islamicate world has to move away from the assumptions that it can be defined by the distortion of features that are considered to be 'normal' within Western history.

It is important to note that this book does not argue that Islam or the West are monolithic homogenous entities. 'The West' and 'Islam' are shorthand expressions for complex and mobile formations, the boundaries of which are not given, but rather are political in nature and the sites of constant struggle. Taking note of the internal differences in Islam or the West does not, however, invalidate the existence of the West or Islam. The logic of collective identities is precisely that they are forged through the erasure of internal differences. This is the case of any collective identity, whether it be a nation state, a local community or a transnational amorphous formation such as the West or Islam. Thus the heterogeneity of Islam is not a sign of the impossibility of Islam; nor is it necessary to ascribe an essence to Islam, to understand it as the product of a continuous attempt to marshal its heterogeneous elements. This marshalling is accomplished by the invocation of the name of Islam. The Islamicate world is a group of cultures, societies, networks and histories, which are attached to the Name of Islam. In *A Fundamental Fear* Islam was conceptualized as a master-signifier. What this means is that there are no multiple Islams, but rather that all Muslims attach themselves, and are attached by others, to one Islam. What that attachment involves cannot be understood outside the struggles and accommodations for an interpretation of Islam that privileges a particular set of relations and practices over another set of relations and practices. In this struggle to establish the meaning of Islam, or to make the name of Islam signify a specific set of values and practices, there are many interventions. For example, currently there are people who assert that 'Islam has been hijacked' by terrorists and others who argue 'Islam means opposing tyranny by any means necessary'. There are also people (Muslims and non-Muslims) who think that Islam is something analogous to a computer programme and that by reading its operating code (the Qur'an and *hadiths*) one can discover who is a Muslim and what they should (or should not) do. For example, suicide is forbidden in Islam, therefore Muslims cannot engage in martyrdom (or suicide) missions. In contrast to such interpretations there are a growing number of Muslims who emphasize the political nature of the relationship between Islam and its signifieds. For these Muslims, Islam does not end in the eighteenth century, or in some metropolitan museum, with (often looted) relics of other past civilizations. For these Muslims, the meaning of Islam must include opposition to repression, and a continual struggle to fashion a just social order. What unifies and holds together the diverse Muslim *Ummah* is the Name of Islam, and the struggles and associated settlements with that Name. The argument for 'multiple Islams' conflates the signifier with its signifieds. There are not many Islams, one for each national or ethnic group or socio-economic group, but rather many interpretations of one Islam. This is because the interpretations of one Islam are locked in relations of co-operation and conflict over what constitutes its heart, what is peripheral and what is outside it. The Islamist-inspired 'awakening' has re-ignited a 'war of interpretation' throughout the Muslim *Ummah*, a struggle for hegemony over the meaning of Islam, a struggle that makes little sense if we presume a world of 'multiple Islams'.

Islamism, Terror of the World

The second edition of this book appears at a time when the world seems to be divided between those who oppose Islamism and those who support it. Many of the world's major powers find themselves confronting restive Muslim populations, whether of irredentist (the Russian Federation, China, India), or diasporic (European Union), or a more conventionally colonized nature (the United States). It is difficult to avoid the conclusion that one of the largest groups of people in the world who *do not* seem to be content with the current division of world power would describe themselves as Muslims. The politicisation of this discontent has taken the form of Islamism. Islamists find themselves in a complex international situation in which their ability to create a geopolitical space for themselves is limited by the ever present possibility of an anti-Muslim united front among the major powers. Any accommodation with a major power has to be bought at the expense of some Muslim constituency. This geopolitical situation not only affects the external possibilities of any Islamist movements, but has also had the effect of encouraging a highly militarized form of Islamism, since diplomatic manoeuvrings tends to mean abandoning some Muslim community to its fate at the hands of one of the major powers. An Islamism that spurns the diplomatic in favour of the military not only appears more authentically representative of the *Ummah*, but seems to be the only route by which a global Muslim presence can be actualized in the face of such a hostile international environment.

The 'war against terrorism', to the extent that it has an over-arching political logic other than an attempt by the American neo-conservatives to discipline the world, is directed towards meeting the challenge of Islamism. Islamism has become increasingly identified with acts of 'terrorism', a process which culminated in the events of 9/11. The association between Islamism and unrelenting violence is presented as a sign of the intellectual bankruptcy of Islamism and its failure to bring about the radical transformations of Islamicate societies. Such linkages between Islamism and violence are made not only by the usual suspects (e.g. Kemalists, Zionists, Islamophobes) but also from within the ranks of those who formerly identified themselves with Islamism. Rached Ghannouchi is perhaps one of the most famous examples of those Islamists who have turned to-wards the idea of democracy as a way of getting beyond the impasse of Kemalist terror and Islamist counter-terror. It is important, how-ever, to place the linkage between Islamism and 'terrorism' in some kind of perspective. A starting point would be to deny that terrorism is a useful category for understanding political violence. Can it really be maintained that Chechens who hold up a theatre in Moscow are terrorists, whereas the Russians who destroyed Grozny and who continue to ravage Chechnya (perhaps killing a third of the Chechen population in the process) are simply doing their job, just soldiers following orders?

One could multiply examples like the above without great effort. Only the naive or mendacious could hold on to the category of terrorism as simply a descriptive term without any polemical charge. One of the consequences of the end of the Cold War has been the disappearance of the category of freedom fighter. During the Cold War, insurgencies, against either the Soviet camp or the American camp, were presented by opposing sides as being the actions of freedom fighters rather than terrorists. The disappearance of the notion of freedom fighter has meant that any sustained challenge to the prevailing world order can now only be considered as an act of terrorism.

In this sense it is important to point out how the 'international community' has been reconfigured, so that it is conceptualized in opposition to terrorism. This means that a charge of terrorism can be used to exclude states and peoples from membership of the 'international community' and thus from being protected by the provisions of international law (see, for example, the US decision to exclude those whom it considers to be 'illegal combatants' from the protection of the Geneva Convention). The articulation of an 'international community' in opposition to (Islamist) terrorism replays the colonial discourse of a world order that is organized in terms of the opposition between civilization and barbarism. By defining the opponents of the current world order as external to that order, the 'war against terrorism' can be waged with a savagery similar to that used by the colonial powers to pacify their 'savages'. (This experience of waging savage wars of pacification is one that the United States clearly shares with more 'conventional' European colonial empires.) By establishing a frontier between the 'international community' on the one hand and terrorists (almost exclusively Islamists) and rogue states on the other, the 'war against terrorism' becomes close to being 'a war without limits', since those who are not members of the 'international community' cannot be considered to be its peers, and thus they have no legitimate right to exist. No doubt the assumption in waging such a war is that Western technology and Western virtue will always trump whatever counter-measures the other side might take. Reciprocity as self-denying ordinance can be abandoned since the other side is incapable of causing the United States equivalent harm (for example, the Geneva Convention can be selectively abandoned because it is not expected that American fighters will ever fall into enemy hands). The danger associated with this 'war without limits' is precisely that the other side will be forced into removing any self-restraints on the conduct of its activities. Thus, the escalation of violence, not only in extent but also in intensity, becomes more rather than less likely. The only obstacle to such a possibility is the belief that the superiority of American military power will be such that its enemies will be crushed before they can mount a significant response.

Another consequence of the end of the Cold War has been the demise of communism as a viable ideology of social transformation. This has meant the loss of a narrative that would explain why the world is as it is, and how to imagine a world where what should be could be. Communist discourses helped to politically educate populations. This included helping to disseminate the idea or suspicion not only that violence was something perpetuated by 'thugs' and 'terrorists', but that the establishment was itself violent and violating. That is, violence could be structural and systemic rather than just the act of an 'evil' or 'mad' individual. The discrediting of communist discourses and the hegemony of neo-liberal values and practices that emphasize the individual's sovereignty and autonomy have, however, made it more difficult to represent the influence of structures. The difficulty of accounting for structures of cruelty and repression means that the condemnation of violence is increasingly skewed towards those who do not have the means to establish their own structures of violence, and those who can only resist systemic violations by ad hoc acts of violence. There is no space for Chechens who resist the Russian army, there is no space for the Kashmiris who fight the Indian occupation, and there is no space for the Palestinians who want to free Palestine. They are all branded as terrorists, since their violence is often visible, while the violence of their oppressors remains complex, structural and veiled in legalese. Such a definition of terrorism reduces the possibility of resistance to the terrible inequities and tortures that many Muslim women and men face. Islamist challenges to the prevailing order can only be represented as acts of terrorism, because there is no space for challenges to the prevailing political order. Thus, in Palestine, in Chechnya, in Kashmir, and in Algeria, to name only the most obvious cases, the legitimacy of the Islamist struggle against repression is denied as the protestors are labelled as terrorists, while those who staff and command the repression machines of the state are presented as reasonable and moderate members of the international community.

The international discourse of terrorism articulated by the United States (and subsequently used by authoritarian regimes) has become hegemonic, with the result that any challenge to any state's authority is considered to be terrorism. This has the effect of de-legitimating any resistance to repressive regimes. Many of these have been very successful in articulating Islamist opposition as 'terrorism', thus creating the excuse for 'dirty wars' against Islamists. Even Islamists who have tried the electoral route have been forced on the defensive by being branded as 'terrorists', thus allowing the ruling elites of the Islamicate world to declare them to be 'anti-constitutional'. Currently, the electoral as well as the revolutionary route to an Islamic state seems to have been diverted or blocked by these Westoxicated elites and their use of death squads and torture centres. The measures used against the Islamists have ranged from campaigns of extermination initiated by Baathists and the Algerian junta to the dirty wars, para-legal violence, legislative prohibitions and smear campaigns of other regimes.

The Islamist Impasse?

Many of the difficulties encountered by Islamists have been common to other historical attempts at transnational social transformations. Specifically, the Islamists face four main challenges to their ambitions to institutionalize a new order. First, in most Muslim societies a large section of the population remains committed to Westernization, and for various reasons Islamists have not been as successful in winning over this group. This section of the population believes itself to be secularist, modern and liberal; it certainly presents itself in these terms to Western audiences. Despite their love of liberalism and democracy, however, many of these people have been willing to support illiberal and anti-democratic measures taken by the state machinery against Islamists. The Islamists need to win over this group without diluting their appeal to their core constituencies. To win this group over, Islamists have to deconstruct the rather benign interpretation by which this group tends to 'understand' the West. This has to be done through a radical decolonization and not a demonization of the West (although it is unlikely that the defenders of Western hegemony will necessarily be able, or even willing, to differentiate between the two).

Second, the current divisions of the Muslim world are sanctioned by an international order enforced by the new concert of mainly Western powers. As such, most Islamist groups are forced into making accommodations to the nation-state, with the consequence that nationalism begins to penetrate their discourse (for example, the parties in Kuwait, who claim to be Islamist, are unwilling to allow non-Kuwaiti Muslims to become members). This nationalization of Islamism means that Islamist groups are prone to being isolated, and often forced into political positions which undermine their Islamist objectives – this can be seen in the way that Islamist groups have to pander to policies of ethnic and cultural homogenization even when dealing with Muslim minority ethnic groups. If the Islamists are to remain a distinct political force, they must continue to focus on transcending the nation-state and contribute towards the formation of a global Islamicate culture. This requires Islamists to engage in intellectual-moral reforms, which are geared towards a critique of xenophobic nationalism, and a celebration of an Islamicate identity. To this end, Islamists need to take a more active part in contributing towards a global all-inclusive *Ummatic* culture which is not reducible to any authoritative national (whether Iranian, Saudi, or Turkish), or sectarian (Shia or Sunni) model.

Third, the current global order is dominated by a discourse that privileges the subjectivity of a sovereign consumer. In this way, all values and convictions become matters for individual choice and consumption. Islamists, despite the energy spent on devising 'Islamic' economics, have largely failed to counter this discourse. Their attacks have been based on questions of moral regulation and rectitude rather than overcoming the fundamental logic of this discourse. In this important sense, they have not yet been able to articulate a counter-hegemonic project for the reorganization of the world political economy.[2] The Islamists have an urgent need to develop a response to the contemporary division of global spoils. A number of alternatives suggest themselves, including joining in with the anti-globalization critique of radical and leftist groups. The recent popular boycott in the Islamicate world of American brand names suggests another possibility. More fundamentally, however, Islamists need to articulate a vision in which conspicuous consumption is not the motor of individual gratification and self-realization. The articulation of desire beyond the logic of consumerism is necessary, and the Islamists have tended to deal with the question of desire in a punitive rather than a productive manner. To construct desire requires enculturation and not simply prohibitions or tighter law enforcement.

Fourth, the major difficulty faced by Islamists, despite all their rhetoric of Islam as a total system, a complete 'way of life', is that when it comes down to it, far too many of them have a very limited idea of what 'a way of life' is. It is not something that can be reduced to mere biological functions and religious rituals – there is more to life than this, for example, questions of aesthetics, joy, solidarity and so on ... Given the limited understanding of a 'total way of life', it is not surprising that so many Islamists are considered to be unequal to the task of managing the complexities of con-temporary governance. Their capacity to make the 'trains run on time' or 'make sure the garbage is collected' is often put into question.

The Islamist groups which seem to enjoy the largest base of support are those who have exercised a social welfare function among their communities, for example, Hizbollah in Lebanon, Hamas in Palestine, and to some extent the AK party (in its various incarnations with its management of municipalities) in Turkey. There is a need for Islamists to demonstrate great skill in dealing with the banality of governing. Islamist parties that seem to offer little more than injunctions to greater piety, without putting those systems and procedures that would encourage such behaviour into place, display a lack of governmental imagination, which restricts their capacity for effective governance. Islamists often give the impression that they have a rather limited conception of the nature and possibilities of the state. This difficulty is partly due to a larger problem in which Muslims and Islamists have tended to privilege a theological reading of their history. As a consequence, their capacity to conduct a conversation with their past is too often a rather terse affair. Thus the Islamists often share a difficulty with rest of the Islamicate world in accessing their own (non-canonical) history as a resource for the future.

Despite these four difficulties, the Islamist project is not necessarily over. The condition of possibility for Islamism was the product of a number of distinct developments and processes: the decentring of the West, a quest for a post-Caliphate order and globalization. It is worth considering whether those conditions that made Islamism possible in the first place continue to prevail.

De-Centred West

In the wake of the US-sponsored war on terror and its seizure of Afghanistan and Iraq (to date), is it still possible to maintain that the West is de-centred? To the extent that the de-centring of the West was one of the main conditions of possibility for the emergence of Islamism, is it possible to see in the US-sponsored crusade on Islam-(ism) the so-called war on terror, as a negation of a de-centred West? Does not the apparent retreat of Islamists in the face of American power point to the restoration of the West as centre? Are we not witnessing a re-centring of the Western cultural formation? Could the gap that appeared between the West and the universal be seen as a temporary blip, the result of decolonization and superpower bi-polarity? There are two factors, however, which suggest that the 'de-

centring of the West' is not over, but rather, since the first publication
of *A Fundamental Fear*, it has become even more intense.

First, the identity and coherence of the West continues to be
contested. The controversial election of George Bush has helped to
highlight the differences between the European and American frac-
tions of what Martin Shaw describes as the Western conglomerate
state.[3] The West was constituted principally by the globalization of
the European formation and its appropriation of the Americas. The
articulation of a substantive difference between Europe and America
presents the possibility of the fragmentation of the unified Western
centre. (While there has been an anti-European strand in both Anglo
and Latin America, particularly during the nineteenth century, this
anti-Europeanism has been subsumed by the idea that America,
particularly the United States, exemplifies the best of a European
heritage.) It could be argued that, given the highly contingent manner
in which the neo-Reaganites have 'hijacked' the American establishment, the subsequent so-called 'Talibanization' of American public
life is ephemeral and does not reflect any long-term strategic or
structural change. Even if this is the case and the social changes in
the US are producing a society less and less like the America en-
visioned by the neo-conservatives, it does not follow that the hegemony of the right is over. Hegemony does not require a consensus or
a majority; it can suffice by preventing dissent from being organized
into what is considered a viable alternative. In other words, hegemony
means that those dissenters who do not or cannot speak through its
language are considered mute and, as such, outside the framework of
public discourse. While, in the long term, a disjunction between the
neo-conservative rule and the more variegated experiences of the
ruled may produce a crisis of legitimacy, it is possible for regimes and
hegemonies to remain entrenched even as the gap between rulers
and ruled expands. There is, however, reason to believe that the
conservative transformation of American political culture is not an
effect of Bush's victory, but rather the consequence of a process that
has been under way for the last thirty or so years. A neo-conservative
hegemony has been established so that public debate is dominated by
neo-conservative tropes, and those who cannot speak through these
tropes are considered to be outside the arena of politics.

As a consequence of these developments, the possibility of two
powerful divergent interpretations and projections of the West comes

closer to actualization. While it is still too early to be able to make a sharp distinction between American and European values and practices, it is, however, possible to imagine the Western conglomerate state becoming bifurcated in the future. This implies the further undermining of the identity and coherence of the West. This weakening of Western identity makes it difficult to maintain the distinction between the West and the Rest as the grammar of world order. The postcolonial dis-articulation between the universal and the West continues apace.

Second, power is at its most effective when it is able to present itself as a natural way of life; in other words, when power has become invisible it is no longer considered to be power, but seen as just the way the world has been and will be. Power finds its legitimacy in the fashioning of a culture in its image. Enculturation and socialization minimize the need for the use of force. Imperial enterprises that rely solely on the exercise of violence are unsustainable. In this light, the war on terror can be read as an admission of the failure of American hegemony over the Muslim *Ummah*.[4] It has failed to legitimize its occupation of parts of the Islamicate lands. It is these failures that necessitate the use of violence on a global scale in order to discipline a world that does not listen to America unless threatened with Cruise missiles and special forces. The crusade on Islam(ism) demonstrates the failure of legitimacy, and the difficulties Western cultural practices and values have in trying to pass themselves off as universal and natural.

Therefore, the de-centring of the West has not been halted. The postcolonial condition has not been, as yet, rolled back. While increasingly public policy and academic commentary suggest re-colonization as a way of restoring the world to order, it is not clear that the publics of the Western conglomerate state would support and sustain such imperial ventures. The postcolonial condition has penetrated Western culture to the extent that such imperial dreaming fails to fire the popular imagination. The project of Eurocentrism, that is, the attempt to suture the gap between the universal and the West, has become militarized in the years after the publication of *A Fundamental Fear*. The militarization of Eurocentrism is a sign not of its imminent success but rather of its current failure to close the gap.

Waiting for the Caliph

The second condition of enabling Islamism was the abolition of the Caliphate and the quest to establish an Islamically legitimate political order in its wake. It seems curious to argue that the institution of the Caliphate should have such political significance; after all, the Caliphate was contested since at least from the time of the Abbassid–Fatmid confrontation (if not from the very beginning of its institution with the Shia critique).[5] There is also a dispute as to what extent the early Ottomans actually emphasized their Caliphal status. Even if we were to accept the relative unimportance of the Caliphate in the past (and it is still far from clear that we should), it does not mean that the Caliphate did not become important in the post-Caliphate period. After all, contrary to the tenets of Orientalism, Islam does not end with the siege of Vienna. The centrality of the Caliphate is not a purely historical matter for which detached historians act as judges and gatekeepers of what is permissible for today's Muslims.[6] I would argue that the significance the Caliphate has had over the period of Islamicate history has not been constant, but that does not invalidate its growing significance in a post-Ottoman universe. The place of the Caliphate can be (and has been) re-articulated at different moments according to different (re-)constructions of the present and projects for the future.

The attempt to restore the Caliphate is not only the direct aim of political parties such as Hizb-ut-Tahrir; more diffusely, one can also see in Khomeini's concept of *veliyat-I-faqih* an attempt to articulate a Caliphate that is acceptable to Shia opinion and thus able to transcend divisions between Shia and Sunni political thought. Khomeini's assumption of the office of *veliyat-I-faqih* and his personal stature provided the Islamicate world with a *de facto* Caliph. His interventions were instrumental in helping to shore up an Islamicate global presence.

The symbolic importance of the Caliphate that is presented in *A Fundamental Fear* tended to focus on its canonical response to the problem of a legitimate Islamic government. Perhaps what was not emphasized then, and needs to be emphasized now, is that the Caliphate also represents the idea of an Islamicate great power. A power that can lead, as well as guarantee, an independent and sovereign Islamicate presence in the world. The absence of an

Islamicate great power points to the way in which Muslims remain unrepresented at the global level. Such a condition did not have much political significance during a period when Muslim identity was considered to be of minor relevance. The assertion of a Muslim identity in a context in which there is no Islamicate Great Power creates a situation in which large numbers of people are marginalized from the international system. The absence of the Caliphate is not only a metaphor for a normative vacuum in which the gap between the rulers and ruled within the Muslim world cannot be closed, it is also a metaphor for the missing Islamicate great power that could represent the Muslim *Ummah* at a global level. The Islamicate world can still be usefully described as being post-Caliphate. The significance of the Caliphate for the Muslim *Ummah* has not diminished, rather it still continues to act as a horizon. It is in this context that Al-Qaeda can be understood as an attempt to create a virtual Caliphate – a diasporic, Islamicate great power, able and willing to impose its will on a recalcitrant international system on behalf of those who it considers to be dispossessed and excluded from it. The politics of the Islamicate world continue to be conditioned by the absence of the Caliphate. The Caliphate represents not only political legitimacy for the *Ummah*, but also the possibility of its global political presence.

Islamism and Globalization

Globalization, or the hollowing out of the Westphalian order, is often represented by two different trends. One trend sees in globalization the process by which an increasingly integrated world is becoming homogenous. The other trend sees globalization as producing greater heterogeneity. In this duel between integration and fragmentation, Islamist projects are seen as exemplars of the forces of fragmentation. Islamism seems to be a retreat from global homogenization and a last-ditch effort to assert particularism in the face of the McDonaldization of the World. The idea that Islamism is a reaction to globalization, however, tends to ignore the way in which Islamism is enabled by globalization. Islam is a universal religion in that it is not specific to any location or any ethnicity. The interpretation of Islam as universal is well established among Muslims, even though, on occasion, parochialism and particularism creep in. For most Islamists, however, Islam is not reducible to cultural or national practices. Islamists in general see Islam as being for all of humankind.

The reorganization of the world along Westphalian lines contributed to the development of Islam that tended to deny its global and political character. The undermining of the Westphalian state system has created a space where an Islam unencumbered by national cultural accretions can operate.[7] Such a space allows for the articulation of Islam unconstrained by national or particularistic concerns, an Islam that is able to embrace the entire Muslim *Ummah*. The creation of a large Muslim diaspora is one of the key developments that has enabled the spread of a pan-Islamicate sense of Muslimness.[8] In the Muslim diaspora in Western plutocracies, Muslims, unified by experiences of racism and Islamopobia, are brought into contact with each other increasingly as Muslims rather than as members of ethnic or national communities. The growth of Muslim advocacy organizations and media outlets all demonstrate the construction of a nascent Islamicate civil society in the Muslim diaspora, which is multi-national and multi-ethnic in character. This can be seen in the way in which many *ordinary* Muslims responded to the Bosnian genocide, and in the way in which *support for the Palestinian cause has become part of the common sense of Muslim public opinion from Indonesia to Canada.* It can be increasingly seen in the way in which conflicts in Kashmir and Chechnya go beyond their specific locations to a find support in a wider range of Muslim public opinion. So the hollowing out of the Westphalian order continues at a pace.

The capacity of national governments to regulate their populations in their nominal jurisdictions, to tie 'their' people in knots of dependency and loyalty, are increasingly limited. This opening of national spaces enables the development of a trans-national Muslim identity. It is this trans-national Muslim subjectivity that Islamism benefits from, since it helps to form an interpretation of Islam, not simply as a social relationship historically associated with particular national societies, but rather as a matter of political choice that seeks to go beyond the conventional boundaries in which Islamicate identity was always considered to be secondary to national identity.

Islamism is a political discourse that benefits greatly from many of the processes associated with globalization. It is able to disarticulate globalization from Westernization, and offer itself as another paradigm of what lies beyond the nation-state. A trawl through the inmates of the American 'concentration camps' in Guantanamo Bay and elsewhere would readily reveal the trans-national nature of Al-Qaeda. This trans-nationality is not unique among some Islamist organizations. There is no reason to believe that Islamism will not continue to benefit from globalization. What remains to be seen is to what extent the regulatory and disciplinary strategies of the war on terrorism will bring about the end of globalization by enhancing the policing powers of national authorities, and strengthening, at least at the level of peripheral states, the Westphalian template.

Islamism and Empire

The symbols of the American Imperium were not attacked because of the virtues of American society. They were not attacked because of resentment at American prosperity. The attacks on the United States were not psychotic or cosmological, but political.[9] To think that attacks on Western targets are simply a reaction to the wonders of Western civilization is to engage in a narcissistic fantasy. The significance of the attacks on the Pentagon and the World Trade Center resides in the way in which it transcended the barrier that separated centre and periphery. During the colonial struggles of the nineteenth century, the 'natives' could rarely, if ever, cross this barrier. Anti-colonial wars were waged, for the most part, on the soil of the colonized and the 'collateral damage' was confined to those residents in the colonies. Post-coloniality makes it increasingly difficult to maintain the separation between centre and periphery. It makes it difficult to enjoy democracy at home and support repressive regimes abroad.

There are voices among the new crusaders who dream of the transformation of the Islamicate world through an occupation modelled on post-war Germany or Japan, and who see Islamism as third in the line of ideologies after Nazism and communism, crushed by American power. Islamism, however, is not analogous to communism or Nazism. It could be argued that communism and Nazism are variants of an immanentist Christian heresy, in which salvation could be immediately found in new social order.[10] Islamism's relationship to Islam is not similar to the relationship of Nazism (or communism) to Christianity. It is not a secularized re-occupation of theological discourse. Islamism is an interpretation of Islam, which emphasizes its social and political import. It is not a replacement for Islam. Further-more, the occupation and reconstruction of Germany and Japan was facilitated by the Soviet threat. The people of Japan and Germany were being offered not American occupation or liberation, but American occupation or the possibility of Soviet occupation. There is no credible geopolitical rival to the United States, the threat from which can be used by the United States to sell its occupation. Despite the nostalgia for empire being exhibited among some circles in Western plutocracies, it is a nostalgia that does not seem to resonate with those who were subjected to Western empires. It remains the case that despite all the disappointments and devastation visited upon ex-colonial societies in the wake of decolonization, there is hardly any popular movement in any major ex-colony demanding the restoration of imperial rule.

The success or failure of the war on terrorism will depend on the extent to which the project of Eurocentrism is able to close the gap between Western cultural formations and universal values. It is not the occupation of countries such as Afghanistan or Iraq (or whichever regime becomes the latest addition to the American government's list of rogue regimes) that is significant; the real challenge for Western supremacists is whether they can occupy the universal.

The challenge presented by contemporary Islamist movements goes beyond 'panics' about terrorism or weapons of mass destruction, for what Islamism points to is the end of 'the Age of the West' and thus the limits of Westernization as the future of the world. In other words, the study of the Islamicate world has to move beyond the paradigm of the 'West and Rest', in which the 'Rest' of the world is reduced to little more than the West's residue. This is the context which allows *A Fundamental Fear* to be situated in a broader set of interventions in various fields (e.g. the so-called 'California school' of world history, some forms of cultural studies and post-colonial dis-course theory), which have (in many different ways) begun to interrupt the West and Rest dyad as a way of apprehending the world.

The political turn of Islam cannot be understood outside the very complex ways in which it relates to the project of Western hegemony. Islamism is a project that draws much of its strength from a con-viction that there is no need for a detour through the labyrinths of Western history, before one can arrive at a vision of the good life and a just order: universal values can be generated from Islam.

Notes

1. For examples, see Georges A. Fawaz (1999) 'Islamists have come to a halt', *Survival*, 4 (1) Spring; Oliver Roy (1999) 'Crisis of Legitimacy in Iran', *Middle East Journal*, 53 (2); Gilles Kepel (2000/2002) *Jihad: The Trail of Political Islam*, Harvard: Harvard University Press.

2. See also Anouar Majid (2000) *Unveiling Traditions: Postcolonial Islam in a Polycentric World*, Chapel Hill, NC: Duke University Press.

3. Martin Shaw (2000) *Theory of the Global State*, Cambridge: Cambridge University Press.

4. One indicator of this failure can be seen in the growth of 'anti-Americanism', not just in Islamicate communities but also in many other parts of the world. See, for example, a 44-country survey with 38,000 respondants on attitudes to the USA in light of the 'war on terror', Pew Global Attitudes Project, 2002.

5. For a discussion of the undermining of Caliphal legitimacy which allowed 'anti-Caliphs' to be established by the Fatimids and Umayyads, see Janina Safran (2001) *The Second Umayyad Caliphate: The Articulation of Caliphal Legitimacy in Al-Andalus*, Cambridge, MA: Harvard University Press.

6. Talal Asad (2003) makes a similar point in his discussion of the role of Muslim reformers in the reconfiguration of the law in colonial Egypt; see *Formations of the Secular: Christianity, Islam, Modernity*, Stanford, CA: Stanford University Press. For further details of this argument see S. Sayyid (2000), 'Beyond Westphalia: Nations and Diasporas' in Barnor Hesse (ed.) *Un/settled Multiculturalism: Diasporas, Entanglements, Transruptions*, London: Zed Books.

8. For details of transnational Islamicate civil society see Peter Mandaville (2001), *Transnational Muslim Politics: Reimagining the Umma*, London: Routledge

9. For an analysis of the way in which the war on terror is based on an attempted disavowal of its political nature see Barnor Hesse and S. Sayyid (2002), 'The "War" against Terrorism/The "War"' for Cynical Reason', *Ethnicities*, June 2 (2).

10. Michael Burleigh (2000) *The Third Reich: A New History*, London: Pan Books, p. 10.

Prologue: The return of the repressed

I am Khalid al-Islambuli, I have killed Pharaoh, and I do not fear death. *Khalid al-Islambuli*[1]

I should prefer a purely rabbinical explanation. *Jorge Luis Borges*[2]

Of the many spectres that have haunted western civilization from time to time, perhaps none is so perplexing or so irredeemably strange as the contemporary resurgence of Islam. The spectral nature of this phenomenon arises not only from the way its emergence conveniently coincides with the approach of the witching hour of the second Christian millennium, but also from the way in which the Muslim presence for the west has tended to be grounded in a 'hauntology', which finds it all too easy to conflate Muslims and ghosts.[3]

Ghosts are the remains of the dead. They are echoes of former times and former lives: those who have died but still remain, hovering between erasure of the past and the indelibility of the present – creatures out of time. Muslims too, it seems, are often thought to be out of time: throwbacks to medieval civilizations who are caught in the grind and glow of 'our' modern culture. It is sometimes said that Muslims belong to cultures and societies that are moribund and have no vitality – no life of their own. Like ghosts they remain with us, haunting the present.

It is argued that ghosts do not really exist; they are but fictions, perhaps just like Muslims who also do not seem really to exist. There are people from the Maghreb, from South Asia, from West Africa – but there are no Muslims. The possibility of a Muslim subjectivity is undermined by notions of class and ethnicity, kinship and caste or tribe and clan. These cleavages are said to demonstrate the hollow nature of Muslim identity.

Ghosts are terrifying. Their bitterness at their incorporeal state, their resentment of the living and their vindictiveness at some ancient wrong that no one can recall – all fuel their unrelenting hatred of us. Even though ghosts do not really exist, they have their uses. When something goes bump in the night we can blame it on a poltergeist. Similarly, you may remember when some good ol' boys blew up the Federal Building in Oklahoma City, how useful it was to have Muslims around to explain bombs in the night. Ghosts, despite not existing, are terrifying. Muslims also generate such fear; even though they are often the lowest of the low, the dispossessed, Muslims are still capable of making even sturdy liberal institutions anxious; and, like ghosts, they seem to appear almost everywhere and any-where.

Ghosts can walk through walls. Boundaries cannot contain them. In the same way Muslims seem to seep through the very fabric of 'our common European' home. They appear in the least expected places: Bradford, Bosnia, in state schools and universities; in secular Turkey and in friendly Egypt; in Chechnya; and there were even rumours they were in Oklahoma City. Muslims transgress state bound-aries, cut across county lines and through disciplinary categories. Their presence marks out a space which seems irreconcilably different and which seems to resist easy absorption within the western enter-prise. The presence of Islam erases time, it marks out an absence from history, but it also seemingly erases the years of western hegemony.

As an increasing number of Muslim communities began to experience changes in what Richard Rorty would call their 'final vocabularies',[4] many Muslims began to narrate their personal identities and the destiny of their communities by referring to a language derived from what they understood to be their Islamic heritage. Organizations demanding that their communities should be organized more strictly around Islamic precepts appeared. Other groups advocated the establishment of an Islamic order. Alongside these party-political activities, the last twenty years have seen a mushrooming of publications (both electronic and printed) devoted to furthering the cause of Islam. The writings of people like Khomeini, Maududi, Sayyid Qutb, Malcolm X, Ali Shariati and others enjoy wide circulation. There is also some evidence of an increased attendance at mosques and a greater emphasis, among both men and women, on what they consider to be Islamic dress. All across the fractured *Ummah* it seems that Islam is becoming increasingly visible and assertive. This assertion of global Muslim subjectivity (or in common journalese: 'Islamic fundamentalism') has aroused a great deal of anxiety among many people. Some of the reasons for this anxiety can perhaps be found in the history of Vienna – the city that marks the most recent high tide of Muslim advances.[5]

Besieging Vienna again

An inhabitant of Vienna forgot the name of the painter of the fresco of Orvieto. This caused him an 'inner torment' and only after a few days could he come up with two names: 'Botticelli and Boltraffio'. Finally, he remembered that the name of the painter was 'Signorelli'.[6] He explained his forgetfulness by arguing that the name of the painter of the fresco of Orvieto had become a substitute for something else (it became a symptom represented by its very absence – the forgetting), and was replaced by distortions. Both Botticelli and Boltraffio were metaphors to re-cover the loss of Signorelli, but the absent Signorelli was itself a metaphor for other repressed thoughts. The repression of the name of Signorelli had become an indicator of something else. The repression was successful because the name of Signorelli was forgotten but, at same time as being successful, the repression was also a failure. For although the name had been forgotten, anxiety remained, and other elements came to signify the loss. So, even when Signorelli was forgotten, it remained as an absence as well as a distorted presence. This Viennese story shows the paradoxical nature of repression and how the very act of repression invites the return of the repressed.[7]

Perhaps the reasons for the fear of 'Islamic fundamentalism' can be found in the metaphors of this Viennese tale. The current Islamic revival and the anxiety it induces can be accounted for in the way by which it marks the return of the repressed. In a political sense this is manifested in the way that resurgent Islam is articulated with political projects which reject the current world order. This rejection can take many forms: global (for example, the rejection of the planetary culture of consumerism); regional (for example, the rejection of Oslo accords and the Middle East 'peace' process); or even locally (for example, the championing of economically marginalized sections of the population or the dispossessed). 'Islamic fundamentalism' seems to threaten the status quo, both internationally and within those states where there are substantial Muslim communities.[8] As a consequence, it has been the cause of national security panics – not just in non-Muslim states but also in Muslim majority states. For various reasons many organizations point to the existence of 'Islamic fundamentalism' as a threatening and disruptive force, against which they have to mobilize resources. 'Islamic fundamentalism' has come to play a similar role to the one that 'red scares' played during the cold war, albeit – so far – on a much smaller scale. Similar kinds of representation are being deployed: Islamic fundamentalists are subversives responsible for every act of 'terrorism'; Muslim 'dissidents' – artists who cannot create in the restrictive climate produced by Islamic fundamentalism – are appearing; and 'the military build-up' by Islamic fundamentalist regimes is understood to be a threat to world order.[9] Islamic fundamentalism is considered to be the vehicle by which many of the victims of the western enterprise seek revenge and redress.

The idea that the Islamic resurgence represents a return of the repressed does not take only a political form. At a more diffuse level, the Islamic revival signals a cultural anxiety in the West. The West sees in Islam the distorted mirror of its own past. It marks the rebirth of the God they had killed so that Man (sic) could live. The Islamic resurgence marks the revenge of God; it signals the return of faith, the return of all that puts into question the idea of the progressive liberation of humanity. These ideas trade on the notion that only in the west are humans truly free, truly human. The articulation of a global Muslim subjectivity threatens human emancipation by trying to make the world a slave to Allah. Islamic fundamentalism arouses such anxiety because it questions a number of assumptions which allow us to continue to see the West as a model of political, economic, cultural and intellectual development. Unlike some challengers to the world order, Islamic fundamentalists seem to make no concessions to the political traditions that have been with us for over two hundred years. The references of Islamic fundamentalists tend to be to the Qur'an, and the formative history of the first Muslim empire (630–61), and not to the rights of man or Marxism in its various forms. Thus, the resurgence of Islam raises questions as to the limits of what has been called the 'legacy of the Age of Europe'. Its appearance seems to challenge the universality of the West, and points to its limitations.[10]

This book sets out to analyse the conditions that have made 'Islamic fundamentalism' possible. The questions posed are fundamentally theoretical ones: why political Islam and why now? What this book will not provide is an empirically rich analysis of how Islamic fundamentalism emerged in particular Muslim communities; there will not be any substantial attempts to examine in detail the organization, recruitment, political strategies, etc. of particular Islamic fundamentalist groups. Nor will this book provide a comparative analysis of the causes of Islamic fundamentalism in its various contexts. For example, I am not going to try to explain the process by which the Front Islamique de Salvation (FIS) has become a significant opponent of the post-FLN regime in Algeria, nor am I going to detail the specific reasons for the success of Islamic fundamentalism in, for instance, Iran. There are two reasons for this: first, this line of enquiry is well represented in the literature on Islamic revivalism.[11] Second (and more importantly) I believe that while this approach, by focusing on individual instances of Islamic fundamentalism, can be a source of many fruitful empirical and historical insights, it cannot provide an explanation of political Islam. What such studies tend to do is to indicate how a series of events challenge the status quo in many Muslim communities. What they fail adequately to explain is why this challenge to the existing order has repeatedly and consistently, over the last twenty years, taken the form of Islamic revivalism. An answer to this question cannot be found by simply itemizing an ever-lengthening list of case studies of Islamic fundamentalism. To account adequately for the emergence of Islamic fundamentalism requires the articulation of a ground in which the various manifestations and causes of 'Islamic fundamentalism' have a coherence that has a wider logic than any particular Muslim community. Such coherence could only be found in a conceptual narrative. The aim of this book is to provide such a narrative.

Ultimately this is a story about change within Muslim communities, about why individuals such as Khalid al-Islambuli chose to kill and be killed in the name of a faith that History had seemingly forgotten. There are many ways this story could be told, I prefer to tell it as a story about the politics of Islam ...

Notes

1. Words spoken by the leader of Sadat's assassins, quoted by Esposito, 1992; Kepel, 1985, p. 192.

2. Borges, 1985, p. 118.

3. For explanation of hauntology see Derrida, 1994.

4. Rorty suggests that all individuals have a set of words and phrases to which they resort when asked to give accounts of their hopes, beliefs and desires. This is a final vocabulary. It is the vocabulary by which we tell a story of ourselves. It is final since beyond it there is only tautology, violence or silence. See Rorty, 1989, p. 73.

5. Toulmin, 1990, p. 5

6. Freud, 1901, pp. 1–7.

7. Psychoanalysis focuses on the moments when the failure of repression is disclosed and what was repressed is revealed but in a distorted form.

8. For some descriptions of this unease, see Esposito, 1992, pp. 168–84; Hippler and Lueg, 1995, pp. 116–59.

9. For example, on 29 September 1994, at a meeting of NATO defence ministers in Seville, François Leotard, the French defence minister, proposed that NATO should direct itself to deterring the threat from 'Islamic fundamentalism'. See *The Independent*, 30 September 1994.

10. For my purposes, the differences between Europe and the West are not important. I am aware that one could make a number of objections regarding the role of Eastern Europe or Mediterranean Europe in the constitution of Europe, and there are arguments for keeping Europe and the West separate. It may be helpful to note that my use of Europe and the West is ideological and not geographical. It should also be noted that 'Islamic militants' make no significant distinction between Europe and the West.

11. For example, Ayoob, 1981; Piscatori, 1983; Cole and Keddie, 1986; Hunter, 1988 provide analyses of various Muslim countries exhibiting the symptoms of Islamic fundamentalism.

1. Framin' fundamentalism

'Islamic fundamentalism' has emerged as a way of representing and analysing a series of events involving Muslim communities. Accounts of 'Islamic fundamentalism' often begin by listing a number of incidents in the Muslim world which show the growing importance of Islam. For example, John Esposito lists the politics of Sudan, Malaysia, post-revolutionary Iran, Pakistan, Bangladesh, Egypt and Libya as all demonstrating an Islamic revival.[1] P. J. Vatikiotis sees 'Islamic resurgence' as a way of conceptualizing the Iranian revolution, 'tribal' resistance to the Soviet invasion and occupation of Afghanistan, and the establishment of the Zia regime in Pakistan.[2] Michael Fischer cites the replacement of the Pahlavi state with the Islamic Republic, the millenarian revolt in Kano (northern Nigeria), the attempted assassination of the Pope, the activities of the Muslim Brethren in Egypt, the assassination of Sadat, and the seizure of the Grand Mosque by anti-Saudi dissidents as being manifestations of Islamic fundamentalism.[3] One could go on extending the list of events which are presented as the empirical referents of Islamic fundamentalism: the civil war in Algeria, HAMAS's activities against Israeli occupation, the Rushdie affair ... and so on.[4]

What then is 'Islamic fundamentalism'? One way of answering this question is to conceptualize it as a strand within a broader phenomenon, a movement which includes political projects represented by organizations such as Gush Emunim in Israel, Shiv Sena in India, or the Christian Coalition in the United States. In this approach, fundamentalism is not specific to Muslims; they are just one example of something that is a general feature of our contemporary world. However, although resurgent Islam may be only one form of fundamentalism, it is the form which is most often cited as an example of it. Fundamentalism itself is made flesh by drawing upon examples of 'Islamic fundamentalism'.[5] Veiled (Muslim) women and bearded (Muslim) men, book burners and suicide bombers have emerged as fundamentalist icons enjoying recurrent Hollywood canonization (see, for example, *Not Without My Daughter* and *True Lies*). Consequently, although representing only one aspect of a global fundamentalism, Islamic fundamentalism has become a metaphor for fundamentalism in general. This would suggest that fundamentalism and Islamic fundamentalism are closely related. To understand Islamic fundamentalism we need a theory of fundamentalism – we need to conceptualize fundamentalism, not just as journalistic slogan, but as an analytical category.

Theorizing fundamentalism

Gita Sahgal and Nira Yuval-Davis[6] are among a number of writers who think it is possible to use fundamentalism as an analytical category.[7] In their opinion, fundamentalism has three main features: it is a project to control women's bodies; it is a political practice which rejects pluralism; and it is a movement that purposefully conflates religion and politics as a means of furthering its aims.[8] Sahgal and Yuval-Davis would have little hesitation in arguing that groups such as Lubavitch Hassids, Hizbollah and the VHP have enough in common to be classed together as fundamentalists. To sustain fundamentalism as an analytical construct, it is necessary to theorize the common features of the various fundamentalist projects, and at the same time to be able to draw distinctions between these and other types of political projects. The three characteristics that Sahgal and Yuval-Davis consider to be constitutive of fundamentalism must, therefore, be common to all forms of fundamentalism and should not be found in other types of political projects.

Problems of governmentality Sahgal and Yuval-Davis consider fundamentalism to be, in many ways, a reaction to the advances of feminism. They argue that fundamentalists see the role of women as having a wider symbolic value, reflecting the morality of their society. This allows them to assert that there is an underlying similarity between, for example, the anti-abortion activities of the Christian Coalition in the United States and the insistence on veiling in many Muslim communities. Despite the many differences between these two groups, they are united by their desire to control women's bodies.

According to Sahgal and Yuval-Davis, fundamentalism of all types aims to exercise control over women's bodies.[9] This argument has great resonance; the subordination of women and/or their confinement to 'traditional' spheres is considered one of the hallmarks of the various fundamentalist movements. Popular conceptions of Islamic fundamentalism all trade on the figure of the veiled, passive and subjugated Muslim woman. But can fundamentalism be usefully defined in this way? Would all political movements which aim to control women be considered fundamentalist by Sahgal and Yuval-Davis? For example, Mustafa Kemal and Reza Khan both considered the role of women to be of central political importance. For them, the role of women had symbolic significance because it signalled the position of their societies upon the ladder of progress, and both introduced measures which exercised control over women's bodies. They demanded that women should not be veiled (on occasion, enforcing their demands by physical force). This would lead us to question whether political projects that prevent women from veiling could be considered fundamentalist.

It could be argued that imposing the end of the veil is not the same, in principle, as enforcing the wearing of the veil. The former is 'liberating' and, therefore, is not an exercise in control but its abandonment; the latter, conversely, is restrictive and, as such, can be considered an exercise in control. In other words, control is only exercised when it is a restriction. But why should the enforced removal of the veil be considered liberating and the enforcement of the veil be considered restrictive? It is only by assuming there is a 'natural' female subjectivity (what Elizabeth Spelman calls an 'essential woman') that it is possible uncritically to equate veiling with a restriction (in other words, the 'essential woman' is unveiled and therefore veiling is a violation of that 'natural' subjectivity).

The consequence of assuming that there is an 'essential' woman is that other women who do not match the ideals of this essential figure are considered 'inessential'.[10] The essential woman has characteristics which are culled from particular historical/cultural formations: she speaks a particular language, eats particular foods, consumes particular products, dresses in particular ways, and so on. Her 'essential' status, however, has the effect of transforming her particularities into universals; her particular way of being becomes everywoman's way of being. The effect of this is that women who do not share the essential woman's particularities become lesser women. As Spelman has so persuasively argued, feminists who fail to address the heterogeneity of women end up underwriting cultural and racial hierarchies.[11] Clearly, Sahgal and Yuval-Davis reproduce versions of feminism which endorse the homogeneity of the female subject.[12] The consequence of such endorsements is erasure.

With regard to the question of the veil, Leila Ahmad's work has shown that the reason for thinking that the veil was more repressive than, for example, Victorian corsets had more to do with the way the veil was used as a marker of particular cultural formation.[13] When white women of the nineteenth century saw veiled women, they understood it to be a sign of cultural backwardness and female subordination.[14] They did not make the same assumptions about their own clothes, which for them did not signify female subordination – because they did not signify cultural backwardness. Cultural backwardness – that is a culture not modelled upon a European template – manifested itself in female subordination. By focusing attention on the veil, the critics of the veil have often neglected far more serious issues.[15]

Unless one assumes that there is an 'essential' woman, one has to accept that control over women is being exercised regardless of whether they are being compelled to veil or unveil. In other words, control is a matter of maintaining and producing subjects. If fundamentalism is to be characterized by the desire to exercise control over women, there should be no difference made between modern Turkey, which prohibits the wearing of the veil in certain situations (or even modern France where Muslim schoolgirls were prevented from wearing headscarves at school), and Saudi Arabia, which prevents women from unveiling in public. It is unlikely that Sahgal and Yuval-Davis would see in the French authorities' resistance to Muslim schoolgirls wearing headscarves a manifestation of fundamentalism.

Fundamentalism cannot be defined in terms of exercising control over women. Exercising control over bodies is the function of governmentality itself.[16] Sahgal and Yuval-Davis seem to have a rather vague notion of governmentality which grants credence to the suggestion that attempts to exercise control over women is a feature peculiar to fundamentalism. It is not only in Muslim societies that control of women's bodies has been considered a matter of political significance, nor is it solely a function of particular types of political movements:

it can be found in regimes as diverse as those of the Nazis, communists, fascists and the most liberal of the North Atlantic plutocracies. Controlling bodies is what governments attempt to do. For example, legislation which very directly seeks to control women, such as legislation governing abortion, is determined in Britain by votes in the House of Commons – a body overwhelmingly made up of male MPs. Nevertheless, it is unlikely that Sahgal and Yuval-Davis would include the mainstream British political parties in their taxonomy of fundamentalism.

Governance involves the control of all bodies – male and female. This does not mean governance is gender blind or that the control which is exercised impacts equally upon men and women, but it cannot be seriously argued that only fundamentalists wish to exercise control over women. The difficulty with Sahgal and Yuval-Davis's approach is that, by assuming 'woman is woman only',[17] they ignore the massive disciplinary techniques of the contemporary state, and only by this act of neglect can they suggest that a common denominator of fundamentalism is the exercise of control over women. In their eagerness to make corporeal the phantasmagoria of fundamentalism, Sahgal and Yuval-Davis are willing to forget the patriarchy that underlies the disciplinary codes of all existing societies.

Styles of political practice According to Sahgal and Yuval-Davis, fundamentalists assert that their understanding of religion is correct and they 'feel threatened by pluralist systems of thought'.[18] In the case of Islam, they note that fundamentalism has taken the form of a return to the Qur'an and the *sharia*.[19] This assertion, however, is countered by many writers who strenuously argue that so-called Islamic fundamentalism is not a retreat into traditional interpretations but an innovative and original reworking of canonical texts. For example, Ervand Abrahamian argues that if fundamentalism means literal readings of canonical texts, this cannot apply to Islamic fundamentalists, since their interpretations of Islamic canonical texts tend to be novel and innovative.[20] This is one of the reasons why, in general, the Sunni *ulema* have tended to oppose Islamic fundamentalists; they regard the 'fundamentalist' interpretations as too allegorical.[21] The way in which Islamic fundamentalists are willing to make pragmatic compromises with programmatic discourses is illustrated by the change in Khomeini's position after he came to power. Previously, Khomeini had argued that only a strict application of *sharia* was legitimate and that activities not sanctioned by the *sharia* could not be undertaken.[22] However, once in power, Khomeini realized that such an adherence would be difficult to implement and he was willing to support the needs of the Islamic Republic above a strict adherence to the traditional interpretations of the *sharia*. The culmination of this process was reached in January 1988, when in letter to Khamenei, the president of Iran, Khomeini declared:

> The government is empowered to unilaterally revoke any *sharia* agreements which it has concluded with the people when those agreements are contrary to the interest of the country or to Islam.[23]

What this makes clear is that the Islamic Republic had the right to abrogate any or all of the *sharia*, in the wider interests of the *Ummah*. There is nothing traditional about this ruling; it is not derived from any canonical text and it actually makes observations of Islamic precepts secondary to state interests.

To be fair to Sahgal and Yuval-Davis, they are aware that many scholars object to their understanding of fundamentalism, especially in relation to Islamic fundamentalism. They acknowledge Abrahamian's disagreement but, alas, do not meet any of his criticisms.

Sahgal and Yuval-Davis seriously underestimate the complexity of the relationship between truth and politics. They seem to have a notion of a normal politics in which truth and politics have a relationship of exteriority, in contrast to fundamentalism in which politics is subsumed under truth. It is only because they assume that politics and truth are distinct spheres at the level of the social that they can suggest that fundamentalism can be understood as a conflation of the political with truth.

The truth is one way of describing statements which we consider to be good or useful. In such a pragmatist definition, truth is constructed and not given. Politics, then, is the process by which societies arrive at a new vision of the truth, a new way of describing the good or the useful. To paraphrase Michel Foucault, '[t]he political question … is truth itself'.[24] As such, truth and politics cannot be separated in the way that Sahgal and Yuval-Davis seem to suggest. Of course, it could be that Sahgal and Yuval-Davis do not share this antifoundationalist vision of the relationship between politics and truth;

they may believe that it is possible to speak truth to power.[25] They may believe in a correspondence theory of truth, which would appear to allow them to maintain the distinction between truth and politics. Even this, however, does not allow them to specify fundamentalism in a convincing manner. For, according to Sahgal and Yuval-Davis, fundamentalists would be those who claim that their beliefs are true and reject alternative beliefs. But this condition is not exclusive to those labelled as fundamentalists; for example organizations such as Women Against Fundamentalism would also claim that their beliefs are true and would reject alternatives offered by those they consider to be fundamentalists. Making truth claims about one's beliefs is a common practice. One may disagree about the content of the projects of various movements but one should not make the mistake that political projects are constructed on any other notion than that they claim to represent the truth. It is not only fundamentalists who claim they hold the truth: Nazis, communists, socialists, conservatives – even the parliamentarians of the North Atlantic plutocracies – all practise politics in the service of truth. 'Fundamentalist' presidents like Carter, Zia-ul Haq, Reagan and Rafsanjani, and secularist leaders like Nasser, Stalin and Hoxha, were equally clear about the truthfulness of their visions.

It seems that fundamentalism is being used here as a substitute for what is more commonly known as dogmatism. Dogmatists, however, can be found in all walks of life; liberals, secularists and scientists can be just as dogmatic as those with strong religious beliefs. The rejection of alternative views is not the monopoly of the groups that Sahgal and Yuval-Davis identify as being fundamentalists – unless you broaden the term to include political figures with tendencies as diverse as Margaret Thatcher (who took pride in the acronym TINA: 'there is no alternative'), Mao Zedong, Abraham Lincoln, and many more. The problem with extending the category of fundamentalism in this manner is it suggests that there is no real reason for confining fundamentalism to religious phenomena in the first place. After all, one can easily follow Shabbir Akhtar and read the Rushdie affair as a clash between two forms of fundamentalism – Islamic and liberal.[26] If the category of fundamentalism becomes simply a description of strongly held beliefs – something akin to the belief of Rorty's metaphysicians,[27] based on a rejection of what Vattimo calls 'weak thought'[28] – then it is clear that even the most 'radical democrats' or postmodern bourgeois liberals have a fundamentalist core. If fundamentalism simply connotes that part of our final vocabulary we are not willing to concede, the difference between non-fundamentalists and fundamentalists collapses.

Combining politics with religion The third feature of Sahgal and Yuval-Davis's definition of fundamentalism is that of a political movement that conflates politics with religion – reiterating a common assertion, especially in relation to Islam.[29] According to Bernard Lewis, to take one example, Islam is by its constitution unable to distinguish between politics and religion.[30] It is the case that Sahgal and Yuval-Davis are alert to various vicissitudes of their examples (the establishment of the Church of England in the UK and the demands in various North Atlantic plutocracies that heads of states should be of a particular religious denomination); however, notwithstanding these anomalies, they are insistent that the use of political means by religious groups is a feature peculiar to fundamentalism. This view, however, assumes that there is a natural division between church and state (or there should be), and that fundamentalism transgresses that boundary.

The difficulty with this argument is that this boundary between religion and politics is not clear-cut. The current definition of religion is the product of a particular history, in which religion is a distinct sphere of life.[31] This has two effects: first, it suggests that religion should be separate from other types of social relations such as politics. Second, it makes it possible to think that religion is simply a self-contained unit of social life, one which can be detached from the social order and considered to be distinct from that social order.[32] It is clear that such a definition of religion allows the theorization of fundamentalism as a violation of religion itself.

This idea of religion is heavily reliant on the use of western Christianity as the model of what a religion is. According to this template, religion refers to specific dimensions of human life as distinct from other dimensions, especially politics.[33] If, however, one models the concept of religion around Mosean Judaism, or Pre-Ummayad Islam, or Christianity of the Byzantine (or if you prefer the East Roman) empire, then the definition of religion would not be so clear about what was religious and what was merely political. Of course, Sahgal and Yuval-Davis could respond that, regardless of genealogical accidents which have produced the current definition of religion, this counter-claim does not invalidate their assertion that fundamentalism is a project that seeks to subvert the 'normal' definition of religion. What does discredit their position, however, is that, as Talal Asad argues, 'there cannot be a universal definition of religion, not only because its constituent elements and relationships are historically specific, but because the definition is itself the historical product of discursive processes'.[34] This line leads to the heart of the problem: where are Sahgal and Yuval-Davis located in their attempt to theorize fundamentalism? While they seem to be aware of this question, they do not really address the problems that it raises; specifically they do not interrogate the effect their location has on attempts to articulate a general theory of fundamentalism.

All definitions are based on the exclusion of some elements and the inclusion of others. I have re-described Sahgal and Yuval-Davis's theorization of fundamentalism in such a way as to show that which is excluded is not same as that which it is claimed is excluded. For example, the reason for excluding French school authorities who ban the headscarf is not based on whether the authorities are exercising control over Muslim schoolgirls, but on prior assessment about what fundamentalism looks like. It looks like 'oppressed' veiled Muslim women, not like the rather selective secularism of the Fifth Republic. The concept of fundamentalism relies not on its internal coherence but, rather, on a 'shared' assumption regarding the role of politics, truth and religion. To make the distinction between fundamentalism and other political/cultural projects, Sahgal and Yuval-Davis rely on commonsensical notions of politics, truth and religion which, they would suggest, are unproblematic givens. However, their common sense – like all common sense – is the dissemination of a particular cultural heritage. In the case of Sahgal and Yuval-Davis, the particular heritage is that of the European Enlightenment. As such, despite their attempts to develop a concept of fundamentalism that is able to include the Christian New Right, the Islamic Republic of Iran, the BJP and so on, Sahgal and Yuval-Davis can only produce a particular cultural understanding of fundamentalism. Their definition of fundamentalism is only made possible by accepting that the site of their interventions is a universal space – where normality reigns – and that fundamentalism marks the practices which disrupt the normal.

My rejection of the category of fundamentalism should not be read as being based on what Lawrence calls 'originist' reasons, that is the argument that a term cannot be transferred from its original context.[35] On the contrary, I think 're-contextualization' is the only viable method of carrying out intellectual inquiry.[36] The problem of fundamentalism, however, is that it is a category which can only be sustained by avoiding a radical re-contextualization. The re-contextualization that the advocates of an analytical fundamentalism seek is that of transcending the origins of the term in Protestant Christian circles. This is a rather limited re-contextualization. What is not re-contextualized is the historical site which establishes the western cultural practices as the template by which the world is described, policed and mastered.[37] The threat of fundamentalism (as a global term) is that it removes from the agenda questions of western identity, by relocating them within the religious-secular opposition. In other words, fundamentalism domesticates radical alterity by making it analogous to a more docile version of the other.

It should also be made clear that my objection is not aimed at the comparative method itself. Comparisons are only useful where similar kinds of things are being compared, and a common terrain exists for comparing them. My criticism of fundamentalism is based on the impossibility of using it as the ground upon which to carry out a meaningful comparison between, for example, the BJP, Likud, the Muslim Brotherhood, the Christian Coalition, and so on. Fundamentalism can only operate as a general category if it situates itself within the discourse of the liberal-secularist enlightenment project and considers that project to be the natural state of affairs. As we have seen, to theorize fundamentalism requires an unproblematic conception of religion and its difference from politics and truth. If one does not accept the hegemony of such a division, then the category of fundamentalism expands to include the political itself. In the end it is difficult not to agree with Nederveen Pieterse when he writes, 'the use of the term fundamentalism signals bad analysis and bad politics'.[38]

The story I want to tell cannot be told from within the demonology of fundamentalism. My concern is to try and account for the emergence of political projects which assert a Muslim subjectivity. The category of fundamentalism forces connections which, I think, are superficial or secondary and which prevent the pursuit of other more fruitful lines of enquiry. I am going to avoid using the label 'Islamic fundamentalism' for the reasons already stated. I want to preserve the specificity of the processes that I am studying from attempts to write a general theory of fundamentalism. Instead, I am going to write about Islamism. In my understanding, an Islamist is someone who places her or his Muslim identity at the centre of her or his political practice. That is, Islamists are people who use the language of Islamic metaphors to think through their political destinies, those who see in Islam their political future.[39] This should not be taken to mean that there are no shades of opinion within Islamism, that it is some kind of monolithic edifice without variation or internal differences. Islamists are no more (or less) identical in their beliefs and motives than postmodern bourgeois liberals or socialists or nationalists.

Islamism is a political discourse and, as such, is akin to other political discourses such as socialism or liberalism. While no one would question that political discourses such as socialism include many varieties and many differences, it is still possible and valid to speak of socialism; it should be similarly possible to speak of Islamism.[40] Islamism is a discourse that attempts to centre Islam within the political order. Islamism can range from the assertion of a Muslim subjectivity to a full-blooded attempt to reconstruct society on Islamic principles. This definition is similar to Oliver Roy's definition of Islamism.[41]

Roy also distinguishes between Islamists and what he calls neo-fundamentalists. Neo-fundamentalists are those whose aim is to see the establishment of an Islamic order in terms of its privatization, in contrast to Islamists who see the establishment of an Islamic order necessitating intervention in public affairs – the capture of the state.[42] Like Roy, I see Islamism as a political project but, unlike Roy, my notion of the political is not limited to projects which aim directly at seizing state power through a singular founding act (revolution). The political is the moment of the institution of the social.[43] It may involve the capture of the state apparatus by a dedicated vanguard, but it may also include a more diffused strategy of 'intellectual-moral reform' of civil society as a precursor to acquiring state power.[44] Thus, within my broad definition of Islamism as a political project there is room for very different strategies of Islamization. My concern is to examine the conditions in which the Islamization of

Muslim communities is possible. Thus, my interest is not centred on any particular strategy of Islamization or brand of Islamism. This is not because I do not recognize the considerable variations between different Islamist movements – but because my current interest is directed towards understanding how, over the last thirty years, Islam-(ism) has come to occupy an increasingly prominent place within Muslim imaginings.

Explaining 'Islamic fundamentalism'

Michael Fischer writes that during the 1930s, Muslim intellectuals and politicians could point to Islam as a force holding back the progress of their societies. In contrast, from the 1970s onwards, no politician and few intellectuals would dare do such a thing.[45] This statement neatly summarizes the kinds of changes that the discourse on Islamism has tried to explain – how is it that Islam has failed to wither away? The attempts to answer this question have resulted in immense quantities of publications,[46] the volume alone making it difficult to present an exhaustive summary. I will not attempt such a summary here, partly because much of the literature is repetitive and partly because my purpose is to configure the discursive economy by which Islamism is described.[47] To this end I focus on themes rather than the authors of this discourse. The selections I make do not depend on the extent to which they are representative of the literature (either as its best or even worst examples); my selection is motivated by a desire to demonstrate the logic of this literature in its attempt to account for Islamism. As such, this not a review of the literature nor a summary of the views of major authors who write about the subject (nor is it a general review of recent scholarship on Islamic phenomena), rather it is an attempt to outline the 'regularity in dispersion' of statements on the causes of Islamism.[48] What follows is a discussion about how narratives on the causes of Islamism have tried to account for its emergence. My aim is to show the logic of these narratives.

There has been much debate about what has caused this explosion of Islamism but it is possible to identify from the literature the following five main points. These are not mutually exclusive and most commentators combine these arguments in a variety of ways, but all are part of the discourse on contemporary Islamic resurgence.

They are the themes most commonly deployed to explain the emergence of Islamism.

Failure of nationalist secular élites[49] For Fouad Ajami this failure owes much to the manner in which the post-colonial élites aligned themselves with modernity and the West, and came to despise their own people for being backward.[50] For Fischer, this is one of the main factors behind the rise of militant Islam. Fischer argues that Islamism is a reaction to the failure of the 'naive liberalism' of the 1930s and Third World socialism in the 1960s and 1970s.[51] The emergence of Islamism is presented as a product of the inability of the secular élites, which succeeded the European colonial regimes, to meet the hopes and aspirations of their people.[52]

Lack of political participation[53] The expansion of the state, both territorially and infrastructurally, makes it difficult for population groups to escape the state.[54] When the infrastructural long arm of the post-colonial state is combined with the heavy-handed despotism of Muslim societies, the result is the erosion of civil society – that is, the authoritarian nature of post-colonial regimes resulted in all legitimate public spaces being restricted.

Michael Gilsenan gives three reasons for the authoritarianism of the post-colonial regimes: first, the personalist nature of the new regimes; second, the expansion of civilian and military disciplinary techniques which came with independence, leading to the 'systematic and unpredictable' intrusion into people's lives;[55] and third, the discrepancies between the ideologies of nationalism and legitimacy on the one hand, and the realities of social inequalities and foreign dependence on the other. A consequence of this expansive authoritarianism is that the mosque emerged as the only arena of public discourse that the state did not fully monopolize.[56]

Ajami also argues that the lack of public participation in the political process was a major factor in leading to the politicization of the mosque.[57] Theda Skocpol uses a similar argument in her study of the Iranian revolution; she emphasizes the role of the institutional networks of the Shia *Ulema* in escaping the Pahlavi dictatorship's control and thus becoming instrumental in the overthrow of the Peacock Throne.[58]

The emergence of the mosque as the only viable public space

politicizes the religious vocabulary as it is increasingly used to describe political problems. It also leads to an increase in the use of religious idioms in making political protests. The absence of democracy and the domestication of spaces where the state could not previously reach (the desert, the mountains), disrupts the previous balance between state and civil society, forcing elements to combine in their opposition to the state's expansion. This combination of elements is possible only on the basis of the widest institutional ensemble that remains semi-autonomous from the state – the mosque.

Crisis of the petty bourgeoisie[59] For Nikki Keddie, Islamism is the ideology of the petty bourgeoisie.[60] Gilsenan is another who sees the origins of Islamism in the crisis of the petty bourgeoisie.[61] The crisis of the petty bourgeoisie arises, according to Gilsenan, from the fact that independence had ambiguous consequences for the petty bourgeoisie, who had come to dominate the post-colonial state through their recruitment into the ranks of a greatly expanded administrative and coercive state apparatus.[62] However, they continued to lack access to power and wealth because of the continuing domination of the ruling élites; that is, the post-colonial mobilization of the petty bourgeoisie did not succeed in giving them power.[63] Thus, the expansion of the role of the petty bourgeoisie, and the inherent contradictions it implies, are responsible for Islamism.

Petro-dollars and uneven economic development[64] There is a very common set of arguments which hinges upon the relationship between economic processes and their political implications: economic growth and development erode traditional social bonds and engender unrealizable aspirations in emergent social groups.[65] Islamism is a reaction to the consequences of rapid economic growth. The destruction of traditional patterns of life and the uncertainty which this implies lead people to assert or reassert their traditional way of life as a way of coping with changes.

In Fischer's account it is 'the influx of rural folk into the increasingly politicised urban sub-proletariat and petit bourgeoisie' which is responsible for the rise of Islamism.[66] Discontent was articulated by the uprooted rural migrants in the language with which they were most familiar – the language of Islamic ethics. The basic argument can be summarized along the following lines: internal migration and rapid urbanization produce a large marginal population; the inadequacy of the urban infrastructure to cope with such a large influx leads to grievances caused by problems such as underemployment and exploitation. However, the deprivations due to internal migration are by no means specific to communities with large Muslim populations. What turns these internal migrants into supporters of Islamism is, the argument goes, that they come from communities heavily imbued with the values and vocabularies of 'folk Islam'.

The movement of members of rural communities from the country to the city leads to a profound change in their experiences. However, the swiftness of the movement is such that the migrants' final vocabulary is unable to adapt to the new modernized, urbanized environment in which they find themselves. They continue to rely on their final vocabulary which is heavily permeated with Islam. Thus, when they encounter grievances associated with life in the slums and shanty towns, the only mode of expression they have is the language of 'folk Islam'. Consequently, ideas such as 'corruption' and 'evil' come to account for underemployment, poor health facilities, and so on. This use of Islamic metaphors to represent their experiences leads to the politicization of Islamic metaphors. The consequence of this is Islamism.

Furthermore, the quadrupling of oil prices by OPEC increased the influence of conservative Arab/Muslim governments and helped to revive Muslim self-esteem and pride. Oil revenues allowed oil-exporting states to embark upon ambitious development projects. They also benefited poorer, more populous Muslim countries (such as Pakistan, Egypt and Bangladesh), who exported labour to the oil-rich states. The remittances of these workers provided the labour-exporting countries with a major source of foreign earnings. The Muslim oil-exporting countries used their revenues to finance Muslim institutions throughout the Muslim world. These institutes, in turn, began to articulate Islamist projects (for example, the Muslim Institute in London). However, greater integration in the world economy weakens traditional economic enterprises and makes them more vulnerable to the fluctuations of the global economy. This affects mainly those population groups which have been the main supporters of traditional religious networks and their opposition to these developments takes the form of Islamism.

Effects of cultural erosion[67]   The integration of Muslim societies into the world capitalist system, dominated by the West, led to
the weakening of 'Muslim' identities; in other words, Islamism is a
nativist response to inclusion in a western-led global system. This
argument is an almost constant refrain in both academic and journalistic accounts of Islamic fundamentalism. (This argument also carries
the greatest weight in accounts written by Islamists themselves.)[68]
Both Gilsenan (1990) and Ajami (1981) make constant references to
the way in which the erosion of cultural identities is the condition of
the possibility of Islamism. Keddie comments on the division in
Tunisia between the Francophone élite, whose lifestyle and values
are based on a western model, and the mass of Tunisians who speak
only Arabic. This, she says, is not simply a socioeconomic gap but
also a cultural one.[69] Fischer, quotes with approval, Barrington
Moore:[70]

> 20th century religious conflict and fanaticism are qualitatively different
> [writes Moore]. They resemble more closely the well known phenom-
> enon of nativism. In many parts of the world, when an established
> culture was beginning to erode, threatening some of the population,
> people have responded by reaffirming the traditional way of life with
> increasing and frantic vigour.

Fischer goes on to argue that Islamism is a reaction to cultural
erosion, manifested in what Marx called 'time-worn disguises'.[71]

These five arguments are those most often deployed to account for
the rise of Islamism.

Processes such as industrialization, urbanization, expansion of
bureaucratic structures and urban population growth cannot tell us
how Islamism emerges. Even something like the failure of the
nationalist regimes does not explain why Islamism, and not some
other political formation, has been able to challenge the post-colonial
order. Why is it that the strains in the current hegemonic order in
the Muslim world lead to the emergence of Islamism, rather than as
elsewhere in the world, where liberalism (of a kind) has often emerged
from the debris of the *anciens régimes*? How do the upheavals associated with integration into the world economy, etc. actually translate
into specifically Islamist projects? What is it that these crises in the
life of Muslim communities actually do?

Narrating Islamism and the crisis of
the political order

Most attempts to explain the rise of Islamism begin with a general process which acts as a fuse to a powder-keg – the powder-keg being some form of Muslim society, the resulting explosion being Islamism. The cause of Islamism is either an external force acting upon some notion of a significant Islamic presence, or Islamism is seen to be a superstructural response to structural crisis. In either case, Islamism is inscribed in the nature of the crisis. These narratives on the causes of 'Islamic fundamentalism' assume that it is possible to understand what emerges from a crisis by understanding the nature of the crisis itself. This is an assumption that I want to test. By questioning the link between the nature of crisis and the outcome of a crisis, I do not propose a 'randomization' of politics,[72] but neither do I subscribe to the view that the nature of a crisis determines political outcomes a priori.

Any social order will include practices that are uncontested and institutionalized. For example, in the North Atlantic plutocracies the distinction between citizens and non-citizens is in many aspects hierarchically arranged; equality is in many cases restricted to citizens. This distinction, however, is taken for granted.[73] This situation corresponds to what Husserl would call sedimentation: that is, the routinization of previous innovative measures.[74] Sedimentation refers to the way in which political issues become part of everyday life, for example the belief that the world is round no longer arouses much political strife – it is a belief that has become sedimented. Sedimentation is contrasted with reactivation. Reactivation refers to the moment of the questioning of sedimentation: the realization of the contingency of what we consider to be 'natural'.[75]

Of course, no network of social relations can be totalized in the form of a structure. The lack of foundations involves the impossibility of closure. This incompleteness will take diverse forms: the interruption of meaning, the endless possibilities of connotation via intertextuality and overdetermination, and ultimately the (non-)presence of something which cannot be said or represented within that structure and which will always come back to haunt it.[76] Society, then, is an attempt to totalize by structuring as many social relations as possible. This structuring or sedimentation is provided by a hegemonic discourse which sutures together the field of discursivity.[77]

Crisis describes the situation in which sedimented relations and practices become unsettled: when the unity of a certain field of discursivity is disarticulated. This leads to the disruption of routinization. As the space of sedimented social relations shrinks, the terrain of undecidability expands.[78] That is, in terrain in which the dislocation of structure introduces a radical ambiguity of identity (identity here refers not only to subjectivity but to all discursive entities), the resolution of a crisis cannot be deduced from the terms of the crisis, since the expansion of undecidability precludes the possibility of deriving outcomes from that crisis. By definition, one cannot predict the undecidable.

There are three possibilities regarding the outcome of any crisis. The first option is that, as predictability and regularity are effects of routinization, the disruption of routine – that is crisis – will inevitably mean the space available for algorithmic solutions is reduced. Therefore, it is only possible to maintain that the crisis will determine its own outcomes if one posits some 'meta-structure' – an overriding construct which encapsulates the crisis within its interior. In this way, the moment of crisis is not a dislocation of a structure but rather it is inscribed in the structure. This is the preferred route of many economistic accounts, which relocate the moment of crisis from one plane (usually the political) to another more fundamental level which is immune to the dislocation. At this deeper level, the 'crisis' is not a disruption of a routine but rather the working out of the logic of the system. This means that there is no crisis, no dislocation, since the 'crisis' is part of the structure which is still operating. As there is no crisis, outcomes are not derived from the crisis but from the routine operations of the 'meta-structure'.[79]

The second possibility would be one in which a crisis is seen as characterized by a struggle for hegemony by various forces. It could be argued that one could determine the outcome of the struggle by calculating the balance of forces, with the greater force having a higher probability of success than the lesser force. In this account it appears that the basic difficulty is an empirical one of assessing accurately the balance of forces. This, however, is not the only difficulty. At a theoretical level – unless one assumes the struggling forces are essentialist – the struggle will modify their identities, in which case, the identity of the successful force will have been transformed during the struggle to establish its hegemony. The

transformations could not be foretold, since they are the product of
the strategies produced in the struggle for power. Again, the outcome
of crisis cannot be derived from crisis.

The third option is that even calculations of the balance of forces
are not possible, since the de-sedimentation is such that undecidability occupies not only the act of calculating, but the very
constitution of what a 'force' is or what 'balancing' would be. For
example, on the eve of the Iranian revolution there was a general
consensus about what a revolution was: what and who were the
main participants, what weight should be attached to the various
forces in play, and so on. Fred Halliday, writing at the time, system-
atically listed a number of future options for Iran. These included
continued Pahlavi rule, a relative liberalization of the Pahlavi mon-
archy, a military dictatorship, a 'bourgeois democracy', and even a
slim possibility of a socialist alternative.[80] What he excluded was the
possibility of an Islamic republic. Halliday's omission is not a matter
of an individual error of judgement – he is not the only person who
failed to note the possibility of an Islamic republic being the outcome
of the crisis of the Pahlavi state[81] – rather the omission was due to
the crisis of the Pahlavi state being such that it de-sedimented even
the pattern of previous Third World revolutions in many important
ways: for example the absence of massive peasant mobilization, the
limited role of leftist ideology, the general absence of a large-scale
and protracted struggle and so on.[82] Again the possibility of de-
sedimentation is such that undecidability expands into the logic of
the crisis, thus making it impossible to derive the nature of the
crisis.

The de-sedimentation of aspects of Muslim communities cannot
tell us why Islamism has emerged. Descriptions of rural–urban migration, rapid and uneven economic development, etc. are more usefully
read as showing some of the reasons for the dislocation of the
political order in the Muslim world. This dislocation of the political
order cannot explain why Islamists have become a significant political
force. Dislocation triggers a struggle: the struggle to reorganize the
field and master that discontinuity.[83] The outcome of the struggle
cannot be settled in advance; it is an open-ended process until a new
hegemonic order is inaugurated. The new order, however, will mask
the contingency of its inscription and will construct itself – retroactively – as a necessary outcome of the crisis. It cannot be deduced

from a regularity; it is an act whereby the new is forced into existence. It implies discontinuity, not regularity.[84]

The de-sedimentation of the political order suggests a situation similar to Gramsci's notion of a crisis of authority.[85] Gramsci defines this as the condition in which:

> the ruling class has lost its consensus, i.e. it is no longer 'leading' but only 'dominant', exercising coercive force alone; this means precisely that the great masses have become detached from their traditional ideologies, and no longer believe what they used to believe previously, etc.[86]

Although I have some theoretical doubts about the traces of classism and economism in Gramsci's definition,[87] I think it is a helpful way of understanding the situation which confronts the rulers of the Muslim world. The various processes associated with urban–rural migration, economic globalization, etc. widen the scope of the un-decidable at the expense of the structural. These processes are in part responsible for the de-sedimentation of the 'ideological cement' that held the post-colonial Muslim communities together, but they do not explain the emergence of Islamism – such processes cannot account for the historical specificity of Islamism.[88] While these nar-ratives help to provide useful descriptions of this crisis they do not provide us with a persuasive account of how the crisis of the political order explains the appearance of Islamism. To do that we need to be able to theorize the 'ideological cement' or hegemonic discourse that constitutes the current political order in the Muslim world.

I think that it is more useful to read the explanations of Islamism as providing a set of empirical descriptions of what is happening to the current political order in Muslim communities. Why do these crises lead to Islamism and not to something like liberalism or social-ism? It is one thing to accept and enumerate a series of structural problems within Muslim societies but it requires that another step be taken to explain why these problems meet their response in the form of Islamism.

Notes

1. Esposito, 1992, pp. 40–41.
2. Vatikiotis, pp. 168–70, in Cudsi and Dessouki, 1981.
3. Fischer, 1982, p. 101. These events marked the beginning of what Fischer

is careful to remind us is the 'fifteenth century of the Islamic era'. What unifies the various elements in this list is that they seem to be inspired by Islamic funda-mentalism – or as Fischer writes, 'class basis and their traditionalising but, non-traditional, ideologies'.

4. Conversely, examples of non-fundamentalist forces are used to illustrate the decline of Islamic fundamentalism. For an example of this see Babeair, 1990.

5. For example, even though an organization like Women Against Funda-mentalism is committed to fighting all kinds of fundamentalism, and is careful not to indulge in Islamophobia, its formation was triggered by the Rushdie affair. That is, it was an episode closely identified with Islamic fundamentalism which led to the creation of an anti-fundamentalist campaigning organization.

6. The reason for selecting these writers is not because they are necessarily representative of attempts to theorize fundamentalism (though the argument could be made that their conceptualization of fundamentalism shares many features with other such attempts), nor because I think their account is paradigmatic, but rather because their work makes clear the conditions of its discursive possibility.

7. For example, Marty and Appleby's (1991) multi-volume fundamentalism project takes a similar approach, as does Bruce Lawrence, 1995.

8. Sahgal and Yuval-Davis, 1992, pp. 3–5.

9. Ibid., p. 8.

10. Spelman, 1990, p. 158.

11. Ibid., pp. 133–59.

12. See Glavanis and Ray (forthcoming). They demonstrate the systematic way in which western feminism has uncritically followed orientalist and racist accounts of Muslim women. They have shown how Sahgal and Yuval-Davis are not im-mune from western feminism's 'selective' blindness in regard to matters Islamic.

13. Ibid.

14. Ibid.

15. L. Ahmed, 1992, pp. 164–8.

16. The notion of governmentality used here is borrowed from the work of Foucault. Foucault made a distinction between the Machiavellian art of govern-ment and the modern science of government. The former was mainly concerned with ways in which the prince could hold on to his principality. The latter refers to the way in which an ensemble of institutions and procedures allow the exercise of power over the population as a whole. This complex regime is no longer motivated by a relatively simple desire to maintain the prince; it is rather a logic that sets out to enframe and regulate all aspects of social life. See Foucault in Burchell et al., 1991, pp. 87–104.

17. See Spelman (1990, pp. 160–86), who highlights the way in which certain types of women (and their experiences) are considered 'unessential' to feminism.

18. Sahgal and Yuval-Davis, 1992, p. 4.

19. Ibid., p. 5.

20. See for example, Shariati, 1979, pp. 97–127; Abrahamian, 1992, pp. 103–5.

21. The position of the Shia *ulema* is slightly different, though it has to be noted that the senior *ulema* in Iran have, on the whole, remained distant from the political process in Iran. As a consequence, on the death of Imam Khomeini, a fairly junior ayatollah had to be made *Vilayat-i-faqih*.

22. Abrahamian, 1993, p. 15.

23. Khomeini, 1988.

24. Foucault, 1980, p. 133.

25. One of the reasons Norman Geras gives for rejecting anti-foundationalism is that it makes it impossible to use objective criteria to check excesses of power. Geras, 1995, pp. 111–12.

26. Akhtar, 1989.

27. See Rorty, 1989, p. 75.

28. Vattimo, in Vattimo and Rovatti, 1990, pp. 31–6.

29. As Glavanis notes, Sahgal and Yuval-Davis's observations on Islamic phenomena (in particular) are heavily indebted to orientalism and neo-orientalism. Glavanis, 1995.

30. Lewis, 1993, p. 4.

31. Ibid. pp. 28–9.

32. Asad, 1993, pp. 27–30.

33. It should be noted this is very partial reading of western Christianity; there are many examples when this idealized division between church and state was absent even in western Christendom.

34. Sahgal and Yuval-Davis, 1992, p. 7.

35. Lawrence, 1995, pp. 91–5.

36. See Rorty, 1991a, pp. 93–110, for an elaboration of this idea of 're-contextualization as inquiry'.

37. Asad, 1993, p. 200.

38. Pieterse, 1994, p. 5.

39. Obviously there is a relationship between Islam and Islamism, but what that relationship is cannot be discovered by reference to an Islamic essence. In the subsequent chapters I will discuss this relationship.

40. This, however, is more difficult since too often any attempt to speak about Islamism leads to charges of essentialism – no doubt an over-hasty reaction to Said's critique of orientalism.

41. Roy, 1994, p. 24.

42. Ibid.

43. Laclau, 1990, p. 31.

44. It should be clear that I assume that Muslims have civil societies – I am aware that this view would not necessarily find general acceptance.

45. Fischer, 1982, p. 102.

46. It is estimated that by the mid-1980s something like two hundred books were being published in English, per year, on topics relating to Islamic fundamentalism. See Haddad et al., 1991, p. ix.

47. The quality of this literature is subject to much criticism: see Said, 1981, pp. 12–26; Al-Azmeh, 1993, p. 103; Haddad et al., 1991, pp. ix–x.

48. Foucault, 1986.

49. Arguments which point to the failure of nationalism as a cause of Islamic fundamentalism are widespread; for some examples see Ajami, 1981, pp. 15, 140–41, 171; Keddie in Halliday and Alawi, 1988, p. 15; Taylor, 1988; Amin, 1989, pp. 131 and 135.

50. Ajami, 1981, p. 171.

51. Fischer, 1982, p. 102.

52. Examples illustrating this point can be found in Ajami, 1981, pp. 15, 140–41, 171; Fischer, 1982, p. 101; Keddie, in Halliday and Alawi, 1988, p. 15.

53. Versions of this argument can be found in Sivan, 1985, p. 83; Ayubi, 1991, pp. 218–19; Gilsenan, 1990, pp. 261–3.

54. See Mann, 1986, pp. 477–83, for a detailed analysis of infrastructures of power.

55. For an extreme example of this phenomenon see Khalil's chilling description of the Baathist state in Iraq: Khalil, 1989, pp. 46–72.

56. Gilsenan, 1990, pp. 261–3.

57. Ajami, 1981, p. 171; Sivan, 1985, p. 83.

58. Skocpol, 1982, p. 275.

59. The main sources for this set of arguments are Keddie, in Halliday and Alavi, 1988, p.14; Gilsenan, 1990, pp. 261–3; Ayubi, 1991, 215–16; Fischer, 1982, *passim*.

60. Keddie, in Halliday and Alawi, 1988, p. 14. But she reassures us that the 'petty bourgeoisie ... is notorious for switching ideologies', the implication being that Islamism is possibly only temporary.

61. Gilsenan, 1990, p. 261.

62. Ibid., p. 262.

63. Ibid., p. 263.

64. Examples of the influence of petro-dollars in generating Islamic fundamentalism can be found in Hunter, 1988, pp. xii–xiii; Al-Azmeh, 1993, pp. 23 and 32. For problems associated with integrating into the world capitalist economy, see Vatikiotis, in Cudsi and Dessouki, 1981, p. 193; Wessels, 1989.

65. See for example Howe, 1992.

66. Fischer, 1982, p. 102.

67. This set of arguments can be found in Ayubi, 1991, pp. 217–20; Ajami, 1981, pp. 50–75; Amin, 1989, pp. 79–123; Wessels, 1989.

68. See J. Ahmad, 1984. Ahmad provides an account of Iran's cultural dependency on the West during the Pahlavi, which was very influential among radical Iranians.

69. Keddie, in Halliday and Alawi, 1988, p. 20.

70. Fischer, 1982, p. 101.

71. Ibid.

72. This is Wood's conclusion as to what are the consequences of anti-foundationalist political theory. See Wood, 1986, especially pp. 76–89.

73. For example Fischer (1983, p. 151; 1990, p. 476) is able to criticize the treatment of minorities within Islamic discourse, pointing to the manner in which minorities are made subordinate to Muslims – an implicit contrast being drawn with the equality of citizens which is guaranteed by the North Atlantic plutocracies. This, of course, takes no account of the way in North Atlantic plutocracies claims of 'equality of all citizens before the law' underpin discrimination against those who are considered to be non-citizens (guestworkers, residents, immigrants, etc.).

74. Husserl, 1970, p. 269–99.

75. Laclau (1990, pp. 33–5) gives these Husserlian categories a political twist: reactivation is synonymous with the political and sedimentation is analogous to the social.

76. On intertextuality, see Kristeva, 1984. On overdetermination, see Freud's 'multiple determinations', 1900, 4, p. 306 or 'superimposed layers of meaning', 1900, 4, p. 219.

77. Laclau and Mouffe, 1985, pp. 93–148.

78. The notion of undecidability draws on the work of Derrida (1978) and its use within political contexts by Laclau, 1990.

79. The possibility of a 'meta-structure' that is immune to dislocation has been thoroughly criticized in recent political theory, see Bowles and Gintis, 1987, pp. 71–9; Laclau and Mouffe, 1985, pp. 75–92.

80. Halliday, 1978, pp. 299–309.

81. See Halliday's reflections on his book and the Iranian revolution (1987, pp. 29–39).

82. Burke III and Lapidus, 1988, p. 32.

83. The category of 'dislocation' used here draws on the work of Jacques Derrida, especially his essay 'Sign, Structure, Play' in *Writing and Difference*. This notion has been given a more political twist by Laclau. See Derrida, 1978; Laclau, 1990, pp. 43–60.

84. Lefort, 1986, p. 202.

85. See also Jessop, 1985, pp. 90–93. Jessop provides a valuable summary of Poulantzas's classification of political and economic crisis. While I have a number of reservations regarding the underlying essentialism of Poulantzas's categories, I think they provide convenient shorthand descriptions of complex processes.

86. Gramsci, 1971, pp. 275–6.

87. For an analysis of the economism at the heart of Gramsci's thought, see Laclau and Mouffe, 1985, pp. 69, 85 and 86–7.

88. Gulalp, 1992, p. 15.

2. Thinking Islamism, (re-)thinking Islam

One way of describing the discourse on 'Islamic fundamentalism' is to call it 'orientalism'. Until Edward Said's pioneering critique, orientalism was simply an academic label describing disciplines that studied 'Eastern' societies, histories and languages.[1] Since then, it has come to denote an exercise in power/knowledge by which the 'non-western' world is domesticated. The debate generated by Said's critique raises several important theoretical points regarding the possibility or desirability of an epistemology that is aware of its site of enunciation. For example, Said argues that the construction of fundamentalism as a key term to analyse political conflicts is derived from the concerns of 'intellectual factories in metropolitan centres like Washington and London'.[2] This allows the 'abnormality and extremism' of fundamentalism to be contrasted with the moderation and reasonableness of western hegemony.[3] As we saw in Chapter 1, attempts to articulate fundamentalism are exercises in normalizing and perpetuating the hegemony of a particular cultural formation. At the heart of this debate about self-reflexive epistemology (that is, an epistemology that does not start by assuming its uncontested universalism) is the question of the status of Islam. Is orientalism able to provide adequate descriptions of Islam?

Said, by combining Foucault's ideas on discursive formations[4] with Gramsci's thoughts on hegemony, built up a powerful critique which questioned the validity of orientalism.[5] Said rejected orientalism's claims to be a neutral scholarly activity that studied the East. He contended that orientalism was made possible by the imperialist expansion into the Muslim world, and, simultaneously, it made such an expansion possible. Thus, the practice of orientalism was inexorably bound up with imperialist domination over large parts of the Muslim world.[6]

Specifically, Said argued that orientalism provides accounts of Islam (and the Orient) which are organized around four main themes: first, there is an 'absolute and systemic difference' between the West and the Orient.[7] Secondly, the representations of the Orient are based on textual exegesis rather than 'modern Oriental realities'.[8] Thirdly, the Orient is unchanging, uniform and incapable of describing itself.[9] Fourthly, the Orient is to be feared or to be mastered.[10] Orientalism operates within several theoretical narratives: it is a theory of despotic power, of social change, of exoticism and of rationality.[11] All these narratives rest upon the assumption that Islam is ontologically distinct from the West. The orientalist approach to Islam can be summarized as 'essentialist, empiricist and historicist';[12] it impoverishes the rich diversity of Islam by producing an essential-izing caricature.

Said's critique flirts with two different forms. In one form it sees the orientalist enterprise from the perspective of a sociology of knowledge: that is, the critique tries to show how western scholarship was subverted by its complicity with western imperialism, and how the reality of the Orient was distorted by orientalism. This is what I call 'weak orientalism'. The best example of this is provided by Said in *Covering Islam* (1981), the telling subtitle of which is *How the Media and the Experts Determine How We See the Rest of the World*.

In its 'weak' version, orientalism remains a discourse of power/knowledge informed by the historically specific conditions of European global expansion. Though Said is aware that there are older precedents which characterized Europe's relations with the 'other' (e.g. Ancient Greeks, the Crusades), he is able nevertheless to date the beginning of orientalism as coinciding with the Napoleonic invasion of Egypt. Although he is equally aware that the question of orientalism raises more general issues about the representation of the other, he is unable theoretically to ground this. As a result, Said's reading of orientalism as an act of violence is limited. For him, the violence of orientalism comes from the power it exercises over 'Islam' – that is, violence is political and not 'philosophical'. In this version, orientalism remains a discursive possibility of imperialism.

The other form Said's critique takes is that of theorizing the orientalist enterprise, not in terms of its validity but with regard to how orientalism actually constitutes the Orient. This is what I call 'strong orientalism'. In this discourse–theoretical approach, the problem with orientalism is not just that it distorts the 'real' Orient but that the Orient itself becomes a creation of orientalism. 'Strong orientalism' is not as developed as 'weak orientalism'. Largely because Said's relative scepticism about Derrida's enterprise prevents him from locating the violence of orientalism – not just in the relations of power, but in the logic of western metaphysics. Said interprets the confrontation between Foucault and Derrida as a struggle about what the text is. According to Said, Derrida sees the text 'as a praxis on whose surfaces and in whose interstices a universal grammatological problematic is enacted'; whereas for Foucault, the text's existence is due to a 'highly rarefied and differentiated historical power associated not with the univocal authority of the author, but with a discourse constituting author, text and subject which gives them a very precise intelligibility and effectiveness'.[13] It is easy to understand why Said should side with Foucault, since his critique of orientalism rests on trying to historicize and implicate orientalists, colonial institutions and the Orient in relations of power/knowledge. However, his hasty (but qualified) dismissal means that he is unable to use the tools developed by Derrida to theorize more rigorously the possibility of 'strong orientalism'.

An indication of some possibilities of 'strong orientalism' is pro-vided by Bryan Turner's reading of orientalism. While Turner agrees with Said that orientalism constructs itself by a number of binary oppositions, he is keen to emphasize the way in which Islam is deployed as a counterfactual possibility. That is, the study of Islam emerges as a contrast to Christendom/the West/modernity. Thus, it is a means of establishing and reinforcing the identity of the West. Orientalism is an attempt to write the history of the West through the history of the 'other'. Orientalist narratives about the 'Orient' function as a supplement to the origin of the West.[14]

For Turner, orientalist narratives hinge upon a bifurcation between the West and Islam. The practice of orientalism established a set of binary oppositions in which the plentitude of the West was contrasted with the lack of the Orient: so that the West had rationality, the Orient was irrational; the West had tolerance, the Orient was fan-atical; the West was progressive, the Orient was traditional; and so on. Islam is consistently identified with the negative and antithetical terms. The similarities between Turner's description of orientalist discourses and Derrida's description of western metaphysics are striking. Derrida characterizes western metaphysics as consisting of a 'violent hierarchy' of binary opposition in which one term is privileged over the other (the pure over the impure; the rational over the irrational; presence over absence, etc.). The subordinate terms are guarantees of the existence of hierarchy; they are outside the system but, none the less, the condition of its very possibility. What is involved in orientalist discourse is the spatial fixing of the metaphysics of presence. The power of 'strong orientalism' does not just come from its attachment to imperial networks of control, it also comes from the organization and sedimentation of particular grand narratives which tell the history of the West.

'Strong orientalism' is the reason why attempts to read Said's *Orientalism* as simply a sociology of knowledge flounder.[15] Attempts to reduce the critique of orientalism to the problems of scholarship and other textual problems is completely inadequate. What is at stake is not whether particular scholars are bad or dishonest, it is not a question of bias; the problem of orientalism is the problem of what space exists for the 'other'. Said's attempt to account for orientalism outside the context of imperialism becomes strained because, by treating orientalism as power over the production of texts, Said has difficulty in explaining how orientalism continues to function outside those particular historical power structures which he examines in *Orientalism* – he has difficulties in coming to terms with the full implications of the constitutive role of orientalism.

Many of Said's critics find it difficult to understand his insistence that there is an equation between power and knowledge. They prefer instead to discuss Said's arguments (regarding how knowledge about the Orient is produced and distributed) without considering what kinds of power structures enable such production and distribution.[16] Thus, the Middle Eastern scholars who have responded to Said's critique have tended to focus on its 'weak orientalism' form. This, as Mani and Frankenberg point out, has the effect of transforming political questions into textual problems.[17] For example, it is alleged that Said seems to confuse the generic boundaries by including political and administrative text, diaries and travelogues within his category of orientalist writing. This lack of respect for genres produces a critique which is undifferentiated.[18] There are also attempts to assert that the descriptions of orientalism are empirically valid, that there is a 'real Orient' which corresponds, to some degree, to the descriptions of the orientalists.[19] There are attempts to show that the 'bias' that Said finds in orientalism is also found in the representation of the 'other' in all societies[20] – that his critique is itself reductionist, historicist and ultimately based on an essential dichotomy between the Occident and the Orient which characterizes orientalism.[21]

These clusters of criticisms are not external to Said's text, or merely the product of antagonistic readings; they emerge from the blank spaces and ambiguities within Said's text. In particular, Said himself is not sure how to respond to the challenge of 'strong orientalism'. This explains the curious reticence about the fate of Islam after *Orientalism*. If Islam is constituted by orientalism, what happens when orientalism dissolves? What, if any, kind of Islam will remain? Said's main concerns are with the struggle against western intellectual and cultural imperialism. He illustrates the hostility of orientalism to Islam, his 'counter-writing' is directed towards negating orientalism, but 'the negation of Orientalism is not the affirmation of Islam'.[22] This has the effect of turning Said's negation of orientalism into a negation of Islam itself.[23] There is nothing to suggest that he believes that Islam can exist outside the discourse of orientalism. As Binder notes, this is the *aporia* which emerges from Said's critique, beyond which it cannot go.[24] This paradox, by which the dissolution of orientalism leads not to a 'liberating interpretation of Islam' but to its dissolution, calls into question the limit of Said's text. Is it really possible for *Orientalism* to go beyond orientalism? For Said, to deny Islam as a meaningful entity would be to threaten his project: how can there be a 'counter-writing' when that which you counter does not exist?

Said seems to sense the ambiguity of his position; he cannot really speak for the subjects of orientalism, since orientalism reduces its subjects to a silence. For Said to speak he has to de-orientalize himself, but this means that Said has to find another place from which to speak. Said seems to understand that orientalism totally constitutes Islam, thus if he starts to speak about Islam, he will be reincorporated into orientalism. Therefore he remains silent regarding the possibility of an Islam outside the field of orientalism.[25] It is my intention to show that it is this impasse which has produced anti-orientalism.

Anti-orientalism and Islam

The implication of Said's argument for the study of Islamism is that there is no correspondence between the orientalist articulation of Islam and the diversity of the world of Islam.[26] Said's contention is that Islamism is neither homogenous nor monolithic in the way that it is represented by academic and popular mediums. Said argues, then, that there are different tendencies and varieties of Islam and Islamism. He writes:

> Thus far from being a coherent movement, the 'return to Islam' embodies a number of political actualities. For the United States it represents an image of disruption to be resisted at some times, encouraged at others. We speak of the anticommunist Saudi Muslims, of the valiant Muslim rebels of Afghanistan, of 'reasonable' Muslims like Sadat, the Saudi royal family and Zia al-Haqq. Yet we also rail at Khomeini's Islamic militants and Qaddafi's Islamic 'Third Way', and by our morbid fascination with 'Islamic punishment' (as administered by Khalkali) we paradoxically strengthen its power as an authority-maintaining device. In Egypt the Muslim brotherhood, in Saudi Arabia the Muslim militants who took the Medina mosque, in Syria the Islamic Brotherhoods and Vanguards who oppose the Baath regime, in Iran the Islamic Mujahideen, as well as the Fedayeen and the liberals: these make up a small part of what is an adversal current though we know very little about it. In addition, the various Muslim nationalities whose identities have been blocked in various post-colonial states clamour for *their* Islam. And beneath all this – in madrasas, mosques, clubs, brotherhoods, guilds, parties, universities, movements, villages and urban centres all through the Islamic world – surge still more varieties of Islam, many of them claiming to guide their members back to the 'true' Islam.[27]

Thus, Said argues that the term 'Islam' has been overused and is an 'unreliable index' of the phenomena that we are trying to comprehend.[28] According to Said the polysemic nature of Islam demonstrates the inadequacy of orientalist descriptions and raises serious questions as to the usefulness of Islam for accounting for recent developments in the Muslim world.[29]

Said's critique has gained some influence in the study of Islamic phenomena, and has been instrumental in weakening the grip of classical orientalism on the study of Islam and the Orient.[30] His reticence about an alternative to orientalism has led a number of writers to formulate an alternative. There has been an attempt to use other theoretical matrices to analyse Islamic societies and cultures which focus mainly on the 'material', socioeconomic forces at work.[31] These theoretical interventions have, on the whole, tended to de-emphasize the concerns of the traditional orientalists on the signifi-cance of Islam. As a result, the role of Islam has been dismissed as simple nominalism.

The anti-orientalists, noting that Islam is empirically diverse and noting that Said's critique concentrates on castigating orientalism for its monolithic caricature of Islamic phenomena, have produced a theorization of Islam which seemingly rejects essentialism. That is, they have produced an account in which Islam is not reducible to eternal fixed substantive properties which define its 'whatness'.[32] This turn towards an anti-essentialist and anti-orientalist understanding of Islam finds its most radical statement in Hamid El-Zien.[33] El-Zien proceeds with a review of various anthropological studies which aim to uncover the 'real Islam'. He focuses on five studies which he uses to represent various positions within anthropology.[34] However, El-Zein concludes that the diversity of practices relating to Islam, as revealed in these studies, challenges the assumption that there is a unity of religious meaning. If Islam is constructed by so many different discourses, can it still be Islam? This ability of Islam to be used in a variety of contexts leads El-Zien to the conclusion that there is no such thing as Islam, but that there are only Islams. Therefore, it is not possible to argue that 'a single true Islam' exists. Thus, El-Zein claims that 'Islam', as a concept, is not sustainable, since the idea of 'Islam' presumes a positive content immune to local articulations.[35] As he declares:

> neither Islam nor the notion of religion exist as a fixed and autonom-ous form referring to a positive content which can be reduced to universal and unchanging characteristics. Religion becomes an arbi-trary category which as a unified and bounded form has no necessary existence. 'Islam' as an analytical category dissolves as well.[36]

This dissolution of Islam as an analytical category is the hallmark of the anti-orientalist approach. The problem with El-Zien's account is that he believes by demonstrating the multiplicity of the uses of Islam he can refute the orientalist idea that Islam is one entity, and that by showing the great variety of Islamic practices he is making an argument against essentialism. Pluralization is not a safeguard against essentialism.[37] El-Zein rejects the totality of Islam in favour of its local articulations. Consequently, anti-orientalists mark not so much a break from orientalism, as its reversal – a reversal centred around the role of Islam. Whereas Islam occupies the core of the orientalist explanations of Muslim societies, in anti-orientalist narratives Islam is decentred and dispersed. In orientalism we encounter a reduction of the parts to the whole (local phenomena are explained by reference to the essence of Islam), while in anti-orientalism there is reduction of the whole to its constituent parts (Islam is disseminated in local events). The space left vacant by the dissolution of Islam as a serious concept is occupied by a series of 'little Islams' (that is, local articulations of Islamic practices). The problem of identifying these 'little Islams' is conveniently displaced to other categories and it is possible to identify two main categories to which the role of Islam is displaced in anti-orientalist discourse.

Islam as ethnicity 'Islamic' identity is located in ethnic solidarities and conflicts. Islam is seen as an ethnic marker – a mark on an already pre-existing ethnic identity.[38] There are two problems here. First, Islam is not a marker of all ethnic identities but only those found in certain contexts. If Islam is not a marker of all ethnic identities, then it is an addition to ethnicity. The nature of the link between the ethnic identities and their Islamic mark is unclear and it is not explained why such an addition is necessary – unless, of course, the ethnic identities are themselves not fully complete. But if this is the case, how can Islam be a mere addition if its presence is necessary to complete an ethnic identity?[39] Second, beyond discourses of biological determinism or nationalist absolutism, it is difficult to understand a priori the primacy of ethnic identities. Ethnic identities are as socially constructed as other forms of identification.[40] The idea that Muslim identity is more artificial than an ethnic identity cannot simply be assumed by examining the nature of these identifications. For example, in the Bosnian conflict Muslim came to denote a community equivalent to Serbs and Croats.[41] In other words, being a Muslim meant being part of a distinct community; what was distinctive about the community was not its ethnicity but its Muslimness. In this sense, the ethnic dimension was secondary.

Islam as ideology   Islam is defined as a system of beliefs which, like any system of belief, in the final analysis is a reflection of socioeconomic processes and struggles. For example, Fischer is convinced that ideologies are covers for deeper structural interests.[42] Here the role of Islam is inserted into a theoretical framework dominated by the opposition between idealism and materialism, in which the material sphere is primary.[43] By regarding ideology and society as two distinct spheres whose relationship is one of mere exteriority (a reflective link between two self constituted unities), this narrative seeks to displace Islam to the field of representation of real subjects (for example classes). The role of Islam is strictly secondary and mystifying. Islam is seen as a mere vocabulary through which legitimacy and representation are mediated. However, even if we consider Islam as a vocabulary, it cannot be simply a vehicle through which a set of secular demands are expressed; it is also the condition of possibility by which a set of demands can be constructed. Vocabularies are not only expressive but also constitutive. The 'material' realm is not just 'expressed' by a certain vocabulary, rather, the representation itself is constitutive of the identity of that object. 'Reality' ('real' subjects or objects) is external to the representation, and the use of a particular vocabulary has a direct bearing on the identities of that 'reality'.[44] This means that Islam is not just the way in which deep structural interests are masked, it is also the means by which interests and identities are formed.

These attempts to account for Islam rest upon the displacement of what is to be explained. What unites these two approaches is their attempt to locate Islam in the contemporary world but, at the same time, displace it to the terrain of surface effects, where various signifieds (ethnicity, culture, class, etc.) bear the burden of explanation. What anti-orientalism produces is a series of 'little Islams' reflecting the various economic, ethnic and social factors of the variety of Muslim communities. What remains to be devised is an account of Islam not reducible to these 'little Islams'.

Said's critique apparently leaves only two options open for the study of Islamic phenomena: either one ignores Said's critique and reasserts the orientalist orthodoxy, or one replaces it with anti-orientalism. Either we follow classical orientalism and assume there is an entity called Islam, so there is no need to worry about the object of our analysis and we can consider Islamism to be simply a manifestation of Islam. Or we can follow the anti-orientalists and assume that the category of Islam is largely irrelevant for the understanding of Islamism.[45]

Anti-orientalists present an approach to the study of 'Islamic phenomena' which emphasizes the role of the political economy. In their framework Islam plays a variety of roles, depending on what socioeconomic context it is inserted into. Their structuralist (economistic) perspective did not allow them to elaborate on the significance of nominal entities, other than as a form of ideologism. Anti-orientalists, by treating Islam as a nominal entity, tended to dismiss its importance. For them, Islam is nothing more than a label and has no importance in itself; any significance it may have comes from the contents that are attached to that label.[46] As such, an anti-orientalist framework is unable to provide a viable alternative for conceptualizing Islam. Islam, however, matters. Even anti-orientalist accounts, which are openly dismissive of its importance, and point to its instrumental use as means of supporting or opposing certain cultural and political positions, spend considerable energies delineating its functions.[47] The question arises, however, if Islam is purely a secondary element, why does it play the role of articulating social/political projects. Enumerating the variety of functions of Islam does not answer the question of why it is that its name is evoked. For anti-orientalists its importance is due merely to its use as a source of symbolic authority and validation – in other words its instrumentality. They, for the most part, do not enquire why it is that Islam is being used in this way.

Islam matters. Therefore, it needs to be theorized. It matters, but not because of the reasons the orientalists give. The anti-orientalists are right to point out the problems of the orientalist construction of Islam and are right to point to the polysemy of Islam. However, despite its polysemy, it retains its singularity. The question remains: why is it that it is the name of Islam, rather than another name, that has become so central in Muslim politics? It is only by theorizing the signifier 'Islam' that one can hope to understand current attempts at Islamization. The possibility of an alternative to the anti-orientalist view is provided by the work of Slavoj Zizek.[48]

The matter of Islam

An anti-foundationalist approach to the relationship between Islam and Islamism would focus on the way in which Islam is deployed in the discourse of Islamism. We have seen that within orientalist discourse Islam is considered to denote a cluster of attributes. For anti-orientalists there is no such thing as Islam, but only the contextual application of the term to denote an ever-changing list of practices. What I want to do is to start with the anti-orientalist description of Islam as a nominal element, and extend that analysis as a way of refining the concepts by which we could identify a discursive object like Islam.

The starting point of an analysis of the political role of Islam must be Saussurean linguistics. The distinction that Saussure made between a signifier and a signified suggests the idea that a sign is a pure metaphor – that is, a sign without a concept is a theoretical impossibility. In Saussurean linguistics the distinction between the acoustic image (signifier) and concept (signified) is based on the idea that a pattern of sound refers to something else (that is, it has meaning because a signifier signifies – is related to a signified). If we say that a signifier has no fixed content (that is, it does not have a signified), we are actually saying that it is an acoustic image without meaning (that is, an acoustic image without any concept). A pattern of sound without a concept (without meaning) would be merely noise.[49] Islam is not noise; it may have many signifieds but it is never without a signified.

The possibilities of Saussurean linguistics were extended by Roland Barthes. In his earlier work, when he was dreaming the dream of semiology, Barthes examined the equivocal nature of the signifier. Semiology was to be the all-embracing science of signs, which would include all kinds of structural systems: fashion, highway code, myths, food systems, etc.[50] He stressed the ambiguous character of the sign and the possibility of polysemy. The issue of polysemy rests on the principle that one signifier has no *single* signified but can refer to a set of signifieds, depending on the context. Polysemy entails the possibility that a signifier can be reattached in different contexts.[51] Barthes also maintained that, at the bases of all sign systems, there is a 'natural' language: an authentic and transparent medium. At the core of this natural language is the closed relation between a signified and a signifier, on which a second order language is built. The first order language is the domain of denotation, against which connotation leans. The closed relation between signifier and signified, however, is abandoned in Barthes's later work, when he criticizes the Saussurean sign and discards the possibility of a first order language.

Jacques Lacan extends the later Barthes's theory of the sign and abandons the idea of the pre-existence – or even the existence – of a signified outside its relation with the signifier. For Lacan (and later for Barthes), the signified is produced by the signifier. The latter is no longer representative of a signified because Lacan abandoned the very notion of representation in relation to the sign. Lacan would then theorize the construction of meaning in discourse as halting the sliding of the chain, or network of signifiers, by the use of a quilting point.[52] It is this quilting point which makes possible the illusion of a referent.[53]

From the above we can argue that Islam is not a signifier without a signified, but a signifier whose meaning is expressed by its articulation. This, however, seems a rather unsatisfactory answer as we are left with two problems. The first refers to the context of any articulation. The second relates to the specific character of the articulation of the signifier Islam: its particular function in the network of signifiers (that is, its status as a nodal point). We should now look at these problems in turn. Even if at the level of theory it is possible to articulate any one signifier (or chain of signifiers) to any signified, no articulation occurs in a vacuum; it always occurs in a terrain where there are already relatively stable articulations (that is sedimented meanings). In other words, signifiers are found in articulated networks.[54]

Moreover, signifiers tend to preserve traces of previous articulations and these traces are organized in chains by the mechanisms of metaphor and metonymy. They refer ultimately to no referent or, rather, they point at something beyond that field and from the field itself. But, these traces can be articulated, and re-articulated in chains. For example, in the case of Islam one can see that 'Islam' connotes many things (Qur'an, Messengership of the Prophet, and so on), which it carries along in any of its articulations within any single Muslim community, and these cannot be disarticulated without dissolving the specificity of 'Islam'.

The inter-discursivity of Islam cannot be erased by its inclusion within any particular discourse. By the same token, Islam cannot be the product of any one discourse (except, of course, its founding discourse). The inter-discursive character of Islam raises the question of what prevents its dissolution: why does it have, not only a specific relevance within a certain context, but also continues to carry some distinctive qualities – for example, its relationship to the Qur'an, to Muslims, etc. Theoretically, there is nothing to prevent Islam from dissolving into its constituent discourses. Islam is saved from dissolution by political action. That is, in the absence of an intrinsic link between signifier and signified, there is a need for that link to be established by a political act and maintained by police actions.[55] The various attempts to reinterpret and re-articulate Islam already carry within them traces of previous articulations and interpretations, to the extent that all attempts at re-articulation must begin where the last articulation left off. This would suggest that, although Islam can be used to suture a large number of discourses, and that in each act of suturing, its identity will be transformed, it still retains traces of its other articulations.

We can see that re-articulations of Islam have a tradition, that is marks of its previous uses. This tradition is not only temporal. Islam does not only bear the marks of its previous interpretations, it also bears the marks of its current articulations in different discourses. Thus, the content of Islam is provided by the contestation between past and present reinterpretations. Behind these various articulatory practices, there is the trace of Islam's inauguration. This foundational moment continues to act as a call to 'return to the origins'. This return is inscribed in the possibility of recovering the 'original meaning' of Islam. This attempt to recover is never a recovery, for the attempt modifies what was to be recovered and forces us to question the status of this 'return to origins'. How can this calling back to the original Islam continue to operate despite its polysemy? Are we not simply asserting an essence to Islam by imparting it with an original content? I do not suggest that Islam has one true meaning outside the political construction of that meaning, but what I do propose is that the sign of Islam carries with it its history of articulations, including the history of its founding. This moment of foundation, however, has its own specificity.

What does Islam found? Tautologically, it founds a community of those who subscribe to it: Islam founds the Muslim *Ummah*. In this act of founding Islam is the means by which a community is unified and established: the unity of a 'Muslim' community comes from retrospectively constructing its identity, through the use of Islam as a nodal point. That is, Islam would not only function to unify a particular community with respect to this signifier, but it is also the name by which the Muslim community identifies and actualizes itself. What unites the various 'Islamic' practices found throughout the world is their invocation of the name of Islam. Islam's relationship with Muslims is unlike any other relationship between any element and Muslims, since, within the discourse of Muslims, Islam occupies a privileged place.[56] The inter-discursivity of Islam is tied up, in a large measure, by its significance for the construction of a Muslim identity.

Does Islam have a different status among the signifiers to which it is articulated? We know that Islam may be used as the means of articulating a multiplicity of positions, but this does not necessarily mean that there are multiple Islams. I would like to recall here the question posed by Zizek: 'What creates and sustains the identity of a given ideological field beyond all possible variations of its positive content?'[57] This is exactly the question we face: Islam has emerged as the means of articulating a multiplicity of positions without losing its specificity. That is why, when much of the literature complains about the emptiness of Islamist programmes and the malleability of Islamic symbols, it misses the point. What is extraordinary about Islam is that, although it can be used to articulate so many divergent positions, it maintains its specificity – it remains 'Islam'. Zizek sets about answering the question he posed by stating that a field of discursivity is unified and bound by the intervention of the Lacanian quilting points.[58] The various elements which are constitutive of the field of discursivity do not have positive identities, but their identities come from their insertion into a relational ensemble. Their meaning is given, not by reference to their positive content, but in relation to other signifiers. The quilting point performs the function of totalizing the field of discursivity (unifying it and drawing its limits), and thus produces a meaningful structure.[59] To put it succinctly, the social is formed by the structuring of a number of 'proto-ideological elements' (floating signifiers) into a unified field, by the arbitration of a nodal point.[60] This knot of meaning fixes the other elements, arrests their floating, and thus gives meaning to the whole ensemble.[61] The floating signifiers acquire their identity in the (never fully closed) ensemble of meaning quilted by the nodal point. The significance of the quilting point is that it gives a retroactive meaning to all the other elements in the system. It is this point which organizes the discursive field by retroactively fixing the meaning of the elements. (One should be clear that a nodal point is a functional category not a substantial one: any element may become a nodal point if it is used to quilt a chain of signification.)

It seems that we can fine-tune our description of Islam by considering it as a crucial nodal point. Nodal points are discourse-contextual but not all discourses have the same nodal points. We could go further and argue that Islam is a nodal point in the discourse of Islamism but, of course, one could easily say that Islam is a nodal point in the discourse of *fiqh* (jurisprudence of Islamic law); that it is a nodal point in the discourse of the various Sufi orders; and is also the nodal point in the discourse of the various practising Muslims. In all these cases Islam performs the function of a nodal point: it retrospectively gives meaning to other elements included in the discourse. Of course, there are other discourses in which Islam is just an element, for example the discourse of comparative world religions.

In a totalized universe of meaning we find a multiplicity of nodal points operating to structure the chains of signification, but among them we find one specific signifier – the master signifier – which functions at the level of the totality (that is, it retroactively constitutes that universe of meaning as a unified totality). This master signifier is a paradoxical signifier in so far as it is a particularity that functions as a metonymy for the whole discursive universe. As such, it acquires a universal dimension and functions as the place of inscription for all other signifiers. It is the signifier of the totality that guarantees and sanctions that unity: it designates the whole by its very presence. It functions as the place of inscription of all other signifiers of that totality.[62] The master signifier is a signifier to which other signifiers refer, and are unified by – and it fixes their identity. It is the unique point of symbolic authority that guarantees and sustains the coherence of the whole ensemble.

But why 'Islam'? Why has it operated as a master signifier in such diverse and multiple discourses? It cannot be due to its substance, since the master signifier does not have a substantive identity. Yet it has something 'that makes people feel that there's something in it'.[63]

That 'something' is its 'itness'. This is what Zizek calls the real kernel that escapes signification of any constructed object.[64] In the case of the master signifier it becomes the 'thing', the relationship which holds a community together.[65] As Zizek says, it is what is accessible only to the members of the community; it is what gives plenitude. It is not a set of features or practices, because there is something 'more' in it – 'something that is present in these features, that appears through them'.[66] It occupies the place of master signifier because it holds that community together for as long as the members of that community believe in it, even though it marks the point where signification is impossible (that is, where signification fails, since the thing cannot find a referent and no signifier or set of signifers can fully define it). As such, it is the paradoxical signifier par excellence for, although it marks the failure of signification, its very presence masks it.

It is in this sense that Islam has become the master signifier in Muslim communities. It is analogous to the way in which the nation occupies that place, in the same way, in many European societies. Islam unifies the totality and is the place that holds the community together. It unifies and totalizes and, at the same time, draws the limits of the community. Yet these limits will become areas of con-tention for any successive articulations of Islam and force us to question whether these limits are marked by ethnic markers (non-Arabs, Arabs), by the post-colonial borders, or solely by its distinction to what it is not – that is, the West.

Islamism: Islam as a master signifier

The relation between Islam and Islamism is not as direct as the orientalists maintain, nor is it, as anti-orientalists would contend, merely opportunistic. Rather, it is constitutive – that is, both Islam and the identity of Islamism are transformed as Islamists attempt to articulate Islam to their project. The ability of Islamists to articulate Islam as a central political category is not due, as some maintain, to the reputed indivisibility of politics and religion in Islam.[67] Rather, it is the function of how Islamists attempt to transform Islam from a nodal point in a variety of discourses into a master signifier. Hence, the often-heard Islamist slogan: 'Islam is the solution'. This is an attempt by Islamists to hegemonize the general field of discursivity by constructing Islam as a master signifier, the point to which all other discourses must refer.

What makes Islam a candidate for a master signifier? Islamists make use of the inter-discursive nature of Islam in three main ways: they define Islam as *din* (faith), as *dunya* (complete way of life), and as *dawla* (a state or political order).[68] Each of these attempts to construct Islam also involves confronting and adapting to other interpretations of Islam. It is not that Islamists simply articulate Islam, but that their articulation already includes both other articulations and traces of Islam's presence in other discursive configurations. The Islamist project revolves around gathering the ways Islam operates in different discourses, and unifying them by using Islam as a master signifier.

The master signifier functions as the most abstract principle by which any discursive space is totalized. In other words, it is not that a discursive horizon is established by a coalition of nodal points, but rather by the use of a signifier that represents the totality of that structure. The more extensive a discourse is, the less specific each element within it will be: it will become simply another instance of a more general identity. The dissolution of the specificity and con-creteness of the constituent elements clears the path for a master signifier becoming more and more abstract, until it reaches a limit at which it does not have any specific manifestation:[69] it simply refers to the community as a whole and it becomes the principle of reading that community. It does this by becoming a manifestation of the impossibility of fullness of any social complex. (This is because no social complex is based on objectivity; the differential moments within the social do not refer to a positivity but, rather, an attempt to constitute a positivity.)[70] The greater the number of elements a master signifier is called upon to muster, however, the more fragile will be the link it has to any particular element. In this case the limits of the discourse will not be provided by an aggregation of antagonistic others, but by an expression of the most general form of antagonism: the incarnation of evil.[71] This is part of the answer to William Connolly's question: why do identities close themselves by defining a range of differences as evil, when there is no apparent threat from the bearers of this difference?[72] It is only through the incarnation of evil that a muliplicity of differential elements are able to be con-centrated in a single point. It is at this point that the political nature of a master signifier cannot be separated from ethics.[73] The operation of a master signifer is an attempt to unify a way of being which is lost and fragmented in its unspectacular mundane daily manifestations.

For Muslims, Islam is the most abstract signifier. This allows it to operate in a most generalized way. It is not that Islam is equivocal or ambiguous and can be articulated to a variety of political tendencies; rather, to make use of the distinction that Rorty draws when describing his notion of a final vocabulary, Islam is the thinnest of phrases in Muslim's final vocabulary. It is this thinness which makes it difficult to contest. Ultimately, for Muslims, Islam is another word for 'Goodness incarnate'. Thus, when Islamists claim that the best government is an Islamic government, here 'Islamic' refers to the incarnation of goodness, so that the claim becomes: the best government is good government. This is a claim which is difficult to refute directly, except by attacking the relation between Islam and the incarnation of goodness. But it is precisely at this point where Islam is strongest, because, for the majority of Muslims, Islam must be the definition of good. It is for this reason that Muslim governments which have been challenged by Islamists have often responded by arguing that Islamists do not represent true Islam, rather than by claiming Islam does not represent true goodness.

Theorizing Islam as a master signifier avoids the essentialism of the orientalist approach, since Islam is not imposed with an historical essence. At the same time this approach rejects the structuralism of anti-orientalist accounts which, by treating Islam as a superstructural moment, minimize its significance, and thus have to resort to categories of 'opportunism' and 'false consciousness' to try and account for the emergence of Islamism. Islamism, then, is a project which attempts to transform Islam from a nodal point in discourses of Muslim communities into a master signifier. In particular, the Islamist project is an attempt to make Islam a master signifier of the political order. It is the struggle to establish which signifiers will constitute the unity and identity of a discursive universe which is central, since the transformation of a signifier into a master signifier is what makes possible the constitution of unity and the identity of the whole and its parts. For Islamists the name of the master signifier is Islam; for their opponents, Islam cannot be the master signifier. The conflict being waged throughout Muslim communities ultimately revolves around this issue.[74] To clarify the contours of this conflict between the Islamists and their opponents I need to outline the identities of their opponents and their relationship to Islam. It is puzzling that Islamist projects aim at Islamizing already existing Muslim societies, since how can Islam not be a master signifier in Muslim communities?

Notes

1. I am very much aware of my intellectual debt to Edward Said and his work, and any disagreements that I express in the following pages should be seen in the light of my acknowledgement of Said's influence in opening up these horizons for me.

2. Said, 1994, p. 375.

3. Ibid., p. 376.

4. Said, 1985a, p. 3.

5. Ibid., p. 7.

6. This does not preclude the possibility that different types of 'orientalism' were deployed in other areas subject to western conquest.

7. Said, 1985a, p. 300.

8. Said, 1985a, pp. 300–301.

9. Ibid.

10. Ibid.

11. Turner, 1989, pp. 631–3.

12. Turner, 1978, p. 7.

13. Said, 1978, p. 703.

14. See, for example, the debate among sociologists trying to write the history of the transition from feudalism to capitalism and the problems presented by the endurance of Asiatic state structures. See Wickham, 1985.

15. For example, Halliday, 1996, pp. 199–207.

16. For example, see comments by Irwin, 1981; Al-Azm, 1981; Lewis, 1982; Hourani, 1991, pp. 63–4.

17. Mani and Frankenberg, 1985, p. 176.

18. See for example, Halliday, 1996, p. 213; Lewis, 1982; Irwin, 1981, p. 106.

19. This line of reasoning is very common among Leftist critics, wedded to a stagist concept of history, who see in orientalism the confirmation of the Marxist reading of historical development rather than a confirmation of the orientalism inherent in Marxism itself. See, for example, Al-Azm, 1981, pp. 6–8.

20. Halliday, 1996, pp. 214–15.

21. This argument has been most forcefully made by Al-Azm, 1981, pp. 18–22.

22. Binder, 1988, p. 120.

23. Ibid.

24. Ibid., pp. 120–21.

25. Ibid.

26. Said, 1981, p. x.

27. Ibid., p. 60.

28. Ibid., p. 61.

29. Ibid., p. xii.

30. Hammami and Rieker, 1988, p. 100. See also the comments by Halliday and Alavi, 1988, pp. 2–3.

31. See Glavanis, 1995, for the way in which political economy-based studies of the Middle East began to proliferate in the wake of Said's *Orientalism* (1985a).

32. For the definition of essentialism used here, see Fuss, 1989, pp. xi and 1.

33. El-Zien, 1977, *passim*. See also Al-Azmeh's discussion of Islam as a political category (1993, pp. 23–31).

34. El-Zien, 1977, p. 227.

35. Ibid., p. 252.

36. Ibid., p. 254.

37. For an elaboration of this point, see Fuss, 1989, p. 4.

38. Zubaida, 1989, pp. 150–51.

39. This is similar to the argument developed by Derrida to theorize the notion of supplement, see Derrida, 1973, pp. 88–104; 1976, 141–64.

40. Benedict Anderson, 1990, demonstrates some mechanisms by which nationalism is constructed.

41. This contradicts Halliday's assertion that it is never valid to consider Muslim subjectivity as being equivalent to an ethnic community (1996, pp. 115, 119 and 215). The primacy of a subject-position is context-dependent: in certain situations, certain subject-positions may have greater salience than others. Underlying Halliday's attempt to argue that Muslim subject-position is by definition secondary is the assumption that ethnic identities are, by definition, primary.

42. Fischer, 1990, p. 189.

43. See Laclau and Mouffe's 1987, pp. 86–92 discussion of idealism and materialism in their defence of discourse analysis from Geras's critique (1987).

44. For further elaboration of this point, see Rorty, 1982, pp. 191–210; 1991b, pp. 21–34; Laclau and Mouffe, 1987, pp. 93–148.

45. For example, see Halliday, 1996, p. 114.

46. This is the position taken by Halliday and Alavi, 1988, pp. 6–7.

47. See for example, Halliday, 1996, pp. 207–10, or Shepard, 1987; or Fischer, 1980.

48. For details see Zizek, 1989, Chapter 3.

49. Laclau (1996, pp. 36–46) makes a similar argument regarding what he calls 'empty signifiers'.

50. See Barthes, 1973, *passim*.

51. This examination of the equivocal nature of the signifier forms the bulk of Barthes's early work on semiology. See Barthes, 1973, especially the last chapter: 'Myth Today'.

52. Lacan's notion of quilting points comes from Freud's nodal points. See Freud, 1900, pp. 388 and 456. According to Freud nodal points in dreams are 'elements upon which a great number of dream thoughts converge ... for purposes of condensation and disguise'. Lacan extends this notion: it is 'around them [that] everything is irradiated and is organised as if there were small lines of force formed in the surface of a tissue by means of the quilting point' (Lacan, 1988, p. 383).

53. The illusion of a referent is produced by the retroactive operation of quilting. For further information on this, see Zizek, 1989, p. 95.

54. We never encounter a field that is either empty or only a possibility, nor do we find a fully determined and closed field. There is always a certain ensemble of

structural limits. The terrain of meaning which is historically constituted is never fully fixed, allowing then a certain play of signification but having a certain stability.

55. Boyne, 1990, p. 105.

56. This privilege is due to its historical circumstances not its essential characteristics.

57. Zizek, 1989, p. 87.

58. See Zizek, 1989, pp. 87–8. See also Laclau and Mouffe, 1985, pp. 111–12.

59. Laclau and Mouffe, 1985, p. 141. Laclau and Mouffe have annexed this concept of nodal points from the work of Freud (see Freud, 1900).

60. Zizek, 1989, p. 87.

61. Laclau and Mouffe, 1985, pp. 105–13.

62. Zizek, 1989, pp. 88–9.

63. Freud, 1900, p. 221.

64. This marks the point of failure of representation and the impossibility of fully suturing any unity, but at the same time the master signifier, by its very presence, masks that impossibility since it creates the illusion of the referent and normativity: i.e. the illusion of the necessity of that inscription.

65. Zizek, 1990, p. 51.

66. Ibid., p. 53.

67. For example, see Lewis, 1976, p. 44; Kepel, 1985, pp. 21–4 and 224–8.

68. Ayubi, 1991, p. 68.

69. Zizek, 1990, pp. 51–2. Zizek makes a similar point in regard to the emergence of xenophobia in former Yugoslavia, in which what he calls the 'nation-thing' is the source of identification beyond any concrete manifestation.

70. Laclau, 1990, pp. 90–91.

71. Examples of this logic at work can be seen in Reagan's notorious characterization of the Soviet Union as the 'evil empire'. It can also be seen in the discourse of Khomeinism in which the United States is reduced to the Great Satan. See Bernard and Khalilzad, 1984.

72. Connolly, 1991, p. 3.

73. Zac and Sayyid, 1990.

74. This is not to deny that many other factors are in play, including greed, vested interest, short-term calculation, personal advancement and so on. The conflict is like any other political conflict into which a myriad of other factors intrude. The point is that confrontation between Islamists and their opponents overdetermines these other struggles.

3. Kemalism and the politicization of Islam

Accounts of Islamism tend to make a major distinction between the Islamists of today and other political movements which came to power as the European empires retreated. These movements have been variously described as 'nationalist', or 'secularist' or 'modern-izing'; another way of describing them is to use the category of Kemalism. The advantages of using Kemalism are twofold. First, it reflects the centrality of Turkey within the Muslim world in the early twentieth century, a centrality symbolized by the caliphate and the fact that Turkey was the strongest independent Muslim state – some-thing that the Arabocentric orientation of Islamic studies tends to forget.[1] Second, to provide an account of Islamism that does not fall into cultural essentialism and particularism, we need to reject the tendency of the literature on Islam and Islamism to privilege Arabness and reduce the 'globality' of the Muslim world to Arab ethnic specificity. The analysis offered here focuses on broad themes and structures rather than on an empirically based detailed narrative of events, its aim being to provide the broad contours of a post-orientalist political history of the Muslim world in the wake of European empires.

In this chapter I do three things. First, I describe how Islam as a master signifier structured the Muslim world after the death of the Prophet, and the centrality of the caliphate in this account. Second, I analyse Kemalism as it emerged in Turkey following the overthrow of the Ottoman regime. In particular, my interest lies in the way Mustafa Kemal and his followers dealt with Islam. Third, I am interested in using the notion of Kemalism as a metaphor to describe the various Muslim regimes that emerged following decolonization. In achieving the above three aims I focus on the central tenets of the modernization programme initiated by Mustafa Kemal, interpreting

Kemalism in terms of its theoretical imports. I have chosen not to focus on providing a detailed analysis of Kemalism's actual status in various historical and political contexts – which I am well aware would demonstrate significant variations – since the purpose here is not to furnish a detailed and exhaustive analysis of Kemalism but to establish Kemalism as a means of reading a wider Muslim political context.

The institution of the caliphate: fixing Islam

Apart from the initial period of Muslim history (632–945 AD), the caliphate does not appear as an important institution in the political history of the Muslim world. Most accounts are highly dismissive of it and, partly as a consequence of this attitude, histories of the Muslim world are rarely told as a unity. The regionalization of Islamic history has the effect of marginalizing the significance of the caliphate. While there is little doubt that the caliph became a mere figurehead for much of Islamic history, it is also clear that from the death of the Prophet until 3 March 1924, there was always a caliph.[2] The caliphate's lack of political power did not lead to its abandonment as an institution. To explain the significance of the caliphate in the Muslim world, we have to examine the structure of authority within Muslim history.

For the original Muslim community the problem of political authority was simple: all authority was invested in the Prophet. The figure of the Prophet dominated Islam. It is the Prophet himself who acts as the nodal point of the nascent *Ummah*. The unity of that community is not centred on the statements the Prophet makes but on the Prophet himself. This does not mean that the message of the Prophet is unimportant in mobilizing support, but that it is the messenger that holds the support together because the message is manifested in the actions of the messenger. In other words, the Prophet reveals what Islam is, but Islam is also what the Prophet does. It was not possible to make substantial appeals against him in the name of Islam. In disputes about the meaning of the message only the Prophet could make a final adjudication. At the same time the Prophet was outside Islam, since Islam was not his creation; he represented himself as simply enunciating it. I do not want to say that Islam is Mohammedism, but rather that it was the figure of the Prophet which unified and represented Islam. During this time the master signifier of the Muslim community was not Islam but the figure of the Prophet. While the Prophet was alive, what he said and did was Islam. When disputes arose, only he could resolve them, and there could be no appeal to higher authorities against his decision.

What is the relation between an enunciator and originator of a discourse and the discourse this person founds? I call the person or group of persons that are responsible for formulating a founding discourse[3] the lawgiver, since it is he or she who establishes the limits of the political community and thus its identity. The work of the lawgiver – that is, the work they produce/articulate – I call the law. The lawgiver enunciates the law, but at the same time he or she incarnates it. This tension between the lawgiver and the law is relatively easy to domesticate as long as the lawgiver exists. Once the lawgiver becomes absent, however, the question of political authority in any community becomes acute.

The centrality of the caliphate as the source of political authority and legitimacy started with the death of the Prophet (632).[4] It is the death of the lawgiver that marks the birth of the law; it is the death of the Prophet which institutionalized Islam. I mean this not simply in an abstract sense but also empirically: the codification and collection of the Qur'an begins with the death of the Prophet, as does the collection of *hadith* (sayings attributed to the Prophet) and the formation of the *Sunnah* (the traditions of the Prophet). If the lawgiver is no longer there to hold together the various discursive strands of a political community, the political community risks disintegration. For a political community to maintain its identity beyond the demise of the point upon which that identity was constructed, it should try to institutionalize that absence. That is, the nodal point of the community shifts from the lawgiver to the work of the lawgiver: the law. The need for the law begins with the absence of the lawgiver.

The death of the Prophet shifted the unifying principle of the *Ummah* from the Prophet to his message. Thus the law took the place of the absent lawgiver. However, the need for the law also gives rise to the need for interpreters of the law, for the law cannot speak. In other words, the community needs those who can reconstruct what the absent lawgiver would have done if he had been confronted with this or that situation. Here we can see the various strategies one could use: analogy, knowing the intentions of the lawgiver, and so on. But this desire to produce interpretations leads to the production of an authority different from the lawgiver, and the appearance of the law also leads to the appearance of an authorized reader/successor.

Thus the appearance of the caliph (successor) involves the recognition of the notion of Islam as a master signifier. It is only with the absence of the Prophet that Islam comes to be the nodal point of the Muslim community. This relationship between the Prophet and Islam can be illustrated with an example in the Prophet's lifetime. At the battle of Uhud, the Meccan armies spread a rumour that the Prophet was dead in the hope that this would demoralize the outnumbered Muslim army. When the Muslims heard that the Prophet was dead, they continued to fight, proclaiming that they were now fighting not for the Prophet but for Islam.[5] If the centre of the Muslim community shifts from the Prophet to Islam, immediately the problem arises as to how the site of Islam is to be occupied: what content is it possible to attach to Islam, and who can do this? The institution of the caliphate is the recognition of the emergence of Islam as the master signifier. It would now be Islam itself that would unify and thus forge the identity of the Muslim community. However, precisely because Islam must act as the quilting point, there must be some mechanism to prevent the quilting point from floating out of control. It is the caliph (aided and abetted as time goes on by the *Ulema*), who will attempt to domesticate and regulate the master signifier by establishing the authority of the succession.

Ira Lapidus suggests that 'the caliphs inherited the Prophet's executive authority ... It was a seamless authority inherited by the men who stood in the Prophet's place.'[6] It could not, however, be 'seamless' because the caliph was not the Prophet. The absence of the Prophet marked a break (for example, there could be no more revelations of the Qur'an); this break could be sutured by the institution of the caliphate. The caliphate, however, could not erase the absence of the Prophet, rather it marked that absence. The authority of the successor cannot be that of the lawgiver, since if that were so the successor would become another lawgiver. The Prophet cannot be doubled, without putting at risk the discursive horizon he has inaugurated.[7] However, the place of the caliph as the site of enunciation of the successor must be privileged enough to allow him to speak on behalf of the lawgiver. Even though the caliph cannot legislate, he must be able to adjudicate. The authority of the successor comes from his understanding of, and familiarity with the lawgiver's work. The successor is the condensation of the traces of the lawgiver. Once the quilting point shifts from lawgiver to law, questions about conformity with the law can arise. Now who is most competent to speak in place of the lawgiver? Who is able to interpret the law? Who should become the successor? The early Muslim community split around this question. One party (the Sunnis) contended that the Muslim community as a whole was able to decide on the succession, and that the rules of succession should follow the sedimented rules of succession developed prior to Islam. Others (mainly the Shia) argued that the succession should be limited to those who were the first Muslims (or in stronger terms, those who, because of their relationship to the Prophet, were ontologically privileged readers of Islam). The Shia–Sunni division revolved around this issue.[8]

From this inauspicious start things got worse, as the historical record shows. The caliphate became emasculated when the caliph became a mere figurehead, while the power slipped to his Khorsani and later to Turkish *ghulams*.[9] In 929 AD the caliphate became fragmented when Emir Abdul-Rahman III of Cordoba proclaimed himself caliph in direct challenge to the Abbasid caliph in Baghdad. Three years after the caliph Muttasim was trampled to death on the orders of Hulagu Khan in 1258 (apparently the Mongols were rather chary about spilling royal blood), the Mamluks in Egypt established one of the Abbasid refugees from the sack of Baghdad as caliph. When in 1517 the armies of the Ottoman Sultan Selim defeated the Mamluks and conquered Egypt, the caliphate passed to the house of Osman. However, it was only in the eighteenth century that the Ottoman sultans began to emphasize their role as caliph.[10]

What is clear from this brief outline is that the caliphate was not the centre of political power throughout its history. What is also clear is that the institution was significant enough for various dynasties to lay claim to it (for example the Fatmids, Hafsids or the Mughuls), and that for most of the time the caliph of Baghdad, and those who could trace their claims to the caliphate of Baghdad, enjoyed a certain precedence over other regional caliphs.[11] The significance of the caliphate was not due to the ability of the caliph to command armies and exact taxes; rather, its significance was derived from its ideological position.[12] The caliphate was the link to the lawgiver and the law, as well as being the nodal point around which a global Muslim identity was structured – a mark of Muslim cultural unity.[13] The caliphate was the centre of the Muslim political structure; as long as there was a caliphate, Islam as a master signifier was attached to the state.[14] The caliph, assisted by the senior *ulema*, was able to limit the possible political articulations of Islam. The institution of the caliphate provided Islam with a relative fixity and stability.[15]

Abolition and reaction: floating Islam

On 3 March 1924, at the insistence of Mustafa Kemal, the Grand National Assembly abolished the caliphate. The actual decision to abolish the caliphate, and thus to decentre Islam, was a protracted and complex affair. It is important to mention the messy character of the decision so that we do not forget that abolition was a historical and contingent event. At the beginning of their struggle against the European occupation of Anatolia, Mustafa Kemal and his supporters claimed that they were fighting to free the caliphate from Christian control. It was only after Mustafa Kemal had defeated the Greek forces in 1922 that he began to make serious efforts to abolish the sultanate. Partly, this was in response to the way the caliph and his court had collaborated with the European powers in opposing Kemal and his followers. At this stage, however, Kemal was wary of moving too fast in the direction of abolition and the reduction of the role of the Ottoman ruling family. It is important to bear in mind that most of the higher ranks of civil and military officials had been formed by their participation in the Ottoman service, and thus retained a strong sense of identification with it. In a gradual process, Kemal first turned the sultanate into a constitutional monarchy, and then abolished it altogether. As Deringil writes:

> the whole period from the abolition of the Sultanate to the proclamation of the Republic (23 April 1923) to the actual abolition of the Caliphate on 3 March 1924, can be seen as a period of preparation during which Kemal was involved in preparing opinion both inside and outside the Grand National Assembly. The Caliphate question became a symbolic issue in the power struggle between Kemal and his opponents, both of them using religious arguments.[16]

It was necessary to proceed in this way because of the hold the office of the caliphate, and to some extent the ruling family, still had over the Turkish people. As a means of discrediting the House of Osman Kemal embarked on a systematic campaign of vilification. He reminded the people how the sultan-caliph had used the 'armies of the caliphate' against the national movement and had used Greek aircraft to drop leaflets which condemned the nationalist forces, and described their leaders as rebels. Mustafa Kemal argued that the caliphate had, in fact, ended in 1258.[17]

During the interregnum between the abolition of the sultanate and the abolition of the caliphate there was much haggling between Mustafa Kemal and Abdulmejed over the conditions of the latter's appointment as (puppet) caliph. When the decision was made to abolish the caliphate, the Grand National Assembly issued a state-ment denying that the caliphate was being abolished; instead they argued that the caliphate was reverting to its original form.[18] Kemal ordered that Abdulmejed could not use the title *Halife-i-Resullulah* (Successor to the Messenger of God) which would link the caliph back to the role's origins. In addition, at his accession ceremony he could not wear a turban or any style of dress that would be reminis-cent of the Ottoman sultanate. The Kemalists were very concerned to maintain the breach between their Ottoman past – which signified a universal and multinational state – and the ethnically homogenous Turkish state they supported.

It is important to note several points regarding the abolition of the caliphate. First, there was a sharp distinction between the House of Osman and their authority to rule (consolidated in the office of the sultan), on the one hand, and the office of the caliph as leader of the entire Muslim *Ummah*, on the other. Thus, it was a relatively straightforward matter to get rid of the sultanate but not so the caliphate. Second, the timing of the decision to abolish was con-ditioned, to a large extent, by the exigencies of the political-military situation on the ground. That is, there was a large element of short-term political calculation involved in the actual decision. Third, the second point does not weaken the claim that Mustafa Kemal, at least, was determined to abolish the caliphate. This is clear from the way he rejected several alternatives to the abolition, such as making the caliph a figurehead (like the Mamluks did in 1261). He also refused to become the caliph himself, as was proposed by members of the Khalifat movement; given his popularity as a 'Muslim' hero it is likely he would have been accepted as caliph.[19]

In the past, as we have seen, the caliphate had often been fragmented, denigrated or reduced to a mere figurehead. Why then was it necessary to abolish the office?[20] A clue to the answer to this question can be found in Mustafa Kemal's marathon speech to the Grand National Assembly, in which (among other things) Kemal tried to justify the decision to abolish the caliphate. For Kemal, the caliphate was a political institution that only made sense in the light of a unified Muslim state. This Kemal rejected as being a practical impossibility, for, 'The goal of creating a multinational political community is attractive – but misleading.'[21] The reason why such a policy is mistaken is due to the fact that the only legitimate political entity is the nation state. Kemal argues that the caliphate had been paid for in Turkish (not Muslim) blood. Other Muslims had left the Turks to carry the burden of defending Islam, and in many cases (for example Arabs under Ottoman rule) they had fought against the Turks. If the new Turkey was to emerge it could only do so by serving its own national interest. This was only possible by rejecting the idea of a universal state and, more specifically, by abandoning the caliphate. Kemal refused to continue with the caliphate, which he felt was an anachronism in a world of nation states. So the set of arguments for the abolition revolves around the political arrangements that were considered possible in the early twentieth century.

Kemal also had another set of reasons for abolishing the caliphate, however, which could be seen clearly in his almost incidental comment on the abolition: 'As for the Caliphate, it could only have been a laughing-stock in the eyes of the civilized world, enjoying the blessings of science.'[22] So the caliphate was dismissed because it was an embarrassment for the civilized world. This theme was repeated by Kemal in many speeches, his programme being continually justified in terms of fulfilling the necessary demands of modern civilization.[23] The equivalence that Kemal makes between science and civilization is quite evident; a much more interesting question, however, is why should the world of science and civilization oppose the caliphate? Obviously this world of science and civilization is the world of Europe and its *outremers*.[24] The caliphate could not be reformed or restructured; it had to be rejected – because the caliphate was not a western institution. Here is a glimpse of the antagonism within Kemalism between the West and Islam. It is this antagonism which leads to the rejection of any possibility of a marriage between an Islamic (that is 'native') culture and western technology, and distinguishes Kemalism most clearly from other attempts at modernizing non-European societies.

The abolition of the caliphate ended the possibility of establishing an 'a-national political space'.[25] The end of the caliphate also signalled the end of a struggle in which other possibilities of constructing political communities (pan-Islamism, pan-Ottomanism, pan-Turanism) were finally suppressed in favour of (Turkish) nationalism. Further, it was a sign of the ultimate fragmentation of Islam, since the caliph could no longer act as a quilting point restraining articulations and maintaining a political identity for Islam. It ushered in a new political terrain in which the Islamic presence in Muslim communities was confined to the private sphere, such as in systems of religious practices and in laws governing personal status.[26] All major remaining Muslim communities were either directly governed by European powers or were under indirect European control. Islam was found to be incompatible with modernity. In the choice between modernity, with its promises of tomorrow, and Islam with its memories of past glories, the rulers of the leading Muslim state chose modernity.

The significance of the abolition of the caliphate for Muslim political theory can be gleaned from the reaction to it. One of the main responses was an attempt to try to reconstitute the caliphate: for example King Fuad of Egypt put himself forward as a candidate for the caliphate, and the Hashemites also tried to claim the mantle of the caliphate. But the reaction to the abolition was not confined to political élites alone. There were popular protests against the abolition in many Muslim areas; in Tunisia, for example, there was wide-scale popular condemnation of Kemal's decision. This happened despite Kemal being admired as a heroic figure for his stand against European imperialists. Newspapers also condemned the abolition, which they saw as the legitimization of the fragmentation of the Muslim world.[27] With the caliph as a nodal point it was possible to think that the divisions of the Muslim world were only temporary; following the caliph's removal there was no possibility of drawing the various Muslim communities together.

A similar reaction can be seen among the Muslims of India, who founded the Khalifat movement in 1919.[28] The Khalifat movement had campaigned vigorously on behalf of the caliph in the wake of the First World War, urging Britain to support the caliphate.[29] This movement had a great deal of influence in articulating Muslim identity in the most populous Muslim community in the world at the time. This movement, motivated by fear of the consequences of the Turkish defeat in the First World War, sought to use its influence in India to apply pressure on the British government to moderate its policies in relation to Turkey. This concern for the fate of the caliphate was common to both Sunnis and Shia (in spite of their ambivalence with regard to the caliphate). Both Sunni and Shia Muslims in British India saw in the defeat of Turkey the danger of Islam ceasing to be a force on the world stage.[30]

The Khalifat movement had made various interventions in support of Turkey, even organizing funds for Mustafa Kemal's war with the Greeks, and opposing Arab independence since they saw that such a development would weaken the caliphate. Thus, when the news of the abolition reached them, the 'Khalifat Committee in India was thunderstruck, their icon, the Khalifat, had been broken and their idol Mustafa Kemal, had been the iconoclast'.[31] They felt betrayed by the Turkish nationalists.[32] The movement's aim of trying to pre-serve the leading Muslim power was subverted, much to its leaders' bewilderment, by Turkish nationalists. The decision by Kemal to abolish the caliphate completely undermined the Khalifat movement. Many of those involved in the movement began to concentrate their attention in trying to champion Muslim political rights in South Asia, and abandoned any quest for global Muslim unity.[33]

Among Muslim intellectuals the response was varied. In May 1926 a group of *ulema* organized a conference in Cairo, where they re-affirmed the legitimacy of the caliphate and the necessity for it. The most common response, however, was similar to the one advocated by Rashid Rida, who thought it was undesirable and impossible to restore the caliphate and that what was necessary was to reform it. Rida sought to re-establish the caliphate in modern conditions, by turning it into an Islamic version of the Roman Catholic papacy.[34]

Mohammed Iqbal accepted the abolition, allowing his realism to overcome his pan-Islamism. He thought that, as the Muslim world was in fact divided into rival states and empires, this reality had to be recognized. In an era when the *Ummah* was at its weakest, the myth of Muslim unity which the caliph embodied was an obstacle to the creation of a new pattern of relations among Muslim communities.[35] For Iqbal the abolition of the caliphate provided an opportunity to free Islam from its associations with dynastic politics and regional chauvinism:

> Islam is neither nationalism or imperialism but a League of Nations which recognizes artificial boundaries and racial distinctions for the faculty of reason only and not for restricting the social horizons of its members.[36]

However, the most radical response to the question of whether such a thing as an Islamic system of government was feasible came from Abd al-Razeq.[37] Razeq began his questioning of the caliphate by examining the role of Abu Bakr – the first caliph. He argued that not all the enemies of Abu Bakr were the enemies of Islam, and that the association of religion and politics worked to the detriment of religion. He concluded with a striking declaration:

> The caliphate has nothing to do with the divine project and for that matter neither does the administration of justice and the other functions of government and state ... Similarly, religion has nothing to do with the administration of Muslim armies, civic amenities or other municipal projects: these are all matters for common sense and experimentation, drawing on established rules and expert opinion.[38]

For these people, the privatization of Islam was the only path to its renewal. They advocated the assertion of an existential Muslim identity rather than an identity based on a sense of community. Islam could be saved by becoming an ethical discourse which informed, in a very general sense, people's political conduct, but did not determine their policies.

It is important to note that the reverberations of Kemal's deed were felt all over the Muslim world and, in a sense, one can configure the boundary (and thus the constitution) of the Muslim world by following these reactions. Why should Muslims in British India, or Tunisia, be concerned about what is done in Turkey? Their concern is a symptom of the sense of belonging which they felt the caliphate symbolized – that is, there was an imagined *Ummah* which transcended political frontiers.[39] The existence of the caliphate made it possible for Muslims to think in terms of a Muslim world; the division of the *Ummah* could be seen as either temporary or secondary. With the loss of the caliphate it was clear that a new game was being played.

The Kemalists, by abolishing the caliphate, disrupted the sedimented relationship between Islam and state authority – a relationship over a thousand years old. Their act of abolition had the effect of reactivating Islam. The master signifier of Islam was no longer fixed to a particular institutional arrangement, which made the task of reinterpreting what its role should be much easier. In the next section I look at the discourse of Kemalism and how it attempted to articulate its relationship to Islam.[40]

Modernizing Islam: Ataturk's way (1923–45)

The disarticulation of Islam from the state created the possibility of constructing a hegemonic discourse that did not need to accommodate Islam. Islam was no longer linked with state power. For Kemal, as he announced in his inaugural presidential speech, the object of his government was to build 'a new country, a new society, a new state ... respected at home and abroad'.[41] What kind of relationship would this new Turkey have with Islam? In the debates prior to the abolition Kemal had given the impression that the main reason for abolishing the caliphate was to preserve Islam as a private code of ethics. He did not want the state to interfere and politicize (and thus contaminate) Islam. Kemal was fully aware, however, that his government could not treat Islam with benign neglect. There was still the possibility that it could be used to mobilize support against the new authorities. Thus (contrary to some of his earlier statements) Kemal did not rest once Islam had been officially removed from the state, and he actively sought to reinscribe it within his own discourse. The reinscription of Islam within Kemalism can be illustrated by the legislative package that the Grand National Assembly passed following the abolition.

The same day that the Grand National Assembly abolished the caliphate, it passed legislation that put all education institutions under direct state control. In April 1924 religious courts were abolished. In 1925 the Hat Law was passed prohibiting the wearing of the fez and other 'uncivilized' headgear, as well as restricting the use of the veil. In the same year *takrit* (mystic orders) were outlawed. In 1926 the Swiss Civil Code was adopted. In April 1928 Islam was disestablished. In 1928 the provision that mentioned Islam as a state religion was abolished and the Latin alphabet was introduced. It was on the basis of this legislation that the main contours of the new Turkey were drawn.

These reforms all functioned to distance Islam and its cognates from the 'new Turkey'. Islam was too important for individuals to be allowed to have their own interpretation of its role in their lives. The discourse of Kemalism was not content with just removing Islam from the public domain; it aimed at excluding it altogether from the new Turkey. The Kemalists' attempt to re-articulate Islam can be read from the point of view of the four strategies they employed for this purpose: secularization, nationalism, modernization and western-ization. The first two themes were clearly articulated in the six slogans that Kemalists drew up to summarize their ideology: the so-called 'six arrows of Kemalism' (republicanism, nationalism, populism, etat-ism, secularism, and revolutionism).[42] The other two themes, modern-ization and westernization, are distributed more diffusely throughout their discourse.

Secularism   Officially the government of Mustafa Kemal described its attitude towards Islam as Laicism (*Layiklik*). Laicism was defined by the Kemalists as the policy of separating 'religion and the world in matters relating to the state and the nation'.[43] Mustafa Kemal saw secularism as a necessary component of modernization and social change: 'Secularism involved not just the separation of the state from the institutions of Islam but also the liberation of the individual mind from the traditional Islamic concepts and practices.'[44] With the exception of communist-occupied Muslim communities in Albania, Bosnia, the Caucasus, the Middle Volga and Central Asia, no other Muslim communities were subject to the degree of secularism that Turkey was. However, secularism was not the exclusion of Islam but the definition of Islam as a religion – and this notion of religion was modelled using the specific characteristics of Christianity as an ex-emplar. This 'Christian' (orientalist) definition of Islam removed it from the public-political domain. As Turner notes, for Kemalists, secularization was modelled on the history of Europe.[45] The Kemal-ists believed that only by excluding Islam from key public sectors could they embark upon the process of modernization.[46] For them, modernization was founded upon secularization.

The Kemalist drive to secularization followed a number of strategies with regard to Islam. First, it advocated that Islam should be simply a code of private ethics. Underlying this was a second strategy which tried to restrict the significance of Islam by actively adopting a hostile policy towards it. This can be seen in terms of their legislative programme: for example, the decision by the Kemalist government that there should be only one mosque for all Muslims living within a 500-metre radius. Any mosque which violated this law was demolished or converted to another non-religious use, for example a warehouse. No new mosque was built in Turkey until the 1950s.[47] The third strategy was the policy of trying to use Islam as the antagonistic other of Kemalism. Islam was continually being described in terms which made it the 'constitutive outside' of the discourse of Kemalism.[48] For example, Mustafa Kemal repeatedly described Islam as 'the symbol of obscurantism'; as 'a purified corpse which poisons our lives'; as 'the enemy of civilization and science'; and so on.[49]

Nationalism The Kemalists understood the Westphalian model of the nation state to be the only legitimate and scientific form of a political community.[50] During the period between the end of the Balkan wars and the establishment of the Kemalist republic, nationalism took two major forms among Ottoman intellectuals: first, there were those whose advocated pan-turanism – the argument that all Turks should be part of single state stretching from the Aegean to Central Asia. Secondly, there were the Turkists, who confined their nationalist aspirations to establishing a culturally, linguistically and ethnically homogenous state within the confines of Anatolia. Mustafa Kemal favoured the second form of nationalism. As a result nationalism in Turkey came to mean a preservation of the cohesion of the Turkish Republic in the face of separatist demands. As Reccep Peker, the party secretary of the Republican People's Party declared:

> We consider as ours all those of our citizens who live among us, who belong politically and socially to the Turkish nation and among whom ideas such as 'Kurdism', 'Circassianism' and even 'Lazism' … have been planted … We want to state just as sincerely our opinion regarding Jewish or Christian compatriots. Our party considers these as absolutely Turkish in so far as they belong to our community of language and ideal.[51]

Nationalism was a principle to be applied only to Turkish people; it was a means of overcoming the multinational character of the Ottoman state and replacing it with something more homogeneous. Mustafa Kemal argued:

> In a state which extends from the East to the West and unites in its embrace contrary elements with opposite character, goals and culture, it is natural that the internal organization be defective and weak in its foundations.[52]

The Ottoman model of political community, with its ability to contain overlapping loyalties, languages and social networks, was contrasted with the Westphalian model in which all social boundaries were supposed to coincide with the political boundaries of the nation state. The ability of the Ottoman model to contain such diverse elements was presented as evidence of its degenerate character, rather than as a sign of its strength. One consequence of this was that Kemalism articulated the exclusion of a Kurdish identity.[53] The Kurds, who could be contained within the 'a-national logic' of the caliphate and the Ottoman state, could not be accommodated within the parameters of the Westphalian model.[54] The Kemalist project not only sought to institute a new constitutional arrangement patterned on the Westphalian nation state, but also to articulate a new subjectivity based around nationalism. For Kemalism, the invention of the 'Turk' was essential to replace the Muslim as a political subject, since a Muslim subjectivity violated 'the logic of the nation'.[55]

To disseminate this new 'Turkish' subjectivity, the Kemalist project sought to inscribe a new temporal order. To this end, the Turkish History Conferences of 1932 and 1937 promoted the 'Turkish history thesis'. Ottoman history based on religious community was replaced by a 'national history' of the Turkish people, stressing the role of migration from Central Asia in the development of the civilizations of Sumeria and Akkad, Islam and western Europe.[56] Historical narratives provide political projects with both a genealogy (explanations of the past, placing the present in the context of a particular past) and a teleology (construction of future horizons as relations of necessity emanating from the moment of origin).[57] The 'Turkish history thesis' provided the Kemalist project with the means to construct a collective memory that erased the Ottoman past in favour of a more ancient, more basic history centred on Turkish national identities.[58] The impact of nationalism on the Kemalist project stretched both backwards and forwards in time, as well as providing a model for the organization of space.

Modernization   There is a debate in modern Turkish history as to the extent to which Kemalism marks a breach with the Ottoman empire. It is easy to see the Kemalist project as a continuation of the various attempts to modernize Ottoman society beginning with the *Tanzimat* (reordering) reforms. These reforms are attempts by which the Sublime Porte tries to arrest the passing of its former awesome glory. They are similar at a superficial level to other attempts by non-western societies (e.g. Japan) to come to terms with the 'European miracle'. But for the Ottoman leadership, dealing with the 'European miracle' was centred on the rescuing of the Ottoman state. That is, the great reforming bureaucrats like Rashid Pasha, Ali Pasha and Midhad Pasha, and the Sultan Abdulhamid II were motivated by a desire to make the Ottoman empire compete successfully in the predatory international climate of the nineteenth century, where the great European powers hovered above the 'sick man of Europe', waiting for it to fall. For the Ottoman reformers the purpose of modernization was to be successful in resisting the demands of the European powers. Thus most of the reforms were concentrated at the military and administrative levels.[59]

Kemalism inscribed Islam in terms of its antagonism to the Kemalist project of modernization.[60] Thus modernization in the Kemalist discourse came to have a very different meaning from that of the Ottoman reformers, who sought modernization as a technique of improving state power. Mustafa Kemal saw modernization not as a technique but as a project. This transformation of modernization, from being just a means to an end to being an end in itself, brought to the surface the confusion between westernization and modernization.

Westernization   The Kemalists had a unilinear view of history, in which history followed a fixed pattern of progress. In this view, the most advanced position was occupied by European civilization.[61] For the Kemalists, being modern meant being like the Europeans. As Turner writes, the reform programme of Mustafa Kemal was 'consciously mimetic in that it took Europe as its specific model of adaption'.[62] Part of the justification for this mimetic quality of Kemalism was the argument that modernization was only possible if you created the conditions that had made European modernization possible. Since the preconditions of European modernization were European cultural practices, to be truly modernized one had to reproduce European culture. In other words, modernization could not be acquired without a social and cultural transformation. For Mustafa Kemal and his acolytes the European miracle could only be imitated, duplicated and doubled; it could not simply be an inspiration, but had to be a duplication. But the Kemalists did not content themselves simply with institutional transformations. Their attempts at westernization did not end just with the establishment of westernizing agencies, as Turner explains: 'The mimetic quality of Turkish secularization had to be carried out in detail at the personal level, in terms of dress, writing and habit.'[63] This is why, for example, the Kemalists made such fuss about introducing ballroom dancing, replacing traditional Turkish music with opera, and so on.[64]

To become modern, the Kemalists believed that they had to become western; one could not be western and at the same time be oriental. Islam was represented in Kemalist discourse as the epitome of the Orient. Kemalist Turks had to stop being orientals and to start being Europeans; they had to eradicate any association with the Orient, and define themselves as being part of the West. This opposition between the West and the Orient, which was constitutive of both the West and the Orient, however, compelled the Kemalists to assert their western identity by denying and repressing the oriental within themselves. The legislation passed in Turkey during the years 1924–28, Kemal's pronouncements on the merits of western civilization, the 1931 manifesto of the Republican People's Party privileging the party programme of Laicism, etc. were all measures that demonstrated how Kemalism operated *via-à-vis* the opposition between the West and its other – and on which side of this 'violent hierarchy' they wanted to position themselves.[65]

To modernize, the Kemalists had to westernize, but the very nature of westernization implied the necessity of orientalization since you can only westernize what is not western, that is what is oriental. Thus, to westernize you had first to orientalize: one had to represent the oriental, before one could postulate westernization as an antidote. To reject the Orient in the name of the West meant the articulation of the Orient as 'the Orient'. That is, Muslim societies had to be described in terms of their difference from western societies – but this description had to be made in terms of the difference between them as articulated by the West. So the Kemalists had to carry out a twofold operation to enable themselves to be modernized: on the one hand they had to represent Muslim societies as being oriental, as suffering from all the ills that the Orient had to suffer to make the West look healthy and whole. They had to speak about the retrograde influence of Islam on development of modernity within Muslim societies.

On the other hand, the Kemalists argued that the cure for the ills of the Orient was the medicine of the West. It was necessary to de-orientalize Muslim societies, and the act of de-orientalization would in itself overcome its primitive nature. De-orientalization in the context of Muslim societies meant de-Islamization. Hence, the Kemalists found themselves in a paradoxical situation: to be western, one had to reject the Orient. The rejection had to be what Derrida calls 'superhard'; it had to have the firmness of a logical or grammatical example, something that could not admit any ambiguity.[66] The Kemalists themselves, however, were the ones who were, to quote Said, 'orientalizing the Orient'.[67] That is, their rejection of the Orient relied on them being able to articulate and perpetuate an oriental identity.

The only way to manage this paradox of westernizing and orientalizing was for the Kemalists to fix upon Islam the representation of orientalness; it was through Islam that the Orient was given shape. Islam then became a marker of oriental identity. Thus the Kemalists could see that in order to westernize they had to de-Islamize – that is, they had to remove the influence of Islam from their societies. It was only by removing Islam that they could cease to be part of the Orient and become truly western.

The impact of Kemalism

Mustafa Kemal's reformist programme had a great deal of influence on other Muslims living outside Turkey. For example, Reza Khan openly emulated Ataturk's policies.[68] A great deal of intellectual energy in the Muslim world was devoted to discussions of Mustafa Kemal's reforms and their general applicability in other Muslim territories.[69] For example, a pan-Arabist ideologue such as al-Husri saw Kemal's reforms as being sanctioned by the advance of history.[70] The Muslim regimes that emerged following de-colonization demonstrated many similarities to the main tenets of Kemalist reforms. So far I have focused on the discourse of Kemalism as it appeared in Turkey during the formative period of the new Republic (1923–45). However, my interest in Kemalism is not to provide an analysis of post-Ottoman Turkey, but rather to demonstrate the wide significance that Kemal's ideas and policies have had beyond Turkey. The abolition of the caliphate and the project of westernizing what had been the most powerful Muslim state in the world meant that Kemalism could not be treated as simply a local phenomenon, peculiar to Turkey. While there has been some acknowledgement of the role of Mustafa Kemal in constituting a new political paradigm for the wider Muslim world, on the whole the study of Kemalism has tended to remain confined to the field of Turkish studies.

I do not describe the post-colonial regimes that came to power in Muslim majority areas, beginning with the independence of Pakistan in 1947,[71] as 'secularizing' or 'modernizing' or 'nationalist', as the literature on Islamic fundamentalism tends to do.[72] I shall describe them as being Kemalist. I am aware that by describing these regimes through the metaphor of Kemalism I am generalizing about many different kinds of political systems, geopolitical situations, etc. In my defence, I would say that Kemalism is certainly more specific than terms such as 'nationalist' or 'secularist', which are habitually used to describe these regimes. Furthermore, there is a certain family resemblance between all these regimes in their policies towards the political role of Islam. These regimes came into being in a world in which there was no caliphate and all of them are unified in that they reject the use of Islam as the master signifier of their political discourse. This transformation of Islam, from the master signifier of a political order into just another element, is what allows me to describe these regimes as being Kemalist. From now on, when I use the term Kemalism I refer not to the specific discursive practices of Mustafa Kemal, but rather to a more general discourse founded upon the perspective opened up by Kemal and sharing many of Kemal's key assumptions. In other words, Kemalism describes a hegemonic political discourse in the Muslim world, within which Islam was no longer a master signifier of the political order.

Of course, not all Kemalist regimes had identical strategies for dealing with Islam. It is possible to identify a variety of stances regarding how Islam was to be inscribed within individual Kemalist regimes.

The Pahlavist strategy In this strategy, Islam is displaced as a master signifier and its displacement reinscribed in terms of its being an 'alien imperialist ideology'. The aim of this strategy is to try to use pre-Islamic elements to narrate a history in which Islam appears as an interruption – a distortion of the 'true' identity of the society in question. The claim to a non-Islamic heritage is used to dis-articulate Islam from civil society's discursive practices. This strategy is best exemplified by the Pahlavis of Iran.

The classification of Iran as an Aryan society helped to highlighted the troublesome aspects of Semitic Islam.[73] For in the racialized discourses which circulated at the time, development and race were inextricably linked and the failure of Iran to develop could only be result of its 'Semitization' – that is, the Islamic conquest of Iran. Such an argument had great appeal for Reza Khan (an avid con-sumer of racial discourses) and his followers as an explanation of Iran's backwardness, and as a prescription for its future.[74] These arguments also built upon certain anti-Arabness that could be found within some sections of Iranian society.

The Aryanist ideology found its most grandiloquent expression in Mohammed Reza's reign during the period 1971–77. During this period Mohammed Reza used themes of Iran's pre-Islamic past to construct its identity in terms of a 'Great Civilization' founded upon Aryan cultural values. To this end, he initiated a number of policies designed to emphasize Iran's pre-Islamic past, for example: support for archaeological projects, such as excavating the Achaemenid and Sassanid sites; the celebrations of '2,500 years of continuous mon-archy' held at Persepolis; the introduction of a new calendar based on the accession of Cyrus the Great to replace the Islamic calendar. In addition, attempts were made to re-describe Islam as the result of a 'Semitic invasion', and the principal cause of Iranian backward-ness.[75]

Apart from the Shah of Iran, one can detect a similar strategy at play in the discourse of Nasserism, in particular, Nasser's turn to-wards Egyptianism following his defeat in 1967.[76] A similar strand can be found in the discourse of some of anti-FIS Algerians, who narrate Algerian identity in terms of its 'Mediterraneanness', as opposed to its oriental/Islamicness. The Baathist regime of Iraq also followed this strategy for much of its history.[77] For example, the regime took a number of measures to emphasize its pre-Islamic heritage including the use of Mesopotomian symbols in the regime's war propaganda, the project to rebuild Babylon, the regime's investment in archaeology, and so on.[78] This policy of Mesopotamianism was a key component in the Baathist regime's shift towards a more nationalistic and less pan-Arabic vision of Iraq.[79]

The quasi-caliph strategy   In this version of Kemalism, Islam is included in the political order. It is articulated with state power, through the institution of what could be called a pseudo-caliphate – that is, the construction of an authorized successor/reader of the Law. This is attained by using various devices, such as making genealogical claims (like King Hussein of Jordan); fabricating genealogical claims and assuming titles metonymical to the caliphate, for example commander of the faithful (like King Hassan of Morocco); or using another institutional device, such as protector of the holy cities (this has been the Saudi strategy). All these attempts to reproduce a situation in which Islam is closely tied to the state remain within the discourse of Kemalism, since the nation is still used as the nodal point of the political order. The notion of modernization is still mimetic (North Atlantic rather than East European state socialism tends to be the dominant model). While a vocabulary of authenticity is used to denounce certain practices as western and therefore inappropriate (such as voting in meaningful elections),[80] at the same time they attempt to re-describe certain western practices in terms of an Islamic discourse (for example the practice of *shura*, by which the ruler consults with the ruled, becomes the model of democracy).

While the above two illustrations do not claim to exhaust all possible strategies of Kemalism, they are sufficient to illustrate that within the discourse of Kemalism there is a fundamental agreement that Islam cannot be the master signifier of the political order. It may be an element (of greater or lesser importance) within the political discourse of the particular Kemalist regime, but it cannot unify the field of discursivity of Kemalism.

The effect of Kemalism on the role of Islam was twofold. First, the policy of the Kemalists reactivated Islam – that is, their intervention revealed the contingency of Islam and its articulation with particular hegemonic structures. It became possible to think about the relationship between what had been unproblematically Muslim communities and Islam. The possibility of a post-Islamic order beckoned. Second, the Kemalists also sought to inscribe Islam as their exterior. It was this antagonism between Islam and Kemalism which gave Kemalism its own coherence. Islam's dissolution was arrested by the attempts of the Kemalists to articulate Islam as an antagonistic element. Islam could become a subject of open-ended interventions, because from the very beginning Kemalism sought to re-articulate it to the chain of signifiers which drew the boundaries of the Kemalist discourse. The Kemalist construction of Islam turned it into a metaphor for primitivism, for tradition, for anti-modernity. This reading of Islam could not become hegemonic due to Islam's significance in a variety of other discourses which the Kemalist authorities could not reach. For example, Islam continued to operate as a totalizing label for Muslims' discourses on ethics. This survival of Islam in other discursive horizons created the possibility of Islam becoming the site of contestation, in which a different discursive configuration of Islam fought for mastery. Paradoxically, the Kemalists did not depoliticize Islam but, by removing it from the centre of their constructions of political order, they politicized it: unsettling it and disseminating it into the general culture, where it became available for reinscription.[81]

The availability of Islam did not necessarily mean it would become the central element in a political discourse that would challenge the Kemalist hegemony. It is only since the early 1970s that Islam has begun to play a part in the political opposition to Kemalism. The rise of Islamism was only possible when the availability of Islam could be articulated into a counter-hegemonic discourse. That is, the availability of Islam cannot tell us about the condition of possibility of a political project which sought to reinscribe Islam as master signifier. It does not tell us how this project came to be the major challenger of the Kemalist hegemony. The mere availability of Islamic vocabularies is insufficient to explain how a discourse which was organized around Islam was able to challenge the Kemalist hegemony. The question that needs to be addressed is how it is that under particular circumstances certain discourses become counter-hegemonic while others continue their politically marginal existence. Is it possible to explain why one discourse and not another becomes politically central?

Availability and hegemony

Working as I am within a broad anti-foundationalist epistemological framework, there are a number of responses to the above question that I do not feel will be very helpful to my case: for example responses that explain the emergence of political discourses in relation to some teleological understanding of politics or some form of economism. These approaches have been successfully criticized.[82] However, even from an anti-foundationalist perspective, the question requires an adequate response unless one wants to fall into the trap which critics of anti-foundationalism have laid for those attempting to approach social analysis through anti-foundationalism – that is, 'anything goes: anti-foundationalism simply means the randomization of history'.[83] To avoid the charge of randomization, I think it is necessary to develop the category of availability.

Laclau uses availability in an attempt to explain how it is that some discourses prove more successful during crises than others. He seems to be suggesting that if a social crisis is severe enough, so that all the discursive order is shaken, mere availability is 'enough to ensure the victory of a particular discourse'.[84] In other words, a discourse may emerge victorious, not because of any of its innate qualities but simply because it is the only coherent structure in an otherwise totally disorganized world. If we accept Laclau's argument, we could explain the emergence of Islamism along the following lines: Islamism emerges as a challenger to Kemalism because the social order of Muslim societies becomes so disordered that Islam remains as the only point of stability. Therefore the discourses built around Islam become the only discourses promising order. This picture would be further enhanced by a qualification that Laclau introduces: 'the acceptance of a discourse depends on its credibility'.[85] From this one could conclude that what is being presented is really another form of foundationalist political analysis. After all, the role of the categories of 'availability' and 'credibility' seem to be very similar to the habitual metaphors like 'tradition' or 'political culture' that political scientists tend to fall upon when their explanations begin to falter.[86] Laclau would appear to be supporting the line that the raw material for a hegemonic discourse is out there waiting to be discovered. Certainly the availability of Islam does not necessarily mean that it would be used as a building block of a (counter-) hegemonic project. If we follow Laclau's argument, we would have to conclude that all the time we spent trying to locate Islam was wasted. Islam is simply 'out there' in Muslim societies and there is little wonder that it has become the centrepiece of political opposition to the prevailing order: it was bound to happen. Rather than random-izing politics, Laclau would seem to be making it secondary to an essentializing notion of 'political culture'.

The problem arises because Laclau's main purpose in the section concerned is to make the case that there is no necessary cor-respondence between the content of discourse and the organic crisis it tries to hegemonize. Therefore, he does not develop the argument sufficiently and, as a result, it becomes the cause of some confusion.

Let us try to clarify the argument in two parts. First, the main source of confusion seems to be that it is not clear what is involved in the notion of availability. Laclau seems to be using 'available' in the ordinary sense, but he is also hinting at its more rigorous connota-tions. In conventional Heideggerese, what is available is what is ready at hand. Now, the ready at hand is determined by the task at hand. There are many things which are standing by, which potentially could be put to some use. In a workshop, a carpenter will have many tools: hammer, saw, chisel, etc.; the availability of any of these tools depends not only on the tools being there in the workshop, but on there being a job the carpenter wants to do. The need for hammering requires that the hammer be available for use. The available discourse for Laclau is not analogous to the presence of tools in the workshop in the above example. It was not the mere presence of the Nazi Party with its members and manifestos, or the presence of texts from Gobineau, the Protocols of Zion, and all the racist narratives floating around the salons and streets of early twentieth-century European society which were decisive in the Nazi takeover. Nazi discourse was not lying around like an unopened book, which the frightened German middle class happened to stumble upon in the long night of the Depression. Such an understanding of the available confuses it with occurrent (presence at hand); the availability of a discourse is not the same as the objective existence of a discourse. A discourse becomes available through its articulation. The existence of Islam cannot account for Islamism.

So how do we know what discourse is available? This is the second main source of confusion: to what extent can the construction of a hegemony be read as implying that there was no alternative to that hegemony? A vital part of any hegemonic articulation is the establishment of an interpretation which sees it as the only possible outcome. This means the suppression of any alternatives. This retrospective construction of a 'no alternative' situation cannot be read as the confirmation of the sole availability of the discourse that has become hegemonic. The absence of an alternative is a reward for victory and not its cause. For example, a communist discourse was also available in the Weimar Republic. The Nazi hegemony could erase the memory of the decision and represent itself as the only and necessary cure for Germany's crisis. To take another example, communist, liberal and nationalist discourses were all available in pre-revolutionary Iran. The emergence of Khomeini's Islamism was not inevitable, and it was not due to the fact that there was an absence of alternative discourses. Rather, it was the product of a political struggle that established Khomeini's hegemony. It is clear from the context of the passage that Laclau is adamant that the formation of a hegemony is a contingent operation. To argue that there is no hegemonic alternative would be to make a particular hegemony necessary.

What is not so clear and needs to be emphasized is that not all discourses are equally available in any social context. It is in this sense that one can better appreciate Laclau's comments on credibility, for the unevenness of the availability of a discourse is constitutive of the social. This unevenness of availability limits the contingency of the correspondence between the discursive space that needs to filled and the discourse attempting to suture that gap. Credibility is a reflection of that unevenness; it is not a static screen acting as a filter which is external to the hegemonic struggle, but is a part of that struggle. As the unevenness of availability changes, so does what is considered credible. We have to be careful not to slip from talking about historical specificity (the unevenness of availability) to talking about cultural essentialism (unevenness as pre-given).[87] The unevenness of availability is only a reflection of a sedimented power struggle rather than the epiphenomena of some essence. Islamism is not the mere reflection of Islam, but rather it is a political discourse that takes the availability of Islam as a means of undermining the Kemalist *anciens régimes*. Islamism makes use of the availability of Islam, but, at the same time, it increases the availability of Islam. In other words Islamism is organized around Islam, but this is a two-way process since Islamism also organizes Islam. The articulation of Islamism as a counter-hegemonic discourse involves the task at hand: constructing order. The availability of Islam and the Islamists' specific inscription of that task (the construction of a new political order in terms of an Islamic state) were not necessary but contingent outcomes. As Gramsci pointed out, the *ancien régime* has to fall before a new order can emerge.[88] The possibility of Islamism depended not only on the availability of Islam, but also it required the erosion of Kemalism. But why should Islamists benefit from the failure of Kemalist discourses? Some scholars have explained this outcome by referring to the fact that the nationalists were in power, the communists were in jail, and so, by a process of elimination, the mantle of revolt fell upon the Islamists.[89] Even if we accept for argument's sake the validity of this description, it is still not clear why the failure of Kemalist regimes does not clear the ground for other discourses, such as liberalism or social democracy.

The crisis of authority of Kemalism has found an increasingly loud response claiming that the only solution to the crisis will be found in Islam. In other words, with increasing certitude and confidence the Islamist agenda for the solution of the crisis of Kemalism appears to be the only viable alternative to the continuation of the Kemalist regimes. In large parts of the Muslim world the political choice has become polarized between Kemalism or Islamism. The question that has to be addressed is: what are the factors that led to this polarization? Or, to put it in another way: how is it that the Islamists have apparently monopolized the opposition to the Kemalists? The failures of Kemalism cannot explain how it is that Islamism has emerged as the main beneficiary of this failure. The reason for the success of Islamism in opposing the Kemalist regimes still has to be explored.

Conclusion

Let us summarize the argument presented so far. I have suggested that it would be more useful to read the literature reviewed in

Chapter 1, as providing accounts for the weakening of the hegemony of what I have called Kemalism, rather than giving any reasons for the emergence of Islamism. I then went on to argue that the relation between Islam and Islamism cannot be theorized in terms of cultural essentialism. However, this does not mean that the relationship between the two is of secondary importance. I suggested that Islam was initially articulated as a master signifier and Islamism is the attempt to re-articulate that master signifier to a political order. This was the subject of Chapter 2.

In this chapter, I made two main points. First, I argued that the abolition of the caliphate had the effect of unfixing the sedimented link between the state and Islam. The effect of this was to reactivate Islam as a political discourse – it was now possible for Islam to be re-described by other political forces. The dismantling of the Ottoman empire – both territorially by the European powers and ideologically by Kemal and his followers – produced the political terrain with which we are now familiar: a Muslim world fragmented between different nation states, ruled by modernizing (that is Kemalist) élites, which see Islam as being peripheral to the concerns of the state. Mustafa Kemal, by abolishing the caliphate, helped to sanction and to legitimize the idea that national identities encased in nation states are the only credible form of political community. Once the caliphate had been replaced by the discourse of Kemalism it became possible to think about the need for an Islamic state. Second, I argued that the Kemalists tried to prevent the reactivation of Islam by attempting to re-describe it as being the obstacle to modernization. In other words, the discourse of Kemalism was based on the exclusion of Islam from the public domain.

What I have not yet done is to account for the emergence of Islamism. All I have said is that Kemalism, to use the Gramscian term, is experiencing a 'crisis of authority'.[90] I have not said why it is that Islamism appears currently to be the most likely beneficiary of Kemalism's difficulties. This is addressed in the next chapter.

Notes

1. See Hodgson's argument for the unity of later Islamic history and his rejection of the regionalization of Islamic history. Hodgson, 1960, pp. 879–82.

2. A useful introductory account of the history of the caliphate can be found in Holt et al., 1970. See also Ayalon, 1960.

3. Compare this with Foucault's 'founders of discursivity'. These are authors who have, according to Foucault, opened up the possibility of producing texts other than their own, but based on their founding discourses. See Foucault, in Rabinow, 1986, pp. 113–14. See also Pitkin on what she calls the 'Founder' – according to her, the heroes of Machiavelli. Pitkin, 1984, pp. 52–79.

4. For more historical details see Vaglieri, in Holt et al., 1970, pp. 57–103.

5. I am grateful to Mohammed Reza Tajik for reminding me of this story.

6. Lapidus, 1996, p. 9. See also Crone and Hinds, 1986, p. 27.

7. Even when the discursive horizon makes it possible for a doubling to take place, it is not a doubling in the strict sense. For example, in the case of the Dalai Lama, he is in fact a reincarnation of himself, and therefore there is no doubling and no succession.

8. From the very beginning the caliphate did not enjoy universal allegiance. Many Muslims were not very happy that the claims of Abu Bakr, Omar and Othman were given precedence over Ali. It is out of this basic constitutional difference that Shia and Sunni tendencies developed. (This is one of the reasons why the Shia attitude to the caliphate has been, at best, ambivalent.) Over time many other elements were later added, including different rituals, different legal codes, etc. However, at the centre remained the constitutional distinction. This constitutional difference between Shia and Sunni dissolves with Khomeini's theory of the *Vilayat-i-faqih*, which actually moves to a position similar to that of Sunni political theory. For Khomeini argues that in the absence of a direct descendant of the Prophet it is incumbent upon Muslims to live under an Islamic government.

9. *Ghulams* were similar to Anglo-Saxon houscarls, or the *comitatus* of the later Roman empire – that is, men-at-arms bound to their chief, normally recruited from outside local kinship networks. See Beckwith, 1980.

10. For further details of the caliphate and its rather turbulent history, see Vaglieri, in Holt et al., 1970, pp. 57–103.

11. For example, Muslim rulers who had recently acquired power would often seek an endorsement from the caliph in Cairo as means of legitimating their position. Mamluk sultans through their control of access to the caliph and thus his endorsements (*taqalid*) gained a diplomatic primacy among Muslim princes. Petry cites an incident in 1471, when Ghiyath al-Din, the new sultan of Delhi, sent a delegation to Cairo, to request his formal confirmation as sultan. See Petry, 1994, pp. 32 and 62. Some of the early Ottoman sultans also turned to the Abbasid caliph (in Cairo) to legitimize their rule; see Har-El, 1995, pp. 66–7.

12. It can be argued that as the Muslim empire gave way to a commonwealth of Muslim states, the role of the caliph become even less governmental and more ideological. See Har-El, 1995, pp. 10–11.

13. Lapidus, 1996, p. 12.

14. Of course, within the overarching structure provided by the caliph a variety of distinct state organizations developed in the Muslim world, but these did not question the relationship between Islam and government. For a contrary view, see Klausner, 1973, pp. 97–100. She contends that as early as the Seljuk period, the caliphal authority had diminished so much that the political order that emerged under various 'Perso-Turkish' regimes was one in which Islam was no longer a 'coordinator of life and society' but just one coordinate among many (p. 100). She projects this conclusion to the present day. Arguments such as this, however, fail to acknowledge the radical nature of secularization. Prior to the discourse of

secularization, Islam could never simply be another coordinate in social life. There is a tendency in orientalist historiography to perceive the period from the Rightly Guided caliphs to the Abbasids as the golden age of Islam. This construction allows subsequent developments to be narrated in terms of 'decline' or 'corruption' of a pure Islam. If one does not assume that Islam exhausted the social from its inception, the case for its Seljuk secularization is considerably weakened.

15. This is not to suggest that there were no challenges to the authority of the caliphate, but they were very rarely made in the name of Islam. When they were, for example, the Mahdiyya Revolt in Sudan (1879–98), they were made in the form of an authority 'higher' than the caliph: the return of the Twelfth Imam.

16. Deringil, 1993, p. 179.

17. Ataturk, 1983, p. 1,058.

18. Deringil, 1993, p. 180.

19. Kemal could have taken up the offer to be caliph in the similar way that his near contemporary in Iran, Reza Khan, took up the offer to be the new shah.

20. Landau makes the point that much of the criticism of the caliphate during the early nineteenth century came from Europe, motivated by geopolitical considerations (principally, attempts to undermine Ottoman pan-Islamic policies). See Landau, 1994, pp. 176–8.

21. Ataturk, 1983, p. 379.

22. Ibid., p. 10.

23. See Mardin, 1993a, p. 365.

24. Ibid., pp. 371–3.

25. Yegen, 1996, p. 225.

26. Zubaida, 1989, p. 42.

27. Sharbabi, 1990, Chapter 1.

28. For details of the Khalifat movement see Minault, 1982; Niemeijer, 1972.

29. See the statement by Mohammed Ali (1878–1931), demanding British support for the caliphate, in Donohue and Esposito, 1982, pp. 48–56.

30. Minault, 1982, p. 73.

31. Ibid., p. 203.

32. Ibid.

33. Ibid., pp. 203–4.

34. Enyat, 1982, p. 43.

35. Ibid., p. 46.

36. Iqbal, 1981, p. 166.

37. For details of some of the debates, see Hourani, 1983; Abdel Malek, 1983.

38. Abdel Malek, 1983, p. 44.

39. B. Anderson, 1990. Anderson's 'imagined communities' precludes forms of communities not centred on vernacular language. This is partly because he identifies a nation as a horizontal community, and partly because he tends to privilege technology as the source of nationalism (e.g. the printing press). I think his notion of 'imagined communities' can work – without these restrictions – to include all forms of political communities. See Richards, 1993, pp. 1–9, for the fictive nature of modern empires.

40. Many themes of what is called Kemalism were the work of a group of intellectuals organized around the journal *Kadro*. These intellectuals were responsible for turning Mustafa Kemal's ideas into a systematic ideology.

41. Quoted by Erlap, in Finkel and Sirman, 1990, p. 219.

42. See Paul Dummont's and Sabri M. Akural's chapters in Landau, 1984, for a detailed discussion of the role of the 'six arrows' in the ideology of Kemalism.

43. Mardin, 1982, p. 174.

44. Shaw, 1977, p. 384.

45. Turner, 1974, p. 168.

46. Esposito, 1992, p. 9.

47. F. Ahmad, 1993, p. 91.

48. The notion of the constitutive outside is a Derridean category described by Staten in the following terms: 'it refers to an anti-essence that violates the boundary of positivity by which a concept has been formerly thought to be preserved as-such, but in violating it it becomes the positive condition of the possibility of the assertion of that positive boundary'. Staten is adamant that this notion cannot be stated in a more commonsensical way because one would lose the connection with philosophical tradition from which this concept emerges. I am prompted by Rorty's comments on Heidegger ('Heidegger was the greatest theoretical imagination of his time ... he achieved the sublimity he attempted. But this does not prevent his thought being entirely useless to people who do not share his associations') to disagree. My interest in this notion is purely pragmatic, and I understand it to be no more than analogous to the frontier of a state which marks both the limit and extent of the state. See Staten, 1984, p. 18; Rorty, 1989, pp. 117–19 (especially p. 118).

49. Quoted in Gilsenan, 1990, p. 261.

50. In 1648, the treaty of Westphalia brought the Thirty Years' War to an end and reaffirmed the principle that the religious allegiance of any given body of people was to be determined exclusively by their rulers. This signalled the end of any possibility of construing an authority above and beyond the state. The state emerged from the treaty of Westphalia as an autonomous and enclosed space, with its exclusive rights to jurisdiction and demands for affiliation. The Westphalian order encouraged the idea that it was possible to make tidy correspondences between state, territory and people. See Toulmin, 1990, pp. 196–7.

51. Quoted by Dummont, in Landau, 1984, p. 29.

52. Ataturk, 1983, pp. 378–9.

53. Yegen, 1996, p. 217.

54. Ibid., p. 220.

55. Ibid.

56. See Lewis, 1961, pp. 262–73; Toprak, 1981 (especially Chapter 3), for details of the Kemalist production of a Turkish culture 'cleansed' of any Islamic influences.

57. I am grateful to Lilian E. Zac for many discussions regarding the role of historical narratives for political projects. See also Zac, 1995, pp. 147–9.

58. For more details on the articulation of collective memories and production of national identities, see Landi, 1988, pp. 63–4.

59. See Ward and Rustow, 1964, for a comparison between Japanese and Turkish attempts at modernization.

60. Cizre-Sakalioglu, 1994, p. 255.

61. It is easy to detect the influence of the French Third Republic in the discourse of Kemalism. The westernizing stance of the Kemalists, however, cannot be reduced to being due simply to the influence of the French model. The Kemalists sought to be western in grander sense. That is, they saw themselves as

westerners, not specifically francophiles. It was the idea of Europe and European civilization that was their model, not any particular European state.

62. Turner, 1974, p. 168.

63. Ibid., p. 167.

64. F. Ahmad, 1993, p. 87.

65. Derrida uses the term 'violent hierarchy' to describe the binary logic of western metaphysics. See Derrida, 1987, pp. 48–52.

66. Staten, 1984, pp. 151–2.

67. Said, 1985a, pp. 5–6 and 65–7. See also Mutman, 1992.

68. See Banani, 1961, pp. 44–5.

69. Cleveland, 1983, p. 15.

70. Ibid., p. 16.

71. By post-colonial, I mean a state of affairs which is purely descriptive. I take it to be the period following the de-colonization of European rule. So that in the case of Turkey, the post-colonial period begins with the victory of Mustafa Kemal over western attempts to carve up Anatolia, and the subsequent repudi-ation of the treaty of Versailles. In the case of Egypt, post-colonial refers to the coup that brought Nasser and the Free Officers to power in 1953, and not the period following Egypt's nominal independence in 1922. The beginning of the post-colonial period varies from place to place, but for the majority of Muslim communities, it refers to the period from 1947–61, during which most of the present-day Muslim states gained some form of real autonomy from imperial centres. See Keddie for a similar understanding of the post-colonial: Keddie, in Halliday and Alavi, 1988, p. 15.

72. For example, see Stowasser, in Stowasser, 1987, p. 7.

73. The discovery of an Indo-European superfamily of languagues in 1787, by William Jones, was a key development in the classification of Iran as an Aryan civilization – a cognate of western civilizations.

74. The allies removed Reza Khan in 1942 from the 'peacock throne' because of his pro-Nazi tendencies.

75. Details of this 'Great Civilization' discourse and its relationship to Islam can be found in Sayyid, 1987.

76. For details, see Hopwood, 1982, pp. 98–9.

77. See Baram, 1991, pp. 61–83, and 97–8.

78. Ibid., pp. 30–37 and 41–52.

79. One of the consequences of Iraq's war with Iran was that the secular Baathists began to make increasing use of Islamic metaphors.

80. See Gosaibi, 1993.

81. Serif Mardin makes a similar point arguing that: ' ... Islam has become stronger in Turkey because social mobilization had not decreased but on the contrary increased the insecurity of men who have been projected out of their traditional setting'. See Mardin, 1993a, pp. 372–3.

82. For example by Bowles and Gintis, 1987.

83. For example, see Wood, 1986.

84. Laclau, 1990, p. 66.

85. Ibid.

86. Elkins and Simeon, 1979, p. 127.

87. See Zubaida's discussion about how this slippage between historical speci-

ficity and cultural essentialism mars much of the writing on the Muslim world. See Zubaida, 1989, p. 161.

88. Gramsci, 1971, pp. 210–12 and 275–6.

89. Clearly, this argument does not hold for all cases. For example, Islamists were the subject of state repression in many Muslim countries including Egypt, Iraq and Pahlavi Iran.

90. Gramsci, 1971, pp. 275–6.

4. Islam, modernity and the West

The political role of Islam was not the natural product of an 'Islamic' culture but, rather, was a consequence of the way in which Islam was inscribed within Kemalism itself. Having said that, we still are no nearer to an understanding of how Islamism – a discourse that is centred around a political role for Islam – has managed to emerge as the main opposition to Kemalist *anciens régimes* in large parts of the Muslim world. I have established that Kemalism was the dominant political ideology of the Muslim world following the retreat of the European empires, and, until some unspecified time around about the late 1960s and early 1970s, the regimes that emerged from colonial control were organized around the principles of what I have called Kemalism. This Kemalist order, since the mid-1970s, has become increasingly threatened by Islamist tendencies. Descriptions of the failures of Kemalism can be found in the literature on Islamic fundamentalism; what is difficult to find are explanations of why only the Islamists among the opponents of Kemalism should benefit from the hegemonic crisis of Kemalism. It is this question that I wish to address in this chapter. In the first part of the chapter I look at some of the consequences of the weakening of hegemony as a prelude to a discussion of why the fruits of a disintegrating order are distributed so unevenly among political rivals.

The weakening of the Kemalist hegemony

We know that before a new order can be established the *ancien régime* has to be in serious crisis itself; a new hegemony can only be established in a space vacated by the old hegemonic order. In order to describe the contemporary situation of the Muslim world in which the Kemalist orthodoxy is under challenge we have to understand what a hegemonic operation looks like once it starts to go awry. To have a clearer idea about the relation between Kemalism and Islamism we have to know what the main features of a breakdown of a hegemonic order are. My answer to the question posed by this situation depends on how we understand the functioning of a fully formed hegemony. What is the actual configuration of a hegemony?

It is helpful to begin by enumerating a number of features regarding hegemony. First, a hegemony is never absolute or total. Laclau and Mouffe provide a number of theoretical arguments in support of this proposition.[1] One could also examine some historical accounts which question the premise that a hegemonic discourse is generally prevalent throughout the great mass of society;[2] for example, Abercrombie et al., in a study of feudalism, suggest that the efficacy of the discourse of feudalism was in fact surprisingly limited.[3] Thus, even though I have described Kemalism as a hegemonic discourse, we have to be aware that at no time could it be considered as successful in constituting a fully formed Kemalist society. The project of Kemalism, like all political projects, failed fully to constitute all social relations and not all subjects within Kemalist regimes fully internalized the discourse of Kemalism – that is, not all subjects gave their full adherence and showed ideological conviction *vis-à-vis* the Kemalist order. This was as true in Turkey as elsewhere in the Muslim world.[4]

Second, not only are hegemonies incomplete, they are also uneven. Machiavelli makes the point that Roman caesars needed to win only the consent of their praetorian guard, the rest of the population they could rule by fear.[5] Samir al-Khalil's study of Iraq under Saddam Hussein makes much the same point, arguing that the Saddam regime depends on the active support of a very small group and on the repression of the rest of the population.[6] Stuart Hall makes a similar point with regard to the ability of Thatcherism to penetrate and recruit key constituencies, while excluding other sections of society which remained immune to the appeal of Thatcherism.[7] Hegemony, then, is spread unevenly throughout social relations. Some institutions within state–civil society are heavily involved in the hegemonic operation while others are excluded from hegemony. Kemalism was not equally and evenly hegemonic in all Muslim societies or even within the same Muslim communities. For example, in Syria it is the army – and in particular its officer corps – which has been most strongly committed to what I call Kemalism.[8]

Third, it would be helpful if we see hegemony not as the organization of consent supported by coercion,[9] but rather as the
disorganization of dissent (supported by coercion). In other words, to
be hegemonic one does not need to secure active support as long as
one can prevent the organization of opposition into any coherent
form. What I am suggesting is that all hegemonies are confronted by
dissenting elements; the ability of a hegemonic bloc to remain in
power depends on its preventing these dissenting elements from
coalescing into a counter-hegemonic force.

A hegemonic bloc has a number of strategies available for this
purpose. It can try to buy off elements of the opposition; it can play
off the opposition factions; it can attempt to suppress some or all
oppositional elements; and most important of all, it can try and
conceal the scale of the opposition. It is this final strategy, the making
invisible of any resistance, that is crucial to a political hegemonic
formation. Hegemony demands and depends on public compliance;[10]
its rituals of power are geared to that end. It cannot penetrate into
the private spaces in which much of everyday life goes on, because
its gaze is directed (and can only be directed) towards overt acts of
resistance.[11] The secret police have not yet devised a way of dis-
covering whether a supine performance while under the watchful
gaze of others (not necessarily those in authority – for anyone can
be an informer) corresponds to a supine personality in all situations.
Public protestations of deference cannot guarantee the absence of
inner defiance.

The relevance of this for Kemalism can be summed up in the
following way. First, the Kemalist regimes were not able to impose
Kemalism totally.[12] As I argued in the previous chapter, the incompleteness of Kemalism manifested itself in the politicization of
the role of Islam, and the inability of the Kemalists to make their
interpretation of Islam appear natural or sedimented. Second, the
weakness of Kemalism varies, not only from country to country or
from region to region, but also from institute to institute. In some
countries the army remains the main bulwark of Kemalism; in others
the professional associations have become Islamized. As a result of
these regional and institutional variations, the overall picture regarding Islamism is very complex. There are a number of Muslim
communities in which the Islamist position is very visible (south
Lebanon springs to mind as a good example), there are other places

in which there seems to be little overt sign of Islamist activity (Albania). There are places in which the Kemalist élites are fighting tooth and nail for their very survival (as in Algeria and, to some extent, Egypt). There are some states in which ruling Kemalists have sought some kind of accommodation with Islamists (for example Jordan). There are yet other places in which, despite the weakness of specifically Islamist political groups, an Islamist vocabulary has become the language of everyday political contestation (Pakistan). But there are very few Muslim communities, with the exception of Iran (and possibly Sudan), where Kemalism has been replaced by Islamism as the hegemonic discourse.

The unevenness of the Islamist presence should not distract us from considering the significance of such a presence in the first place: that is, in most Muslim communities Kemalism is having difficulties concealing the existence of an Islamist opposition. This itself points to the weakening of Kemalism's hold as a hegemonic discourse. In spite of the unevenness of the Islamist presence, it is clear that it is the only emergent counter-hegemonic discourse. Between the Kemalists and the Islamists, there are no other politically significant tendencies or alternatives. Again this is puzzling, since the unravelling of a hegemonic discourse usually unleashes a proliferation of movements and political alternatives – the situation accompanying the fall of the Soviet Union is a prime example.[13] The contemporary situation of the Muslim world is marked by two features: the inability of the Kemalists to disarticulate the opposition and the emergence of Islamism as the only serious rival to the Kemalist *anciens régimes*. The literature on Islamic fundamentalism has concentrated on explaining the first characteristic in its accounts of the various weaknesses of Kemalism, assuming, for the most part, that once the first problem is dealt with, the second feature would be resolved automatically. The literature could do this because much of it relied either on forms of cultural essentialism, or on its theorization of Islam to carry the explanatory burden. I have previously discussed my difficulties with this approach. It is clear that most accounts of Islamic fundamentalism cannot explain satisfactorily why it is Islamists and not others who seem to be the main beneficiaries of the misfortunes of the Kemalists. The reason why Islamism has come to secure this position is examined in the rest of this chapter.

Given that for a variety of reasons Kemalism was weakened, why was it that Islamism managed to secure for itself the role of opposition? The alternatives to Kemalism included not only Islamism but also liberalism, socialism, democratization, etc. But it is Islamism which has emerged to challenge the prevailing hegemonic order. One way to explain this would be to find the common denominator between Kemalism and other alternatives such as liberalism. What is it that Kemalism and other discourses do not share with Islamism? This seems to be an impossibly huge question. Fortunately the secondary literature on Islamic fundamentalism provides a possible avenue of enquiry. When all is said and done, one of the most enduring descriptions of the conflict between Islamism and Kemalism is that it is a battle between modernity and its 'other'.[14]

Islam as a symbol of the anti-modern is also one of the dominant constructions of the Kemalist discourses, which, as we have seen, aligned Islam with 'obscurantism', 'superstition' and the rejection of modernity. This convergence between Kemalism and some analysts of Islamism suggests that, if we can establish that Islamists are in fact motivated by the desire to go against modernity, we could conclude that it is the anti-modern character of Islamism which distinguishes it from all other alternatives to Kemalism and Kemalism itself.[15] If the success of Islamism is due to its anti-modern character it is easy to understand why other discourses such as socialism, liberalism, etc. could not benefit from the problems of Kemalism, for they too are organized around the principles of modernity – principles not very different from Kemalism itself. By organizing our reading of the conflict between Kemalism and Islamism as a conflict between moderns and anti-moderns we can understand, perhaps, how it is that only Islamism seems to have benefited from Kemalism's difficulties.

Modernity and Islamism

One way of examining the conflict between Kemalism and Islamism, as the conflict between modernity and its others, is to focus on the figure of Khomeini. There is little doubt in the literature on Islamism about the significance of Khomeini.[16] The great majority of scholarly studies dealing with the phenomena of Islamism will at some point or other refer to Khomeini and the Iranian revolution.[17] The significance of Khomeini lies not only in his opposition to Pahlavi Iran specifically, but in more general terms in his opposition to the prevailing order in the Muslim world.

The diversity of Islamist movements is sometimes cited as evidence that the project of Islamism is incoherent.[18] It is the case that various Islamist thinkers disagree about many important issues; however, disagreement between western political theorists has never been cited as evidence of the incoherence of western political thought or even its sub-branches. Marx, Lenin, Gramsci and Mao, to a name a few theorists working within a particular branch of western political thought – let's call it Marxism – disagree on many fundamental issues (the role of the proletariat versus the peasantry; the possibility of revolution in less advanced capitalist countries, and so on) and their disagreements were often part and parcel of the polemics of inter-state rivalries. Despite this, it is possible to argue that a Marxist political thought exists.

It is Khomeini's political thought that best articulates the logic of Islamism. It is only with Khomeini that Islamism makes the transition from an opposition and marginalized political project to a counter-hegemonic movement. There are a number of reasons for this. Until the Iranian revolution, the hegemony of Kemalism had not suffered any serious setback. Even the formation of Pakistan – a state which seemed to based around a logic that rejected Kemalism – was very quickly reconfigured as a Kemalist republic.[19] The founding of the Islamic republic was overdetermined in the figure of Khomeini. Thus even Islamist movements holding very different views from Khomeini were enabled by the establishment of Iran's Islamic republic. In this sense, while Islamism cannot be reduced to Khomeinism, Khomeini does mark a watershed. Within the literature on Islamism, Khomeini has come to occupy the place of an almost paradigmatic representative of Islamism.[20] He seems to be a symbol of what Islamism means. Therefore, discussions of what Khomeini represents have broader significance as they become interpretations of what Islamism is. If Kemal Ataturk can be presented as an icon marking the culmination of various projects of westernization, then the figure of Khomeini marks the end of Kemalism.

One of the dominant themes in the descriptions of Khomeini is his anti-modern character. Khomeini is often presented as a medieval cleric, removed from the modern world and committed to 'turning back the clock of history'.[21] This representation has been attacked by Sami Zubaida, who argues that it is difficult to see Khomeini as an anti-modern caricature. According to Zubaida, Khomeini is not outside modernity and, in fact, only makes sense in the context of modernity.[22] This is a very important point since, if it is sustained, it would force us to reconsider the relationship between Islamism and Kemalism. If the prime representative of the logic of Islamism cannot be outside modernity, then the conflict between Kemalism and Islamism cannot be glibly read as a conflict between modernity and tradition.

Zubaida's reading of Khomeini is supported by other recent writings on the Iranian revolution, which also consider that Khomeini represents a modern political trend and not some atavistic revival of traditional belief.[23] According to Mansoor Moaddel, the Iranian revolution and the subsequent Islamic republic do not 'represent the triumph of traditionalism over modernity'.[24] He describes the Iranian regime as a form of Third World fascism.[25] Moaddel demonstrates his argument by focusing on a number of key features, such as ideology, autonomy of the state, and the system of police repression. In all three features he finds similarities between a fascist state and the Islamic republic.[26]

There have been many attempts to produce a generic theory of fascism; on the whole such attempts have been largely unsuccessful.[27] Fascism as an analytical category has remained too nebulous and too particular to permit a general theory. Its use as a pejorative term, even in scholarly accounts, has further hindered any attempts to use it in a theoretically rigorous manner. Moaddel's attempt to describe the Iranian regime as a form of Third World fascism is not immune to general difficulties that have beset attempts to use fascism as an analytical category outside its very specific historical and geographical location. The three dimensions which he uses as means of making the linkage between the general theory of fascism and the specificity of the Iranian case are inadequate to the task.

According to Moaddel the fascist nature of the Islamic republic is shown by ideological similarities with fascism. In contrast to the fascists of Mussolini, the fascist character of Iran has to be derived not from their subjective proclamations (they do not claim to be fascists) but from an analytical standpoint. Given that such an analytical consensus is missing, and the prevalence of fascism as a pejorative category, there is a risk of circularity in trying to determine the fascist character of Islamism. An attempt to define Islamism in terms of its ideological equivalence to fascism confronts a number of major obstacles. First, the ideology of fascism is intimately related to discourses of nationalism. Islamists explicitly reject nationalism, declaring that 'an Islamic state is not a nationalistic state because ultimate allegiance is owed to God and thereby to the community of all believers – the *Ummah*. One can never stop at any national frontier and say the nation is absolute, an ultimate end in itself.'[28] There is no Islamist equivalent to the valorization of the nation found in fascism, even if the structure of the global international system forces their activities into the 'container' of the nation state.[29]

Secondly, and more importantly, within a theoretical perspective in which the economy is primary, the role of ideology cannot carry the major burden of giving shape to a particular political formation, since by definition ideology is superstructural and, as such, could only have a role which is superficial. The fascist nature of Islamism must rest on grounds which are distinct from the assumed convergence between the two ideologies. This means that if Islamism is to be considered a form of fascism it must be on structural grounds which are distinctive to fascism.

Moaddel's second dimension is based on the argument that the Islamist control of Iran is an expression of the 'relative autonomy' of the state. This set of arguments is found in theoretical frameworks in which the state is a dependent (or secondary) institutional complex in relation to the economic structure. The number of problems with this type of theory of the state have generated a considerable literature. Briefly, unless one assumes (and sustains) the primacy of the economic dimension, the entire theoretical edifice collapses. If the economy is not primary, the state cannot be assumed to be secondary; if the state is not secondary, the question of its 'relative autonomy' does not arise. In other words, the notion of the 'relative autonomy of the state' logically rest upon the idea of economic determination 'in the last resort'.[30] Definitions of fascism favoured by Moaddel have as one of their central pillars the notion of a state exercising 'relative autonomy'. Without this, the idea of fascism as a structural analytical category collapses.[31]

Moaddel also makes the point that the system of police repression exhibited in the Islamic republic is another defining feature of fascism. While the regimes of Mussolini and Hitler may have been innovative in introducing certain techniques of repression, these in themselves cannot be markers of fascism. This is the case not only because Lenin and the Bolsheviks were also pioneers in repressive technology, but because such technology is more usefully seen in terms of the development of a disciplinary society rather than as a feature specific to a particular form of political regime.[32] Fascism as an analytical tool is of limited help in understanding the Islamic republic, and it is even less useful for any general consideration of Islamism.[33] Moaddel is helpful in pointing out the non-traditional character of Islamism, but his commitment to an economistic theoretical schema produces internal inconsistencies which make it difficult to accept that any purpose (other than rhetorical) is served by using fascism as an explanatory category for Khomeini's discourse and for Islamism in general.

Abrahamian also rejects the idea that Khomeini's ideology is some kind of reassertion of traditional Islamic values. His thesis is that what he calls Khomeinism is akin to populism. Populism is for Abrahamian 'mainly a middle-class movement that mobilized the masses with radical-sounding rhetoric against the external powers and entrenched power-holding classes, including the comprador bourgeoisie'. Abrahamian goes on to list some of the main features of populism – such as its 'vague aspirations and no precise program', etc. – which he argues characterize Khomeini's ideology. For him, Khomeini is best understood as an Iranian caudillo.[34]

The notion of populism as an analytical category shares some of the difficulties discussed above in relation to fascism. Populism occupies a rather vague space within both Marxian and liberal theoretical frameworks. Within the liberal political tradition it is used to describe circumstances which arise when broadly democratic mobilizations produce results which are non-liberal. Thus, in liberal political theory the significance of populism is that it marks a political possibility in which the link between democracy and liberalism is broken – thereby questioning the axiomatic nature of the assumption that democracy and liberalism are somehow synonymous. The idea of populism touches upon a broader conception of the political in which the distinction between republicanism and despotism is a marker of more than just political practices, it is a marker of cultural formations.[35] Abrahamian plays on liberal connotations of populism, even though his actual use is more indebted to Marxist analysis, and shares its economistic and class reductionist prejudices. For Abrahamian and other scholars (including closet foundationalists) who share similar views political practice is best understood as a gathering of existing political actors. In other words, politics is about mobilizing the various sections of society. The identities of various constituent parts of a society are most commonly identified by economic or social criteria (for example class), or sometimes by ethnic criteria (for exapmle 'immigrants', 'minorities'). Regardless of the matrix which is used to identify them, these actors are considered to be fully formed. Therefore the relation they have with political practice is considered to be external. The political act is understood as the art of forming coalitions by mobilizing these actors.[36] Populism, then, is a particular form of strategy of mobilization and coalition-building.

An anti-foundationalist approach to political practice would see it, not as a process of gathering already existing actors but rather as the formation of new political subjects. In other words, the primary political task is not merely amalgamative but constitutive. All societies are ultimately political creations – the results of previous successful hegemonies. The aim of the political is to create sedimented, 'naturalized' subjectivities.[37] An anti-foundationalist notion of the political would not see it as a process of mobilization but as a process of construction of political subject(s).

There is no doubt that during the Iranian revolution there were various ways of describing and constructing political identities, including those which relied on notions of class, nation and race. There are, however, no a priori grounds for privileging discourses of class as Abrahamian does. One of the most remarkable things about the Iranian revolution was the extent to which the discourse of Islamism was able to constitute a new subjectivity – that is, a Muslim as a political, anti-monarchic and anti-imperialist subject. Being a Muslim meant being against the Pahlavis, against America, against Zionism, and eventually in favour of Khomeini and the Islamic Republic. The Iranian revolution was the event that marks the consolidation of a Muslim political subjectivity. By attempting to describe the Iranian revolution in terms of populism, Abrahamian marginalizes the significance of Islamism within the events of the revolution. After all, the classical paradigm of Latin American populism was provided by Peron in Argentina, or Vargas in Brazil, and neither of these populists made much use of Christian discourse in their attempts to build a new political order.[38]

Both Moaddel and Abrahamian are confronted by the problem of including Islamism and more specifically the Islamic republic of Iran within western political thought. Their difficulties are the result of the way in which western political theory has been structured around an opposition between republicanism (democracy) and despotism. This division, however, is not, as Noberto Bobbio points out, simply based on a set of different political and governmental practices. The 'great dichotomy' between democracy and despotism defines mutually exclusive and hierarchically ordered cultural formations.[39] Despotism is associated with the 'Orient' and democracy is considered to be the patrimony of the West. Accordingly, within western political thought 'oriental despotism' remains a residual category or rather a negation of all that is claimed as being characteristic of western republicanism. So, for example, Adorno's work on authoritarianism regarded the authoritarian personality as merely the distortion of the normal personality characterized by the liberal bourgeois individual.[40]

Patricia Springborg has shown how the articulation of western republicanism and oriental despotism was a product of a western political discourse that was largely ignorant of the governmental procedures of the Orient.[41] Despite this, it was possible to represent good government as western republicanism, and corrupt government as being essentially despotic. These associations remained largely constant even though the opposition between western republicanism and oriental despotism has taken many diverse forms (the Persian empire for the Ancient Greeks, the Ottoman empire for Renaissance Europeans, the Soviet Union for the North Atlantic plutocracies for much of the twentieth century). This is because, ultimately, the distinction between despotism and republicanism was a distinction between the West and its other. The figure of the Islamic republic of Iran and the Islamist dream of an Islamic state appear merely as a contemporary supplement to this 'great dichotomy'. Islamist political projects cannot be simply inserted within the framework of western political thought without contextualizing the way in which cultural, historical and governmental structures are conflated to produce accounts in which western republicanism is privileged and considered to be the ideal. If by definition (good) governance is western republicanism, then any different political practice can serve only to affirm the ultimate necessity of western republicanism, for any other governmental practice must be a deviant or repressed form of republicanism. Thus, by definition any Islamic state must be repressive, since being it cannot take the form of (western) republicanism. The polarization between oriental despotism and western republicanism leaves no space for any Islamist project.

Neither Abrahamian nor Moaddel contextualizes the dichotomy between republicanism and despotism; as a consequence, they need to draw on problematic concepts like populism and fascism as way of accounting for the 'scandal' of the Iranian revolution. That is, a popular political transformation that neither accords with the ideas of western republicanism, nor can be seen simply as a continuation of a stereotypical model of 'oriental despotism'. Both Abrahamian's and Moaddel's analyses are based on an epistemology which has been the subject of much criticism in recent years. Both are unable to transcend the dichotomy between republicanism and despotism.[42] Both are involved in a form of class-based analysis which considers it possible to read political behaviour in terms of class location.[43] Both, however, offer important correctives to the idea that the rise of Islamism is the manifestation of some traditional pre-modern phenomena, but alas they have limited value as conceptual descriptions of Islamism. Given their epistemological model and my anti-foundationalist prejudices, it is not surprising that I find them unconvincing.

So I am going to focus on Zubaida's arguments regarding the modernness of Khomeini. I do this for two main reasons. First, Zubaida constructs his study by making a close reading of Khomeini's political writings. Therefore, the position he arrives at is based on the logic of Khomeini's argument and is not distorted by consideration of the broader political processes of managing revolutionary politics. Second, Zubaida is willing to read Khomeini as a political theorist, which means that the points that Zubaida makes have greater general relevance to other Islamist trends. Zubaida's sociological reading avoids the temptation to see Khomeini simply as the crystallization of a mere superstructural moment.

Zubaida's general thesis is that, even though Khomeini conducts himself in terms of traditional Islamic rhetorical practices, his conclusions cannot be understood without placing them in the context of modernity. Khomeini's political theory only makes sense in relation to a number of categories such as 'people', 'state', etc. that are the products of developments in western political theory. In other words, for Zubaida, western political theory is the necessary precondition for Khomeini's *Al-Hukumah Al-Islamiya* (Islamic government).[44] Zubaida argues that Khomeini's political theory is not a reiteration of traditional Shia political thought; rather, it is a radical and novel reinterpretation of Shia political doctrine, even though couched in the language of traditional Islamic jurisprudence.

Khomeini's later theoretical writings and political statements are replete with examples in which the notion of the people as an active political agent is central. As Zubaida writes: 'What makes Khomeini's theory plausible is the idea of *the people* as a political force which can effect revolution and transformation.'[45] Even though this idea of the people as a political agent is not theorized in any detail, it is none the less, in Zubaida's opinion, crucial.[46] Having argued cogently for the centrality of the notion of a people as a political agent, Zubaida goes on to show that such an understanding of people is a hallmark of modern political thought. He demonstrates this by drawing a picture of an ideal pre-capitalist state and contrasting it with an ideal modern nation state.[47] The purpose of this contrast is to show that in pre-capitalist states the scope of the political was limited to those who lived off the surplus of subsistence agriculture (for example the aristocracy, the military and the higher echelons of the bureaucracy) and excluded, for the most part, the producers of that surplus. On the other hand, in an industrialized state, the scope of the political includes all the population as potentially politically active. It is for this reason Zubaida concludes that the notion of the people as a political force is founded on the modern state–civil society nexus. Thus, even though Khomeini does not argue for a modern nation state, Zubaida concludes that his reliance on the category of the people presupposes it.[48] From this conclusion, Zubaida draws the lesson that Khomeini (and by extension other forms of Islamism) are not to be dismissed as movements or trends out of time, but rather are swimming in the broad currents of modernity.

If Islamism is a modern phenomenon, then the issue of modernity cannot be used to distinguish between it and other political discourses, such as liberalism or Kemalism. If we follow Zubaida we have to conclude that Islamism is also a phenomenon of modernity, and as such it cannot be described in any meaningful way as being anti-modern. Such a conclusion would also gain from a number of political theorists who also argue that there is no way to stand outside of modernity. For example David Kolb, drawing on the work of Hegel and Hiedegger, argues that it is impossible to step out of modernity, since any attempt to be 'un-modern' is based on the logic of modernity which allows for the possibility of cultivating certain identities.[49] If Khomeini – the epitome of a figure who rejects modernity – cannot do without modernity, then surely it follows that modernity is something that cannot be escaped. Modernity is able to recuperate any attempt at defiance or rejection. I examine the consequences of such a move in the next chapter, but the main conclusion I want to draw for the purposes of this chapter is that either the non-availability of rival discourses to Islamism cannot be explained in terms of modernity, or Islamism's relation with the modern is radically different from that of other discourses.

The first possibility would suggest that we must look elsewhere for the reasons why the crisis of Kemalism has met its most compelling response in Islamism. As I have already noted, there is no other clue in the literature to the 'uniformity' of the response to the crisis of Kemalism being met by Islamism. Apart from the supposed anti-modern character of Islamism, there is nothing much to account for why it is Islamism that has emerged to challenge Kemalism unless we resort to cultural essentialism, which understands Islamism teleologically. I have indicated previously the main reasons for the lack of success of such descriptions.

The second alternative is to explore the possibility that the relationship between modernity and Islam cannot be one of total exclusion. Islamists may reject some aspects of modernity and embrace others, and, by working out what they reject and what they accept, we could draw up a matrix which allows us to distinguish between Kemalism, liberalism, socialism, etc. on the one hand, and Islamism on the other. In other words, rather than abandon my intuitive response that it is the question of modernity that makes Islamism the main beneficiary of the difficulties of modernity, I will try and make my analysis more sophisticated by using a more rigorous notion of modernity. This possibility raises a number of interesting points. If Islam and modernity are not external to each other, then what kind of relationship do they have? Is there one modernity or many kinds of modernities? If there are modernities and not a modernity, what is involved in being modern? What does modernity mean, and what would an Islamic modernity look like? There are a number of trends within the Muslim world which advocate 'Islamic modernization'. I have called these projects Kemalist, because I have argued they understand modernization as being identical with westernization. In other words, Kemalism is not the same as modernization; it is a historically and culturally situated discourse of modernizing particular societies in particular ways. What Zubaida's reading of Khomeini seems to suggest is that there may be other ways of understanding modernization. If this is the case, conflict between Kemalists and Islamists could be seen as a conflict about which type of modernization strategy to pursue, rather than a conflict about whether or not to modernize. If we accept Zubaida's conclusions on Khomeini, there is a possibility of describing Islamism as a species of political modernity, but one that is different from Kemalism, liberalism, socialism, etc. in the way it distinguishes between modernity and the West. This would perhaps help us to understand the very vocal anti-western character of Islamists. The Islamists' attack on westernization could be separated from questions about modernity; their rejection of westernization would not imply a rejection of modernization. Such a reading would be helpful in understanding the Islamist phenomenon.

Unfortunately, a closer reading of Zubaida reveals a fundamental difficulty with his conclusion which puts into jeopardy the ability to develop this second possibility. The problem is that Zubaida is not consistent in his usage of the terms 'modern' and 'western'. Zubaida describes some concepts as being modern, and then goes on to describe the same elements as 'western-inspired political paradigms'.[50] The result of using 'modern' and 'western' interchangeably suggests the impossibility of divorcing the modern from the western. The consequence of equating modernity with the West is to suggest that being modern also means being in some sense western. So that, if we agree with Zubaida that Khomeini's project is modern, we must conclude that it is also western. It is clear that rather than disarticulating the relationship between westernization and modernization, Zubaida's usage of the two terms would lead us to the conclusion that there is no difference between the West and modernity.[51] If we follow Zubaida, it seems that there are not different kinds of modernity, and the conflict between Kemalists and Islamists could not be about the different approaches to modernity. In fact, it makes it difficult to agree with Zubaida's earlier contention that Islamism is modern since we can only assert the modernity of Islamism by discounting its self-proclaimed anti-westernism. If Islamism is just another variant of modernity, which itself is part and parcel of western discourse, then what are we to make of the virulent anti-western stance of so many Islamist movements? Clearly, the re-description of Islamism as a western-inspired phenomenon is leading us into terrain that would be difficult to sustain. If we accept Islamism's anti-western stance, then we have to reject its modern status. This is the consequence of using western and modern as synonymous terms.

Modernity and the West: the West and the 'Rest'.

Zubaida, by using the terms 'modern' and 'western' as being equivalent, clouds the relation between Islamism and the West. I would contend that Zubaida's conflation of the modern and the West is not by itself exceptional; rather, this kind of slippage between the two terms is common in everyday speech. This slippage is an indicator of a confusion which lies at the heart of the identities of both modernity and the West. It is only by trying to clarify some of this confusion that I can proceed to try and situate Islamism. I am aware that the literature about the relation between modernity and the West is vast, and my purpose is only to sketch out the main points of this relationship. At stake are questions about what is the West and what is modernity? If there is no equivalence between modernity and the West, then it is possible for us to allow for different forms of modernity. This would lead to questions as to what are the different forms of modernity, and to an exploration of the possibility of Islamism being modern without being western. If, on the other hand, modernity is equivalent to the West, then the only way one can be modern is by being western. Such a position would endorse Kemal-ism, but it would also create a crisis concerning the notion of the West. If we want to argue that a seemingly anti-western project such as Islamism is just another form of western discourse, we have to examine the implications of such a statement, for the identity of both Islamism and the West itself.

To study this theme I start off by presenting a series of arguments made by Stuart Hall regarding the formation of modernity.[52]

To investigate the links between the West and modernity it is
necessary to enquire into the way in which they are constituted as
discursive objects. Hall identifies various discursive horizons which
are centralized around the category of the 'West'.[53] The West is not
constituted as a single solid entity, rather it operates at a number of
levels, in a number of discourses, performing slightly different functions. In other words, the West is a master signifier – a label that
fixes a variety of discursive chains. Hall lists four main areas in
which the category of the West circulates and coordinates.[54] It
functions as an analytical category which allows us to map out the
world in terms of the West and the non-West.[55] Second, it is a
criterion by which we can make judgements about the rest of the
world – both spatially and temporally.[56] Third, it marks a frontier
around which a number of positive and negative qualities are sorted
and then gathered.[57] For example: Europe is innovative, the Orient is
stagnant; Europe is decentralized, the Orient is centralized; Europe
is geophysically stable, the Orient is geophysically unstable, etc.[58]
One can easily see a logic of equivalences at work here, demarcating
a frontier between the West and the 'Rest'. Finally, it is a term that
represents a particular way of life 'that is developed, industrialized,
urbanized capitalist, secular and modern'.[59] This, I think, is crucial:
for the use of the term 'the West' to stand for a particular form of
socioeconomic organization means reading that socioeconomic ensemble in terms of its cultural identity.

This link between cultural identity and particular social and economic practices is further examined by Agnes Heller. She suggests
that European (or western) cultural practices are intrinsically involved
with the identity of Europe.[60] Her argument is based around three
main propositions: first, the formation of a culture is inscribed in an
awareness of a culture. In other words, a culture becomes a culture
only when there is a consciousness of belonging to that culture.[61]
This argument is clearly in opposition to an essentialist account of
identity.[62] A cultural identity is formed by articulating a cultural
identity and not by utilizing some ostensive notion of identity, for
example language or ethnicity.

Second, the awareness of culture is only possible if there are
transmitters of a culture. This point follows from postulating a relational theorization of identity. If identity is not something discovered
it has to be made. The making of an identity requires the activity of

some agency; in her account Heller refers to Homer, Hesiod and Mozart as carriers of their respective cultures.[63]

Third, the transmitters of a culture have a specific identity, an identity that they impart to the culture. The articulation of cultural identity is itself a political act; it requires, therefore, the intervention of political agents. These political agents are found in various forms of social networks (occupational, geographical, ecological, linguistic, etc.). Even if these agents wish to represent some universal interest, they can only do so by expanding an aspect of their identity. For example, the Emperor Caracalla by granting citizenship to all free male inhabitants of the Roman empire made them *Roman* citizens. Even though Rome was a universal state – which theoretically in-cluded the best part of the world[64] – it was still centred on a par-ticular city, which had its own history and culture.

Heller's argument is that there was no such city for Europe. According to Heller, a European identity was a fragmented affair: the inhabitants of the western extremity of the Asian land mass referred to themselves as Christians. Their home city was Jerusalem, (as well as Rome). Their language was Latin.[65] She clarifies her point by contrasting Hellenism and European culture: Hellenism could be identified as being Greek because the principal carriers of that culture were aware of themselves as being Greek. This is not the case with European culture, the carriers of which did not think of themselves as European; their identity was far too fragmented to allow for such a uniform characterization.[66] It was modernity that aggregated the various disparate elements (the various successor states to the Roman empire) into a consolidated form under the name of Europe, as Heller declares: 'Modernity, the creation of Europe, itself created Europe.'[67] What Heller seems to be suggesting is that modernity is Eurocentric because it is an ideology of the formation of Europe.

As I have shown, Hall would agree with Heller's characterization of the link between modernity and the West. What is so striking about Hall's description of the four levels at which the category of the West operates is that one could substitute the category of modern-ity for the West, without altering the basic lines of the discursive configuration of what he describes. Both Hall and Heller also agree on what the effect of conflating Europe and modernity is on Euro-pean identity. The concept of the West comes to refer to a project.[68] That is, European identity is not structured around a geographical or ethnic complex, but is rather an ideological construction of a very special kind. As Hall writes: 'the idea of the West once produced became productive in turn ... It has become *both* the organizing factor in a system of global power relations *and* the organizing concept in a whole way of thinking and speaking.'[69] Europe is an ideological formation centred on the discourse of modernity. There was no European identity outside the project of modernity. The contrast between modernity and non-modernity is also a description of the contrast between what constitutes the West (civilization, democracy, rationality, freedom) and its 'other' (barbarism, irrationality, despotism, slavery). The difference between the modern and the non-modern constitutes a frontier between the West and the Rest. It is important to note that this division between the modern and non-modern, and the West and the non-West, is not causally arranged. One set of these binary oppositions does not have precedence over another. The West and the Rest dyad provides a content to the differentiation between modernity and non-modernity. The frontier between the West and the Rest is populated by metaphors that describe Europe and non-Europe. The sparsity of modernity is filled by drawing on the cultural reservoir of Europe. When we need to illustrate modernity in the concrete, European culture and European history provide us with an apt and authoritative illustration: the official version of modernity. But these theories of modernity also help to reinforce the distinction between the West and the Rest, as many writers have pointed out.[70]

According to Hall, conventional accounts of the formation of modernity have been organized around this notion of the West to produce a discourse that sees modernity as internal to European culture.[71] That is, the reasons for European expansion over the globe are to be found in the peculiarities of European civilization itself – it is the transformation *in* European culture that inaugurates the modern age.[72] The often-quoted remark from Weber's preface to *The Protestant Ethic and the Spirit of Capitalism* provides a paradigmatic example of the blending of European cultural development with notions of modernization:

> A product of modern European civilization, studying any problem of universal history, is bound to ask himself to what combination of circumstances the fact should be attributed that in Western civilization

only, cultural phenomena have appeared which ... lie in a line of development having a universal significance and value.[73]

Weber goes on to discuss the idea that only in the West has there been the development of rationality, science, etc.[74] Weber is not the only one who sees in the development of Europe the origins of modernity, and thus he defines modernity as being European. 'It seems clear that for the majority of European historians and archaeologists who expressed a view on the subject, from Hegel to Marx and beyond, the basic concern was to find an explanation of the uniqueness of the capitalist West and its role in world history.'[75] Turner has pointed out how both Hegel's and Marx's accounts of history were organized around the linkage between modernity and the West. This confusion between the modern and the West is not just a nineteenth-century phenomenon. Recent popular macrohistories have made the same kind of assumption. For example, J. M. Roberts sees the process of modernization as one of 'europeanization' since, as Roberts writes: 'modernization is above all a matter of ideas and techniques which are European in origin'.[76] The effect of this internalist historiography is, as Hall clearly states, that the West becomes identical with the modern.[77]

To conclude, modernity is a discourse about western identity. It is a narrative about the exceptionality of the West, which presents itself as an explanation of exceptionality. Hence its tautological structure: the essence of what made modernity possible is the retrospective abstraction of what is supposed to be found in the West: feudalism, benign climate, recovery of Greek philosophy, etc. Modernity positions itself as a ruptural moment which divides history in two. It is this rupture that gives birth to the West and marks it off as being unique. Modernity is radically different from all that has gone before. The universalization of modernity facilitates and is facilitated by the globalization of Europe and its transformation into the West – a West that refers not to a geographical entity but to a project.[78] It is this intimate relationship that is to be found in most accounts of the 'rise of the West'.[79]

I seem to have come full circle. I started by agreeing with Zubaida that Khomeini's project was modern, but disagreeing with him that Khomeini's project was western. I sought to separate modernity from European identity but failed. Following the arguments presented

above, it would seem that the West cannot be separated from
modernity. There are, however, some possible alternatives. Islamism
can been seen as a variant of western discourse, in which case it
would be necessary to deal with the problems associated with making
Islamism (and by extension Islam too) part of western civilization.
Turner, for one, seems to favour such an option. His argument is
that we should see the historical Islamic presence in Spain and Sicily
as being western; likewise we should see Christian communities in
what is now Syria and Iraq as being oriental.[80] The problem with
this approach is that it relies on geographical descriptions to do the
work of boundary construction. There are no natural geographical
regions; such regionalization is itself a product of geographers who
were not immune from the discourse of modernity. This problem is
especially stark in relation to the consideration of Islam and the
West, since it is precisely by excluding areas formerly under the
jurisdiction of the Roman empire and occupied by Muslim forces
that the identity of Christendom – and thus Europe – was formed.[81]
As Judith Herrin writes, the term 'Europa' was first used in the
eighth to ninth centuries to designate the area over which Charlemagne held sway: areas outside the nominal control of the caliph
and the emperor in Constantinople.[82] It was the inability of the
emperors of the Second Rome and the caliphs to lay claim to the
old boundaries of the Roman empire that allowed Charlemagne to
forge a distinctive European identity.[83] So by bringing Islam into the
interior of the West one is inevitably going to raise very serious
questions about what the West is – questions that cannot be resolved
by reference to an atlas.

A second possibility would be to reject Zubaida's argument that
Islamism is founded upon modernity. I am loath to reject Zubaida's
argument about the modern nature of Islamism as it seems very clear
that the kind of political projects that Islamism articulates can only
be carried by a number of categories which were not present before
the modern age. This is not just in the banal sense of the dependency
of Islamists on modern technology to disseminate their message (for
example the use of cassettes by the supporters of Khomeini to
disseminate his works), but also at the level of political theory. That
is, there are a number of political concepts (revolution, people as
political agents, types of political mobilization and organization)
without which the Iranian revolution would not have been possible.

A third option would be to see in Islamism an attempt to articulate modernity that is not structured around Eurocentrism. That is, to take seriously the Islamists' claims to being a movement dedicated to a denial of the West, but not to read in this rejection of the West an attempt to re-establish 'traditional' agrarian societies. To do this means renegotiating the identity of modernity as well as that of the West. It is an option which is implicit in some of the recent debates regarding the relationship between modernity and postmodernity. This is the option I am going to pursue in the next section of this chapter: that is, to examine the main currents in this debate as they relate to the western identity of modernity.

Modernity: anti-, post-, counter-

It is often argued that modernity has reached its end in the post-modern condition, or that at least it has been transformed. The question of whether the world is characterized by 'high modernity', 'late modernity' or 'postmodernity' has generated much debate.[84] This debate has been further complicated by serious disagreements about what is actually entailed in postmodernity. For example, Ernest Gellner in his examination of 'resurgent Islam' understands postmodernity to be simply relativism.[85] According to Jameson, postmodernism is a manifestation of the postwar consumerist boom.[86] Given this proliferation of the term postmodern it is hard not to sympathize with Rorty's despair: 'In the past I have used the word post-modern … Now I wish I had not.'[88] The only reason I am entering this debate is because, among all this confusion, there are a number of important points that need to be rescued since they help us better to understand Islamism. I would like to add that I am going to look at postmodernity only in relation to its impact on politics, and ignore its impact in the fields of the arts and literature despite various trends in architecture, literature, art, etc. being labelled as post-modern.

Jean-François Lyotard, whose *The Post-Modern Condition* is one of the main attempts to articulate a comprehensive view of post-modernity, sums up postmodernity as the 'incredulity towards meta-narratives'.[88] He refers to Nietzsche's European nihilism as being a description of the postmodern condition, albeit in a different vocabulary.[89] European nihilism is the nihilism that comes about from the

development of Europe's own critical facility. It is an 'incredulity towards meta-narratives' (Lyotard, 1992) arising from the development of certain interpretive techniques which reveal truth to be a fable.[90] Lyotard contrasts this postmodern condition with modernity. For Lyotard, modernity was characterized by 'a desire to systemize and capture the world, to free human beings by using calculative thought to master and manipulate the conditions of life'.[91] Modernity is based in the belief in meta-narratives (such as 'the dialectics of Spirit, hermeneutics of meaning, the emancipation of the rational or working subject, or the creation of wealth') to legitimize its claims to knowledge.[92] The history of modernity (the Holocaust, the corruptions of empires, mutually assured destruction, ecocide), argues Lyotard, has subverted the promises of its grand narratives (reason, enlightenment, progress), thus calling them into question. In the wake of these grand narratives, Lyotard goes on to say: 'We are left with many small narratives legitimizing all sorts of practices ... but we have no general agreement on the rules for settling disputes among multiple narratives.'[93] For Lyotard, changes in technology and cultural artefacts are producing a fluid world in place of traditional fixities which have now vanished. In the light of these changes and inadequacies of the old grand narratives, Lyotard ends his report on knowledge with a call to arms: 'Let us wage a war on totality, let us be witnesses to the unrepresentable, let us activate the differences and save the honour of the name.'[94] This new state of affairs is what Lyotard calls postmodernity. It can be seen from this brief outline that within Lyotard there are two tensions: on the one hand he wants to describe the postmodern as an epoch, and on the other hand he sees in postmodernity a manifesto. That is, not only is postmodernity a description of the contemporary state of affairs, it is also a celebration of it.

The theorization of postmodernity relies on a notion of modernity that has a certain uniformity, one which can be encapsulated. This is not such an unproblematic operation. Rorty, for one, is not convinced that such efforts are possible; for him any attempt at trying to encapsulate modernity is doomed to failure.[95] The only way for us to describe all the various shapes modernity can take is if we can find its inner core – a kernel that allows us to identify modernity in all possible worlds. In other words, to be able to describe modernity, we have to be clear in our minds when modernity ends – we have to be

able to draw the limits of modernity. Writers who see in postmodernity the limits of modernity remind Rorty of Heidegger's claim
that the West has exhausted its possibilities. Rorty does not feel these
declarations about large and complex discourses are really very
useful.[96] These declarations, he feels, are hangovers from the days
when philosophers considered themselves to be legislators. (There is
a sense in which the crisis of modernity is better understood as the
crisis of the role of the intellectual.)[97] To announce the 'end of
modernity' or the 'end of philosophy' is another example of the
conceit of philosophers who like to see clean beginnings and endings,
and feel that the world can be reduced to and by intellectual
tidiness.[98] Pragmatists like Rorty are more inclined to feel that life is
a little more messy than the tidy minds of philosophers would allow
and that one just muddles along, always in the middle of one thing
or another. For Rorty, if one is going to use the label postmodern, it
should stand for an agenda for change, or a manifesto, or an attitude,
rather than heralding the dawning of a new age.[99] He likes the idea
of having an attitude of 'incredulity towards meta-narratives' but he
does not think that this attitude signals the end of an epoch.[100]

I have a great deal of sympathy for Rorty's views: all the concepts
and descriptions used by people in the academic business tend to
obliterate differences. When we talk about 'Europe' or 'postmodern
bourgeois liberalism' or 'Islam', we are implicitly erasing the internal
differences that constitute these entities. Modernity and postmodernity are no exceptions to this fuzziness. But Rorty is not saying that
modernity is difficult to sum up because it is fuzzy; he is actually
making a larger claim: modernity does not have any uniform theme
from which we can abstract its logic. If I have read Rorty fairly, I
think he is wrong. I think Hall's account of modernity does exactly
that. By treating modernity as political phenomena, Hall is able to
give its diverse strands a certain unity: as a representation of European identity.

Modernity can be described as a discourse which formed and
consolidated Europe. Therefore, would it not be possible to see the
limits of postmodernity in terms of its relation to the West? This is
the strategy followed by, for example, Gianni Vattimo and Robert
Young. In his book, *The Transparent Society*, Vattimo gives a historical
account of the emergence of the postmodern condition. For Vattimo
the advent of postmodernity is the product of a crisis in the two

main ideas which organized the discourse of modernity: first, the idea of history as a single unified sequence, and second, progress as an idea about the direction in which history moves. Vattimo sees in modernity a cult of the new and original; according to this view, human history is an ongoing process that moves towards the perfection of the human ideal. Each phase in history is more advanced, more cultured, more civilized than that which came before it.[101] Such a conception of history, that sees it as a progressive realization of the perfection of humankind, requires that history be unilinear. There must be History, if you want to speak of Progress.[102] To conceive of history as History requires:

> the existence of a centre around which events are gathered and ordered. We think of history as ordered around the year zero of the birth of Christ, and more specifically, as a serial train of events in the life of peoples from the 'centre', the West, the place of civilization, outside of which are the primitives and the developing countries.[103]

According to Vattimo this view of history came under sustained attack by western philosophers in the nineteenth and twentieth centuries.[104] He argues that the emergence of the idea that history is a representation of the past constructed by a dominant group began to disrupt the idea of a History. If the past was a reconstruction of particular historians representing the interests and prejudices of the group to which they belonged, was it really possible to think of a universal history? In other words, without a centralized perspective on history all we are left with are particular representations of the past projected from different positions; and these particular histories cannot be unified into a History. With the disruption of the idea of a unified history, Vattimo argues that it is difficult to maintain the notion of progress. This is because a progressive conception of history requires a criterion, a touchstone – something against which to measure progress. According to Vattimo, for the Enlightenment thinkers this criterion was provided by Europe; Europe was the most advanced, the most modern civilization and history was directed towards a greater realization of this ideal. We can see that there is great deal of overlap between the account of modernity I presented above and Vattimo's account.

In Vattimo's account the centre of history and criterion of progress is occupied by western civilization. The resistance to the West is one of the factors behind the erosion of modernity. Vattimo sees in decolonization a de facto displacement of a centralized history. It is not entirely clear what the relation between the decolonization struggles and the western philosophers who criticize the notion of 'history' is. So, even though Vattimo is willing to share the 'credit' for the advent of postmodernity with the Third World, he is not very clear as to what extent it is the internal critique of the West or 'external' critique by the Rest which is decisive in the erosion of modernity.

This ambiguity between the internal critics of Europe and its external critics can also be found in the work of Robert Young. Young describes postmodernity as: 'European culture's awareness that it is no longer the unquestioned and dominant centre of the world.'[105] Young understands postmodernity as a 'de-centring of the West'.[106] I understand this to mean that postmodernity is the condition in which the intimate relationship between modernity and the West becomes untangled. The West is no longer the axiomatic centre of modernity's meta-narratives; its position as the criterion of progress, as the medium of history, is put under pressure.

According to Young, the emergence of postmodernity can be traced to the fallout from the Algerian war of independence.[107] Young points to a number of French writers who have been influential in the development of modern French thought, and who were either from French Algeria or were marked by the liberation struggle in Algeria: for example, Sartre, Althusser, Derrida and Lyotard, among others.[108] Young goes on to describe postmodern thought as an attempt to decolonize European culture.[109] In his book, a number of figures are examined who have been at the forefront of this task of decolonizing European thought. In a later work, Young argues that postmodernity owes much of its development to a group of diasporic writers, whose work has helped demonstrate the provincialism of European thought.[110] These diasporic writers problematize the whole notion of internal and external critics; for, although they are part of diasporic communities, they are also members of privileged élites entrenched in European academies.

Young's description of postmodernity is similar in many respects to Vattimo's. Both acknowledge the role of the non-West (via the process of decolonization) in helping to form the postmodern situation, but their descriptions of the experience of postmodernity focus on the West.[111] Neither Young nor Vattimo has very much to say about the consequences of postmodernity for the 'Rest'. Their gesture to the Rest extends only as far as to concede the constitutive role of the colonized in postmodernity, but there is no discussion of how postmodernity will affect the very same colonized.

The postmodern critique of modernity seems to disarticulate the West from modernity. Only with the advent of postmodernity can we break the relation of substitutability that exists between the western and the modern. The decentring of the West means the weakening of the narratives that constructed western identity. We can see the effect of this in terms of the proliferation of identities and the 'recovery' of lost histories of Europe which all serve to weaken the bonds of European identity. If the West itself is no longer a unified entity, it cannot provide the unity to modernity. The fragmentation of a western identity means that the strategy of filling out the content of modernity by reference to Europe becomes very difficult – the fragmentation of Europe entails the fragmentation of modernity. If there is no one Europe there can be no one modernity. Modernity itself becomes pluralized into a diverse number of narratives reflecting the diversity of Europe, so that modernity is not just the rationality of the Enlightenment but also the savagery of the Holocaust. Modernity is not only yuppies embracing consumerism, but also the rejection of consumerism by hippies.

Decentring does not refer solely to the unity of the West, but also to the relation between the West and the Rest. If the West is decentred, it must be decentred in relation to the non-West; without a centre, there can be no periphery. The decentring of the West means that the non-West cannot be treated simply as the periphery: the decentring of the West involves the deperipheralization of the Rest. This means the dyad that has organized the global discourse for the last two hundred years becomes superfluous.[112] The identity of the Rest also depended on the constitution of a unitary Europe; a Europe that was at the heart of the world. What kind of identity is possible for the Rest, living in an empty-hearted world? If the West can no longer act as the nodal point of the discourses of modernity, the unity of modernity can only be preserved if another centre is found to replace the West. Without such a centre, modernity as a grand project gives way to strategies for coping more or less successfully with the world.

Islam and postmodernity?

The political effect of postmodernity on the advanced capitalist countries has been the subject of much debate, but in general there has been very little discussion about the effects of postmodernity on the Rest. One of the reasons for the neglect of the Rest is that many of the writers on postmodernity have been very clear that only the 'most highly developed societies' can be a party to the postmodern condition.[113] This view is not only held by Lyotard; it is also shared by Giddens and by Rorty, among others.[114] As a consequence the literature on postmodernity has a tendency to replay the modernist narrative. That is, the West preserves its vanguard role as the incarnation of the postmodern, while the 'Rest' are relegated to being just modern. It is very similar to the way in which, in the past, the West would be represented as the beacon of the light of progress amid the darkness of tradition that hung over the rest of the world. (This division between the postmodern West and the modern Rest can be glimpsed in the struggles generated around the Rushdie affair, where a postmodern text was confronted by 'immigrants' in Britain who were neither traditional, as they had forsaken their rural lifestyles, nor postmoderns comfortable with hybridity.)[115] An example of this is provided by Akbar S. Ahmed's book, *Postmodernism and Islam*.[116] It is worth looking at Ahmed's self-consciously Muslim account of postmodernity, which is generally sympathetic to Muslims but is structured around the postmodern/Islam divide. Ahmed provides a useful illustration of an argument that I am rejecting.

Ahmed's book is promisingly titled and attempts to discuss postmodernism side by side with a discussion about contemporary Islam. Ahmed sees the omnipresence of the media as one of the defining features of postmodernity – in fact he goes further and equates postmodernity with the ubiquity of the media.[117] He indicates that western postmodernism and Islamic postmodernism are the not same thing, but can be found running concurrently. This clear statement, however, is not elaborated and Ahmed succeeds only in muddying the waters when he tries to bring out some of the main features of postmodernity. For example, he argues that loss of faith is one of the key features of postmodernity. At the same time he quotes with approval an encounter on the *Late Show* in which Gellner rises to his defence by arguing that Islam has not lost its faith. Fundamentalism for Ahmed is an attempt to cope with the radical doubt engendered by the postmodern condition. He is aware that fundamentalism is used as a euphemism for Islam and is careful to add that fundamentalism is not simply based on religion but also includes secularist ideologies like free market liberalism. Ahmed mentions the proliferation of 'ethno-religious revivalism' and cites it as being the 'cause and effect of postmodernity'.[118]

After this rather unclear attempt to situate contemporary Islamic movements within the context of postmodernity, Ahmed spends the rest of his book attempting to answer questions such as why Muslims do not wear jeans,[119] and what the significance of Madonna is for the Muslim world.[120] Ahmed's comprehensive survey of the main media events involving the Muslim world produces a set of neat journalistic oppositions, such as the opposition between the mall and the mosque.

What is striking about Ahmed's account of postmodernity is the omission of decolonization as a factor in the very constitution of the postmodern. The absence of decolonization leads Ahmed to the deproblematization of identities. For Ahmed the identity of the West remains as constant as the identity of Islam. Thus, postmodernity becomes a game of surfaces where real objects maintain intact their integrity even though telematics puts them in very different relations. Ahmed's attempt to analyse postmodernity in relation to Islam does not go beyond a simple juxtaposition of postmodernity with the contemporary Islamic world. This is not sufficient, because the identity of Islam and the West is not put to the test. Islam remains a paradigmatic example of the other of postmodernity. Thus, Ahmed's apologia for Islam ends in establishing Islam as the other of postmodernity.[121] In fact there is no hint in Ahmed's book that postmodernity is something to which the periphery is a party, except as a spectator. In this he is not alone, among the main writers on postmodernity (Giddens, Lyotard, etc.) there is a similar lacuna regarding the periphery's experience of postmodernity. Ahmed's account falls squarely into this tradition; he simply reinstates the conventional duality between the postmodern and Islam, so that while we in the West play with the new possibilities created by the ending of the old certainties of modernity, Muslims who cannot bear the world without foundations retreat into 'ancient' myths – they search for a rock upon which they can base their identity.

Decentring of the West and Islamism

The reason why we looked at the current debates on modernity and postmodernity was that by identifying Khomeini as being modern, we also located him (and by extension Islamism itself) within western discourse. Having seen that postmodernity refers to a decentring of the West, this opens the way for us to understand Khomeini's political discourse as a manifestation of the decentring of the West. One of the most interesting observations that Zubaida makes is that, despite Khomeini's dependence on modern political concepts, his discourse is conducted exclusively in the idiom of Islamic political theory without citing any modern political doctrines.[122] This, as Zubaida rightly argues, distinguishes Khomeini from all the recent Muslim political thinkers.[123]

From approximately 1870 onwards there developed in Muslim communities an apologist discourse which sought to reinscribe the achievements of modernity as being originally found in Islam.[124] This discourse was motivated by the desire to defend Islam from the consequences of European global ascendancy. It was devoted to arguing that there was nothing intrinsic to Islam which prevented it from being reinterpreted in such a way that it would become compatible with the modern world.[125] Originally, this apologist discourse was associated with Muslim liberal thinkers (for example Mohammed Abduh).[126] By the 1920s, however, it became the dominant mode of expressing Muslim political thought, including even Muslim thinkers who subsequently were considered to be the principal ideologues of Islamic fundamentalism. For example, the work of Shariati[127] and Maududi[128] clearly shows that even when they advocate Islamist solutions, they do so by using elements of this apologist discourse.

In contrast, Khomeini totally rejects this apologist discourse. He makes no attempt to try and locate Islam within a tradition of progressive history, in which major developments are re-described as being originally inspired by Islam. Khomeini does not try to claim that Islam is 'real democracy', or that Islam anticipates socialism, or that Islam is compatible with science, etc. There is no obvious attempt to incorporate or even engage with political concepts associated with the discourses of nationalism, Marxism, liberalism. It is only with Khomeini that the role of western discourse as universal interlocutor appears to be shaken. Khomeini's political thought, alone among Muslim thinkers of the last hundred years, does not try to have a dialogue with western discourse. He does not try to argue with or against western political theory. Given that since at least the 1870s Muslim political thought has actually been a one-sided dialogue with western discourse,[129] and given that (as we said in the previous chapter) the Kemalists felt it necessary to align their projects continually in terms of a western discourse, it is surprising that Khomeini does not try to justify himself in terms of western discourse. As Zubaida points out, Khomeini writes as if western thought did not exist.[130]

Khomeini seems to realize that:

> The trouble with arguments against the use of a familiar and time-honoured vocabulary is that it is expected to be phrased in that very vocabulary. They are expected to show that the central elements in that vocabulary are 'inconsistent in their own terms' or that they 'deconstruct themselves'. But that can *never* be shown.[131]

The possibility of Islamic political thinking can only be undertaken by disengagement with the problems and perspectives of western political thought. As long as Islamic political thinkers are locked in a (one-sided) conversation with western political thought, they remain locked in a logic in which there is no space for anything other than the West. The envisioning of Islamic political order finds itself in a parasitic relationship, dependent upon a western republicanism/ oriental despotism divide. In contrast Khomeini does not offer a point-by-point consideration of why an Islamic republic would be better than western governmental practice, he does not offer arguments against western political theory; he simply states the virtues of an Islamic political order. Khomeini's strategy is emulated by Rorty who declares: 'Conforming to my precepts, I am not going to offer arguments against the vocabulary I want to replace. Instead, I am going to try and make the vocabulary I favour look attractive by showing how it may be used to describe a variety of topics.'[132]

The absence of western citations does not hinder Khomeini's political project; in fact it seems to be the major source of his success. The possibility exists that Khomeini is operating in a terrain in which references to the West are not necessary and may even be counter-productive. An investigation is needed into the extent to which the existence of Khomeini's articulation of an alternative to Kemalism rests upon the ability to articulate projects without referencing the West, in the form of a citation.[133] That is, to what extent can we see the phenomena of Islamism operating in a terrain in which the West is no longer the centre?

This means arguing that postmodernity is not an exclusive domain of the West; the experience of the 'decentring of the West' can be found not only in the 'most highly developed societies', even though the literature on postmodernity is rather sparse concerning its implications for the 'Rest'. It is still possible to present a postmodern experience in terms of the 'Rest'. Nietzsche's writing on nihilism presents a convenient starting point for a 'peripheral' reading of postmodernity. As I noted earlier, Lyotard refers to Nietzsche's account of European nihilism as a precursor of what he describes as postmodernity.[134] The affinity between Nietzsche's European nihilism and Lyotard's postmodernity is too clear to require further comment.

European nihilism, however, is not the only form that nihilism can take. In Nietzsche there is another account of nihilism: ancient or original nihilism. This original nihilism occurred during the transition from pre-moral to moral culture. The cause of this nihilism is the experience of slaves and their oppression in ancient class societies.[135] Ancient nihilism came about as a result of the heightened sense of suffering caused by political subordination. As Nietzsche writes: 'for it is the experience of being powerless against men, not against nature, that generates the most desperate embitterment against existence'.[136] This type of nihilism arises from the experience of political repression; it is a nihilism that contextualizes and historicizes the subordinated. Mark Warren, in his attempt to construct a Nietzschean political theory, makes much of ancient nihilism:

> original nihilism will manifest itself wherever political oppression is coupled with cultural exclusion. ... Within the structure of Nietzsche's world view, one can further conclude that the original nihilism is a transhistorical possibility for humans *just in so far* as one understands the social and political relations that generate the experience of oppression to be transhistorical.[137]

This sense of nihilism, I think, encapsulates the effect of European domination on the subjects of that domination, in that European colonialism was structured around cultural exclusion and political domination. This is exactly the thrust of Hall's argument that the creation of the West implied the creation of a 'Rest' and its inclusion in a relationship of political subordination. The experience of colonization brings forth the contingency of the world of those who have been colonized: their sacred narratives become (for the colonizer) just another collection of stories. In other words, the experience of political oppression forces the oppressed to recognize their contingency. This is an asymmetric process: it is only the colonized and the defeated who are forced to suspect the significance or the usefulness of their final vocabularies – an 'incredulity towards meta-narratives' is imposed on them. It is the meta-narratives of the subordinated that appear to be incredible and seem to inspire suspicion in the face of the grand narratives of the West.

It is possible to expand on Nietzsche's comments on the original nihilism to produce a 'peripheral' account of postmodernity, in which the 'incredulity towards meta-narratives' arises not as a consequence of self-criticism but as a result of a confrontation with a more powerful meta-narrative which judges the meta-narrative of the 'natives' not to be a meta-narrative. This would be the scenario, for example, when traditional healing is confronted with western medicine and found to be nothing more than superstition. There are three key points that need to be emphasized in this relation: first, that this suspicion of meta-narrative is specific. It is restricted to meta-narratives of the subordinated culture: it is not a universal questioning of all the meta-narratives that there are. Second, this suspicion of a meta-narrative is produced by an asymmetric power relationship. Thus 'incredulity' is proportional to the confidence of the stronger meta-narrative. If the stronger discourse (the meta-narrative) begins to weaken, it will reduce the suspicion of the subordinate discourse, because the ability of the stronger discourse to produce 'incredulity' in the subordinate discourse is a function of its power. Third, the imposition of the 'incredulity towards meta-narratives' is unevenly distributed in the colonized community. For example, in the Muslim states the experience of this imposed 'suspicion of (native) meta-narratives' first found converts among upper-class men and (to a lesser extent) upper-class women.[138]

The argument I present is that colonialism produces among the colonized a questioning and weakening of their own meta-narratives. This makes it possible to question whether postmodernity (incredulity towards meta-narratives) is found only in the 'most highly developed societies'. To use the example of the Muslim world as an illustration, the impact of European indirect and direct colonization began a process of questioning of the certainties of Islam, Islamic societies and beliefs. It is this questioning which produced the various reformist thinkers in the Muslim world during the period of the late eighteenth century, such as Afghani[139] and Abduh.[140] The point of this is that experience of contingency (by 'native' narratives) is also the experience of powerlessness.

If this criterion of contingency is used as a way of describing postmodernity, the non-western world cannot be excluded. Of course, when we talk about postmodernity, we are talking about a suspicion of meta-narratives that come after modernity. This means that these examples of colonial instances of suspicion of meta-narratives are not part of the postmodern condition because they represent a questioning of indigenous (or traditional) narratives, and not modern or western narratives. In other words what is happening in these colonial cases is the replacement of one set of meta-narratives with another. Traditional meta-narratives are replaced by 'modern' meta-narratives. This process reached its height in the Muslim world with the development of Kemalism: a meta-discourse that seeks to replace traditional Islamic discourses with a discourse that finds its legitimacy within the meta-narrative of modernity. The replacement of one meta-narrative with another only demonstrates a very partial incredulity towards meta-narratives. Kemalism centres itself on the West, and this is the meaning of its modernity. In contrast, Islamism is based on the possibility of decentring the West: in other words Islamism is based on the suspicion of meta-narratives that it considers to be western.

Is this the same kind of 'incredulity toward meta-narratives' that Lyotard and other postmodern thinkers have in mind when they talk about the postmodern condition? Their descriptions of postmodernity tend to use words and phrases like 'abandonment of foundationalism' and 'hybridity'. Surely, Islamism is attempting to replace one set of meta-narratives with another. Even a cursory knowledge of Islamist discourse would reveal that Islamists do not use the vocabulary of 'death of God', 'hybridity', etc. to narrate stories of their identities.[141] Islamism is presented with all the certainty of a meta-narrative. The content of Islamist discourses is replete with grand claims and essentialist categories marshalled in an uncompromising absolutist language.

At the very basic level a meta-narrative refers to a narrative about narratives. In the view of Lyotard, it is not just any narrative about narratives but rather the narrative by which other narratives are adjudicated. What enables a discourse to be a meta-discourse? How does a discourse achieve the position of being able to act as judge of other discourses? One condition that such a discourse would have to fulfil is the ambition to act as discourse that could resolve disputes between other discourses. In other words, it must attempt to be totalizing. Given several totalizing discourses, how does one emerge as a meta-narrative? The short Nietzschean answer to this very big question is that a meta-narrative establishes itself as such by the exercising of power as a discourse capable of judging others. As Nietzsche writes:

> All values by the means of which we have tried to render the world estimable for ourselves and which then proved inapplicable and therefore devalued the world – all these values are, psychologically considered, the result of certain perspectives of utility, designed to maintain and increase human constructions of domination – and they have been falsely *projected* into the essence of things.[142]

Ultimately, a meta-narrative is a construction of domination, 'a regime of truth'.[143] By politicizing the status of meta-narrative, we are able to contextualize the meta-discursive status of Islamism.

It is true that Islamism is totalizing and does not use the vocabularies of 'hybridity', 'just gaming', etc., which characterize postmodern discourse. However, it is also true that Islamism is only possible in a world in which there is suspicion of a western meta-discourse. It is based not on the rejection of modernity but on a rejection of westernization. The possibility of the rejection of westernization depends on the recognition that there is no historical necessity to the western hegemony. There is a convergence between 'internal' critics of the West and the Islamist critique of western hegemony. Islamism seems to have an ambiguous status: it is not a luddite rage against modernity, but is an attempt to decentre the West, an attempt that is similar to some aspects of the postmodern condition. At the same time it is a totalizing discourse that does not have much room for incredulity about its own meta-narrative.

As argued above, contrary to many accounts of Islamism the Islamists are not anti-modern, and thus their supposed anti-modernity cannot be used to account for the way in which they have managed to bypass other political discourses. Islamists do articulate their identity in opposition to the West, and, by so doing, they associate with Kemalism the discourses of liberalism and socialism. For Islamists the West is not just liberal democracy or the market economy, but it also includes the socialist tradition of state capitalism.[144] Islamist discourse is constructed by articulating a connotative totality in which the West came to represent a denial of Islam, imperialism, state repression, economic mismanagement, cultural erosion, etc. It is this metaphor of the West that is the centrepiece of Islamist discourses. Islamists articulate themselves in opposition to Kemalists, and identify the Kemalists and their policies with the West. The ultimate antagonist for the Islamists, however, is not Kemalism but the West, an 'overarching imperial formation'.[145] The Islamist critique of Kemalism is not restricted to the particular inability of Kemalism to provide better services, to cope with the world economic system, and so on, but a critique of the way in which Kemalism articulated its reforms and practices with western discourse.

Kemalism was founded on the equivalence between modernity and the West; for them modernization and westernization were fundamentally the same thing. One of the implications of the post-modern critique of modernity is to call into question whether there is anything specific about European culture that made Europe a global hegemony. Can it be that, as Rorty once put it, Europe just got lucky?[146] If it is the case that there is no necessity to European ascendancy then the Kemalist attempt to westernize as a way of enhancing their geopolitical position becomes suspect. All westernization does is to produce what Jalal Al-i Ahmad referred to as 'Westoxicated' societies; it does not necessarily produce societies able to compete with Europe on equal terms.[147]

The Islamist rejection of westernization was re-described by Kemalists as a rejection of modernization. Approaches that maintain that Islamism reflects a traditionalist opposition to modernization share with Kemalism a meta-narrative which endorses the idea that westernization and modernization are synonymous.[148] This view was sustainable only as long as the central tenets of the discourse of modernity remained largely uncontested – that is, as long as the West remained the criterion of human progress; as long as it could be represented as the 'most successful, most advanced' civilization; and as long as it could project its hegemony into the future, and could continue to play the role of a centre. In this universe, there could be no *significant* place for political movements or tendencies which denied the centrality of the West within their own discourse, since the West represented the very idea of what was political success. It is the deconstruction of the relation between modernity and the West that produced a space into which Islamism could locate itself; and it is this positioning that can account for its emergence as a politically significant discourse. The appeal and power of Islamist projects are due to the way in which they are able to combine the deconstructionist logic of the postmodern critique of modernity with an attempt to speak from another centre, outside the orbit of the West.

Notes

1. Laclau and Mouffe, 1985, p. 112.
2. Abercrombie et al., 1980, p. 3.
3. Ibid., Chapter 3.
4. For an illustration of the limited appeal of Kemalism outside the ranks of a 'tiny but influential minority', see F. Ahmed 1993, p. 92. See also Lewis, 1961, p. 287.
5. Machiavelli, 1979, p. 113. I am grateful to Albert Weale for pointing out that Hume made much the same point. See Hume's 'First principles of government', in Hume, 1993, pp. 24–5.
6. Khalil, 1989, pp. 3–45.
7. S. Hall, 1988, pp. 262–3.
8. See Hinnebach, in Hunter, 1988, p. 40.
9. Simon, 1982, p. 21. This is similar to Gramsci's formulation of the integral state, see Gramsci, 1971, pp. 239–40.
10. This argument has been fully developed by James Scott, 1990. I am indebted to Scott's book in which the interplay between overt public power and what Scott calls 'hidden transcripts' is explored. Scott provides a fascinating account of how peasants and slaves would behave in front of their 'betters' and how they would act once the gaze of the master was gone. Scott's work cautions us not to believe that hegemonic descriptions of the subaltern are swallowed whole by the subaltern. For a useful review and critique of Scott's work, see Gutmann, 1993.
11. Scott, 1990, pp. 45–69 and 108–34.
12. The places which experienced the most pronounced de-Islamization were in the Communist bloc, for example, Albania and the Muslim majority regions of the former Soviet Union: Caucasia, Middle Volga and Central Asia.
13. For descriptions of some of the political movements that developed in the wake of the crisis of the soviet system, see Hosking et al., 1992.

14. See, for example Watt (1988), who argues that Islam's essence is unchanging and thus it is anti-modern. See also Lawrence (1990), pp. 23–42, who sees in the clash between modernity and fundamentalism the dynamics of Islamist politics.

15. See also the article by Shepard, 1987 (especially, pp. 307–8), where he tries to construct a typology of Islamic movements based on a two-dimensional scale, in which one axis measures the degree of modernity and the other the degree of totalism. This allows him to produce the following variants of Islamic ideology: secularization, Islamic modernism, traditionalism, re-traditionalism and radical Islamism. The first two types of ideologies would correspond roughly with what I call Kemalism and the last with what I would call Islamism.

16. Esposito (1990) considers Khomeini to be a central figure in the contemporary Islamic world; see pp. 12, 31 and 317–23. Sachendina, in Marty and Appleby, 1991, refers to Khomeini's role as innovator; see pp. 403–57. Halliday notes that Khomeini presents the epitome of a charismatic leader; see Halliday and Alavi, 1988, p. 49. These writers are not isolated in their estimation of the significance of Khomeini.

17. See for example, Esposito, 1990, pp. 17–39.

18. Ahady, 1992, p. 240.

19. The debate about the creation of Pakistan/partition of India, is far from resolved. What is clear is there is an inconsistency at the heart of the project of Pakistan. The case for Pakistan was based on the need for a Muslim homeland. The Muslim homeland, however, was to be realized in the form of a Kemalist republic rather than an Islamist state. Thus, the politicization of Muslim identity which was necessary to make the case for a Muslim homeland was incompatible with the Kemalist state that was institutionalized in 1947. As a consequence, the formation of Pakistan also meant the depoliticization of a Muslim subjectivity. It is only with the emergence of Islamism in the *Ummah* that the first post-colonial state founded upon the idea of a Muslim identity began its rather stuttering attempts at Islamization.

20. This is so, even though there is broad acknowledgement that Islamism (like communism before it) does not have a monolithic unity. In fact, as I pointed out in Chapter 2, much is made of the 'internal' differences between various Islamist thinkers and movements. See, for example, Babeair, 1990, pp. 133–4.

21. See Abrahamian (1993, pp. 1–2) for some examples of colourful descriptions of Khomeini.

22. See Zubaida, 1989, Chapter 2.

23. For a contrary view see Rahnema and Nomani, 1990 (especially pp. 3–18). Rahnema and Nomani argue that the Khomeini regime was 'anachronistic' and the vocabulary 'used by the Islamic leaders had its roots in Islamic tradition and was not applicable to the modern world' (p. 3).

24. Moaddel, 1993, p. 257.

25. Ibid., pp. 257 and 262.

26. Ibid., pp. 257–62.

27. For a recent example, see Gilroy (1996).

28. Turbani, 1983, p. 242

29. Giddens, 1985, pp. 12–17.

30. For further elaboration of this point see Laclau and Mouffe, 1987, pp. 92–3.

31. There are of course other theories of fascism, based around psychological

explanations or theories of despotism. Moaddel (1993), however, is mainly interested in the Marxian conception of fascism; such a conception is vulnerable to
a critique of economism.

32. Rejali, 1994, provides a Foucaultian type of analysis of the relationship
between the development of repressive technologies and the development of the
modern subjectivity in Iran. He points out the use of torture was linked not to a
particular political regime but rather to the development of the modern state
itself.

33. Bernard and Khalilzad also discuss the possibility of the Iranian regime as
a fascist state, but conclude that there are important differences between classical
European fascism and the situation in Iran. See Bernard and Khalilzad, 1984, pp.
71–2.

34. Abrahamian, 1993, p. 38.

35. See Springborg (1992) for an elaboration of the way in which republicanism
and despotism end up denoting western and oriental cultural spaces respectively.

36. Compare this to Fischer's quaint vision of politics as: 'a give and take
between conflicting yet just group interest within society', in Esposito, 1983, p.
171. Fischer seems surprised to note that such a (western-liberal) conception of
politics is absent from Khomeini's political thought.

37. This, of course, does not mean that all societies consist of atomized beings
– awaiting identification and socialization. For more details on this point, see
Laclau and Mouffe, 1985, pp. 134–45.

38. It could be argued that liberation theology is an example of a Latin American populism that was based around Christian discourse. However, liberation
theology was never able to take state power and there are questions about the
degree to which it was able to carry a popular mass mobilization.

39. Bobbio, 1989, pp. 1–2.

40. Zizek, 1991, p. 14

41. Springborg, 1992, p. 20.

42. In this they are not alone. See, for example, the collections of essays by
Gassam Salame (ed.) (1994) in which most of the contributions continue to perpetuate this uncritical division between western democracy and oriental despotism,
without problematizing the theoretical framework that establishes these polar
oppositions.

43. Some of the weakness of the kind of approach that Moaddel and Abrahamian offer can be gleaned from Laclau and Mouffe, 1985. See also Bowles and
Gintis, 1987.

44. This monograph can be found in Khomeini's *Islam and Revolution*. See
Khomeini, 1981.

45. Zubaida, 1989, p. 18.

46. Ibid.

47. Ibid., p. 19.

48. Ibid., p. 20.

49. Kolb, 1988, pp. 261–2.

50. Zubaida, 1989, p. 33.

51. Binder, 1988, pp. 120–21.

52. The text by Hall and Gieben, 1992, provides a valuable introduction to
this debate; see especially the section: 'The West and the rest: discourse and
power', pp. 275–332.

53. Hall, in Hall and Gieben, 1992, p. 277.

54. Ibid.

55. Ibid.

56. Ibid.

57. Ibid.

58. See Jones, 1988 (pp. 9, 13, 24 and 225) for examples of these polar oppositions which differentiate Europe and Asia. They are not peculiar to Jones and can
be found elsewhere, for example in Weber, 1957.

59. Hall, in Hall and Gieben, 1992, p. 277.

60. Heller makes no distinction between European and western identity; in
her account the terms 'Europe' and the 'West' are used interchangeably. See
Heller, in Heller and Feher, 1991, pp. 150–51. I will follow Heller's example and
make no substantive differentiation between the two terms.

61. Heller and Feher, 1991, p. 146.

62. For a critique of essentialist construction of identity, see Laclau and Mouffe,
1985, pp. 114–22. Though their criticism relates mainly to class identities, it can
be broadened to include all forms of identity.

63. Heller and Feher, 1991, p. 150.

64. Polybius, 1975, Book I, s. 1.

65. Heller and Feher, 1991, p. 147.

66. Ibid., pp. 146–7.

67. Ibid., p. 146.

68. See Hall, in Hall and Gieben, 1992, p. 276. See also Heller and Feher,
1991, p. 146.

69. Hall, in Hall and Gieben, 1992, p. 278.

70. I refer here, not only to the work of Said, 1981, 1985a, but also to similar
work done on orientalist type constructions of India (Inden, 1990) and Africa
(Mdiumbe, 1988). There is also literature which has come to criticize increasingly
the founding fathers of western social sciences as being implicated in this double
game: their theoretical investigations also serve as political interventions in policing
and settling the frontier between the West and 'the rest'. In this regard, see the
work of Bryan S. Turner (1978) on orientalism within Hegel, Marx and Weber,
and Patricia Springborg's scathing criticism of Weber (1992, pp. 6–7).

71. Hall, in Hall and Gieben, 1992, p. 278.

72. See, for example, the assertion by Roberts, 1976, p. 557.

73. Weber, 1957, p. 25. It is also quoted by Habermas, 1987, p. 1; Robert
Bocock, in Hall and Gieben, 1992, p. 255.

74. See also Gramsci's comments: 'Even if one admits that other cultures have
had an importance and a significance in the process of "hierarchical" unification
of world civilization … they have had a universal value only in so far as they have
become constituent elements of European culture.' Gramsci, 1971, p. 416.

75. Larsen, in Miller et al., 1989, p. 233.

76. Roberts, 1976, p. 577.

77. Hall, in Hall and Gieben, 1992, p. 277.

78. Laroui, 1976, pp. 113 and 165.

79. See, for example, Baechler et al., 1988; Mann, 1986 (especially Chapters
12–15); J. Hall, 1985.

80. Turner, 1989, p. 633.

81. See Herrin, 1989 for a detailed account of the emergence of Europe.

Compare this with Tilly's view that Europe did not exist in the first millennium of Christian history. See Tilly, 1990, pp. 38–45.

82. Herrin, 1989, p. 295. Of course, Europe was originally the name of several creatures in ancient Greek mythology. It was used by the Homeric author of *Hymn to Apollo* to refer to the region north of the Peloponnese. This meaning is retained in Herodotus and in Aeschylus. It is only with Isocrates that Europe begins to develop a more specific spatial and political shape as it is contrasted with Asia. For further details, see De Romilly, 1992. Herrin's attempt to locate the origins of Europe to Europa are based on the argument that between the time of Isocrates and Charlemagne the formation of the Roman empire had radically transformed the frontier between Asia and Europe which had been so central to the Greeks. So while it is perfectly possible to trace the origins of Europa back to the Greeks, it only with Charlemagne that Europe began to have its modern connotations. See also Davies, 1996, pp. 7–16.

83. Herrin, 1989, p. 477.

84. The whole set of debates around modernity and postmodernity has been conducted in a variety of forms, using a wide range of vocabularies, so that it is not always clear that everyone involved in the debate is actually talking about the same thing. Surprisingly, given this lexical overproduction, it is possible to see these exchanges as forming a 'coherent series'; see Gilroy, 1993, p. 41.

85. Gellner, 1992, pp. 22–40.

86. Jameson, in Foster, 1983, p. 125.

87. Rorty, 1991b, p. 1.

88. Lyotard, 1992, p. xxiv.

89. Ibid., p. 39.

90. For details, see Warren, 1988, pp. 35–8.

91. Kolb, 1988, p. 257.

92. Lyotard, 1992, p. xiii.

93. Kolb, 1988, p. 257.

94. Lyotard, 1992, p. 82.

95. Kolb makes a similar point: 'if modernity is less unified, if there is internal multiplicity, then it may not be necessary always to work outside', see Kolb, 1988, p. 259. Giddens, 1990, also makes the same point, pp. 46–53.

96. Rorty, 1991b, p. 67. Though Rorty provides theoretical grounds for avoiding terms like 'the West', he himself is not very consistent. His work is littered with references to 'we Americans', 'North Atlantic democracies', and note his use of the 'West' to denote his culture/society (p. 66). See also Billig, 1993 (especially pp. 76–80).

97. See Gilroy, 1993, p. 43.

98. Rorty, 1991b, pp. 71–2.

99. Ibid.

100. Ibid., pp. 66–72.

101. Vattimo, 1992, p. 2.

102. Ibid.

103. Ibid., p. 4.

104. In this regard, Vattimo considers the work of people like Nietzsche, Marx and Benjamin as being instrumental in problematizing the idea of History.

105. Young, 1990, p. 19.

106. Ibid., pp. 19–20.

107. Young (1990, p. 9) uses the term post-structuralism rather than post-modernity; he argues that this, unlike post-structuralism, includes an awareness of the questioning of western culture. But in this context both postmodernity and post-structuralism can be used interchangeably.

108. Young, 1990, p. 1.

109. Ibid., p. 19.

110. Young, 1994.

111. For example, even though Vattimo concedes the significance of de-colonization in the formation of postmodernity, he argues that what is much more crucial to the crisis of history is the advent of mass communication. He sees in the spread of newspapers, radio and television, the dissolution of the possibility of sustaining the centrality of grand narratives like History or Progress. The spread of technology leads to the proliferation of worldviews which, because they are always juxtaposed with other worldviews, cannot succeed in their claims to exclusivity or universality. The spread of telecommunications, however, is not even; there are still those who consume and those who produce, and the proliferation of jostling worldviews does not by itself eliminate global hierarchies. To put it more succinctly, the conditions that Vattimo describes are not the conditions of a dialogue. Vattimo, 1992, pp. 4–7.

112. Hichem Djait maintains that the absence of a politically unified Islam and the recognition of the composite nature of Europe mean that the old antagonism between Islam and the West is now largely redundant; see Djait, 1985, pp. 168–9.

113. Lyotard, 1992, pp. xxiii, 7 and 11.

114. Rorty, for example, confines his remarks to the North Atlantic plutocracies. See Billig's remarks on Rorty's nationalism: Billig, 1993, pp. 71–2.

115. In particular, see Fischer, 1990, who emphasizes that the postmodernist novel *The Satanic Verses* was being confronted by modernist (Muslim) incomprehension.

116. Turner, 1993, p. 897.

117. Ahmed, 1992, p. 2.

118. Ibid., p. 13.

119. Ibid., pp. 192–3.

120. Ibid., pp. 214–20.

121. Ahmed's view comes very close to endorsing Gellner's understanding of postmodernism (as fashionable relativism) – see Gellner, 1992, p. 22 – and to accepting that Islam is simply anti-relativism writ large. Even though Ahmed demonstrates a far greater awareness of the literature about postmodernism he still falls into the trap of associating postmodernism with 'anything goes'.

122. Zubaida, 1989, p.13.

123. Ibid., p. 13. See also Fischer, 1982, p. 125.

124. Keddie, 1983, pp. xiv–xviii.

125. Hourani, 1983, pp. vi–vii.

126. Hourani (1983) includes some of the main themes and thinkers of Muslim liberalism.

127. For example, see Shariati, 1979, pp. 39–57.

128. For example, Maududi, 1992, pp. 7–12.

129. Muslim interest in, and referencing of, the western political canon was not reciprocated by western political thinkers. During this period, western political thinkers did not have any kind of dialogue with a Muslim political canon; they

ignored Muslim political thought except as an anthropological curiosity. In this, of course, Muslim political discourse was not unique: the West ignored (and by large continues to ignore) the political thinking of the rest of the world.

130. Zubaida, 1989, p. 13.

131. Rorty, 1989, pp. 8–9.

132. Ibid., p. 9. Rorty does not cite Khomeini in this context; no doubt his reticence can be explained in terms of his American patriotism.

133. The references Khomeini makes to the West (and the United States in particular), are purely to a geopolitical adversary. That is, for Khomeini the West is an arrogant and arrogating civilization whose judgements on Islam are irrelevant. The representation of the United States and its allies as the Great Satan (and a variety of little satans) helps to articulate the conflict between the United States and Iran as a conflict between two hermetically sealed blocks. For previous Muslim political leaders (such as Mustafa Kemal), even though specific western powers were adversaries, western civilization was still a source of emulation and inspiration.

134. Lyotard, 1992, p. 39.

135. There is a great deal of debate about the extent to which pre-capitalist societies were class societies and the extent to which they depended on slavery. With the exception of Athens and Rome, it is difficult to treat other ancient societies as slave societies. See Hopkins, 1978, pp. 99–102. I think that it is more useful to read Nietzsche's arguments as metaphors rather than anthropological accounts.

136. Nietzsche, 1968, note 55.

137. Warren, 1988, p. 25.

138. L. Ahmed, 1992, p. 165.

139. See Keddie (1983) for a collection of Afghani's writings.

140. See Hourani (1983, pp. 130–60) for a summary of Abduh's thought.

141. Islamism is not the only example of this tendency of the peripheral discourse to use language of exclusionary absolutism: the discourse of the BJP in India, or the discourse of the Likud in Israel and perhaps even some examples of Afrocentrism in the United States, display a similar kind of logic of exclusion.

142. Nietzsche, 1968, note 12b.

143. For the notion of a truth regime, see Foucault, 1980, pp. 130–33. See also Foucault's use of 'truth regime' to describe Iranian culture (1988, p. 223).

144. See, for example, Shariati, 1980.

145. I borrow this term from Ronald Inden, who uses it to describe 'a complex agent consisting of overlapping and contending polities that more or less successfully relate to each other in what they consider, or at least concede as constituting a single way of life, one that its more active proponents seek to represent as potentially universal in extent' (1990, p. 29). For a fuller discussion of imperial formations, see Inden, 1990, pp. 29–33.

146. Rorty, 1991b, p. 48.

147. Ahmad, 1984.

148. For example, see Choueiri, 1988.

5. Islamism and the limits of the Invisible Empire

> But if you claim you are opening up a radical interrogation, if you wish to place your discourse at the level at which we place ourselves, you know very well that it will enter our game and, in turn, extend the dimension that it's trying to free itself from. Either it does not reach us or we claim it.
>
> *Michel Foucault*[1]

Previously, I have talked about eurocentrism without elaborating what I mean by it, in the hope that some sort of commonsensical fudge would get me by. This, however, will no longer do. One of the problems of defining eurocentrism is noted by Samir Amin: 'eurocentrism like all dominant social phenomena is easy to grasp in the multiplicity of its daily manifestations but difficult to define precisely'.[2] According to Amin, eurocentrism is best understood as a cultural phenomenon based on the principle that 'the West knows best' and which projects progressive westernization as the destiny of the world. In particular, he emphasizes the way in which historiography is dominated by eurocentrism.[3]

Given that Amin's theoretical practice is based on historical materialism, a number of difficulties arise from his insistence that eurocentrism is primarily a culturalist phenomenon. The most significant of these is the way in which he reduces the cultural to a superstructural moment, as a consequence of which eurocentrism emerges as the superstructural adjunct to capitalism. By conceptualizing eurocentrism in such a manner, Amin is able to suggest that socialism is a solution to both the iniquities of capitalism and eurocentrism.[4] The effect of this is to turn the problem of eurocentrism into a sub-species of the general problem of capitalism.

This can be seen in the way in which Amin tries to locate what I have called Islamism (what he calls 'Islamic fundamentalism') as a rejection of 'eurocentrism and imperialist universalism' based on affirmation of 'Arab-Islamic specificity'. Amin's treatment of eurocentrism sets it apart from the discourse of modernity, so that he is able to write:

> the modernity requires an abandonment of metaphysics. The failure to recognize this leads to a false construction of the question of 'cultural identity' and a confused debate in which 'identity' (and 'heritage') are placed in absolute contrast with 'modernization', viewed as synonymous with 'Westernization'.[5]

It is clear that Amin is totally within the discourse of modernity and, therefore, he is unable to recognize the way modernity itself projects its identity as a reflection of its western genealogy. By developing his critique of eurocentrism within the discourse of modernity, Amin reproduces the logic in which modernity and western culture are conflated. For example, his notion of eurocentrism preserves the idea of history as having a (progressive) direction, which can be read back as the history of Europe. His dismissal of Sayyid Qutb's views on secularization illustrate this. Amin rejects Sayyid Qutb's assertion that there is no secularism in Islam by arguing that this was also the case in early Christendom, when there was no separation between church and state – a separation which only developed later. Amin seems to be implying that the history of Christendom becomes a criterion for understanding the history of Islam. Clearly, such an argument is based on the notion that the history of the world is about progressive westernization – a notion that Amin, himself, contends is the hallmark of eurocentrism.

I define eurocentrism as the discourse that emerges in the context of the decentring of the West; that is, a context in which the relationship between the western enterprise and universalism is open to disarticulation and re-articulation. The discourse of eurocentrism is an attempt to suture the interval between the West and the idea of a centre (that is, a universal template). Eurocentrism is a project to recentre the West, a project that is only possible when the West and the centre are no longer considered to be synonymous. It is an attempt to sustain the universality of the western project, in conditions in which its universality can no longer be taken for granted. Eurocentrism is thus only possible when the relationship between universalism and the western project has been problematized, that is, when the West cannot be subsumed with universality. The logic of eurocentrism is committed to closing the gap between the West and the centre; it is opposed by and opposes projects which widen this gap and operate in space created by the gap. As I have argued previously, it is precisely in this space created by the decentring of the West where Islamism emerges. The logic of Islamism necessitates the provincialization of the West and its relocation as one centre among many. It is no longer considered to be the cultural formation that all other cultures must attempt to imitate. Europe is just one culture among others.

It is clear that my view of eurocentrism differs from Amin's, since I locate it in the context of the decentring of the West, while Amin's notion remains within the discourse of modernity. Like Amin, however, I maintain that the logic of eurocentrism is currently hegemonic. Its hegemony has political/cultural significance for the planet. The discourse of eurocentrism is one of the major strands with which the network of western global power is held together. With the dismantling of the overt means by which the West exercised *imperium* over the rest of the world, the logic of eurocentrism is the invisible empire which keeps the 'Rest' in its place.

I argued in Chapter 4 that one of the reasons that Khomeini does not cite the West is due to the provincialization of Europe. In other words, Khomeini exemplifies the logic of Islamism. The argument that I have been developing rests upon the extent to which the logic of Islamism disrupts the logic of eurocentrism. I have argued that the emergence of Islamism is only comprehensible in a terrain in which the West has been decentred. I have also said that it is precisely this terrain where the logic of eurocentrism operates. This is one of the reasons why Islam(ism) is often cited in debates regarding particularism and universalism. This is in contrast to other recent geopolitical rivals of the United States and its clients (for example, the cold war did not generate an anxiety about *western* universalism). This is why attempts to read 'the Islamic threat' simply in geopolitical terms are inadequate: the logic of Islamism is not threatening because of the way in which Islamist forces are able to threaten mutually assured destruction, rather the logic of Islamism is threatening because it fails to recognize the universalism of the western project.

There are a number of objections one could advance against this view. First, one could argue that there is no provincialization of

Europe. Second, one could argue that eurocentrism is justified. Third, one could argue that, irrespective of whether the West has been decentred or not, there is little significance in the fact that Khomeini does not explicitly refer to Marx or the rights of man. The reason for this, according to Zubaida, is that his narrative is still heavily dependent on western categories. These objections are the means by which the western hegemony is projected in the context of the 'decentring of the West'.

The triumph of the West

The denial of the provincialization of Europe can take two main forms. It can be argued that, since the fall of communism in 1989, we are witnessing the final victory of the West rather than its demise. This set of arguments has been put forward in its most sensational form by Francis Fukuyama.[6] Fukuyama's thesis is based on the argument that the end of the cold war signals the final triumph of the West.[7] Fukuyama defines the West as politically based on liberal democracy and as economically based on the market allocation of resources. He makes the observation that, even though there is a resurgence of Islamism, this cannot 'challenge liberal democracy on its own territory on the level of ideas'.[8]

The arguments for the triumph of the West, while seemingly convincing, are based on the distinction between capitalism and communism as also being the difference between the West and the non-West. Certainly, within the cold war discourse, the conflict was seen as one between the capitalist West and the communist East. There is not much doubt that the rhetorical devices of orientalist discourse were redeployed to describe Soviet politics and society. (It is also the case that the 'totalitarianism' of the Soviet model was used to describe the Orient. For example, Wittfogel's *Oriental Despotism*.)[9] Despite this reconfiguration of the Soviet camp as representative of the Orient, there is a case for arguing that the Soviet system was simply a branch of western discourse. That is, despite its opposition to the United States and the capitalist order, the Soviet Union was part of the heritage of the West.[10] The Soviet system can in many senses be seen as a self-conscious attempt to construct an entire social order on the basis of some of the grand narratives of the Enlightenment. While it is the case that within Russian political discourse there has been a great deal of ambiguity about the identity of Russia *vis-à-vis* western Europe,[11] its relation with Central Asia falls firmly within the pattern of the European imperialism of the 1880s.[12] More important than whether western European discourse includes Russia or not, is whether Islamist discourses consider Russia as a representative of the Orient. Here the answer is fairly clear-cut: for Islamists the Soviet model and its cognates are clearly part of the West; for them, Moscow is not an alternative to the West but rather an opponent of Washington. From the Islamists' perspective, both socialism and capitalism are part of western philosophical traditions, based on materialism and the rejection of the divine. This was the substance of the message Khomeini sent to Gorbachev in January 1989:

> Of course, it is possible that due to incorrect methods and wrong actions of the former communist strongmen regarding economics, the grass might seem greener in the Western world. However, the truth lies elsewhere. If at this juncture you wish only to undo the blind economic knots of socialism and communism by taking refuge in the bosom of Western capitalism, not only will you not have cured any of the ills of your society; on the contrary ... Because whilst Marxism is today facing a dead-end in economic and social issues, the Western world is also afflicted with the same issue, of course in a different shape, as well as in other issues. The main difficulty of your country is not the issue of ownership, economics or freedom. Your difficulty is the lack of true faith in God, the same difficulty which has also dragged the West towards decadence and a dead-end, or which will do so.[13]

Khomeini, like other Islamists, saw in Soviet and capitalist societies a culture of materialism founded on common European roots, which is distinct at its most basic level from Islam. From the perspective of Islamists the collapse of Soviet-style socialism is not read as the failure of viable alternatives to the West. Rather it is seen as a sign of the weakness of European ascendancy, especially because of the way in which Islamist narratives of the Afghani *jihad* establish a causal link between the defeat of the USSR in Afghanistan and the subsequent collapse of the Soviet empire.

The second way of rejecting the decentring of the West is by querying whether it is the relevant cardinal point on which to focus our attention. As long as the global political economy, the planetary telematic systems, and the world military order are still hierarchically organized, and as long as that organization is structured around a North–South axis, the 'decentring of the West' makes no concession to that vertical axis at the centre of the distribution of global power. Given that the primary division in the world is between the powerful rich North and the have-not South, there is little to show that the decentring of the West has had any serious effects on these fundamental inequalities.

One of the consequences of the development of the global economy has been the complication of the North–South hierarchy. This does not mean that the world has became a more equitable place: globalization does not alleviate poverty. However, what globalization has done is to make the relationship between the Rest and the West less clear-cut – a less straightforward relationship between poor and rich. Too often the relationship between the West and the Rest was read as purely a relationship of economic dependency. Countries such as Brazil or Argentina were thus considered outside the West, because of their political support for non-alignment and their status as developing countries.[14] Globalization necessitates the discourse of eurocentrism, since it helps to weaken notions of the economic centrality of the West, and thus contributes to its decentring.

There is no doubt that the international system is still hierarchically organized, but it is also true that the emergence of oil-exporting economies and the ever-increasing industrialization of the Asian-Pacific rim indicate that the division between North and South, while still important, is not as rigid as it was once considered to be. In addition, the success of various national liberation struggles in the 1970s and 1980s demonstrated that global hierarchies can be overturned, to some extent at least. The relevance of these developments should not be discounted or exaggerated. There are still great structural inequalities between North and South. However, these inequalities have been affected by the retreat of European power. The decentring of the West has had an effect on the organization and maintenance of North–South hierarchies. In 'Black culture and post-modernism', Cornel West characterizes the contemporary world in the form of three main coordinates: the aftermath of the European Age (1492–1945);[15] the 'precarious but still prominent' hegemony of the United States; and the second phase of the decolonization of the Third World,[16] 'a rather paralytic' process directed at challenging ruling élites in post-colonial states and the global status quo.[17] This seems a useful way of understanding the current world order. It allows for the continuing dominance of the West but in the context of the provincialization of Europe: the West may still be dominant in many ways but it is not hegemonic (in the Gramscian sense).[18] This loss of hegemony can be seen in the way the cultural leadership of the West has been challenged by groups who have an 'undecidable' relationship with the West.[19] The 'victory' in the cold war has not been sufficient to protect the western canon from the questioning of its canonical status.

Eurocentrism and ethnocentrism

There are a number of ways in which the discourse of eurocentrism can be justified. One could follow Halliday (among others) and assert that 'eurocentrism is a valid starting point'; it is the description that best suits the current world. One could also argue that all human societies produce stereotypes, therefore there is nothing very extraordinary about eurocentrism; in fact one could argue that, compared to the ethnocentrism found elsewhere, eurocentrism is fairly benign.[20] Eurocentrism could also be justified by arguing that what it produces has an objective validity;[21] for example, Halliday points to the experience of imperialism as producing such valuable knowledge. Alas, he does not stop to question who or what determines the objective validity of knowledge. This, of course, raises a number of interesting moral dilemmas. Would knowledge gained from experiments carried out on inmates of a Nazi concentration camp have objective validity – if the knowledge produced a technique to alleviate tonsillitis? If objective validity of knowledge is the end which apparently justifies the means, what are we to make of Halliday's principled opposition to various forms of tyranny, particularly since the claim that ends justify means is one the main characteristics of what Halliday would consider to be repressive regimes? Perhaps, it is easy to make assessments of the objective validity of knowledge if one is not involved in having to pay the price for that knowledge. (Anthropological excavations may seem a reasonable price for the knowledge gained if it is not your great-grandparents' graves which are being desecrated.) To illustrate this argument Halliday uses an example of a bank robbery, arguing that the intelligence needed to carry out a successful bank robbery is capable of producing useful knowledge. Halliday neglects to mention that by viewing a bank as a building to rob, the knowledge that will be produced will be partial at best; and it is highly unlikely that the best way to understand a bank (or banking) is from the perspective of bank robbers.

The attempts to justify eurocentrism are based on the notion that eurocentrism is no more than ethnocentrism. So that racism is countered by reverse-racism, orientalism is countered by occidental-ism, and so on. Such reasoning is sustained by transforming an asymmetrical relationship into a relation of symmetry. This has a number of effects. First, it constructs the subordinate subjectivity as an inversion of the dominant subject position. This obscures the possibility of any autonomy of the subordinate. The subaltern only exists as an effect of the hegemonic discourse. It is not that sub-alternity is merely the result of hegemony, but rather the status of subalternity exhausts the subjectivity of the subordinated subject. Second, it erases the dimension of power from any relationship. Orientalism is not simply the stereotypical or essentialist view of the Orient/Islam. It is not just a discourse about knowledge, it is also a discourse about power. To propose occidentalism as its counterpart is to ignore the intimate relationship between power/knowledge. No doubt, the 'Rest' have stereotypical representations of the West, but the source of these representations is often the West itself. A relation-ship of power is a relationship of unevenness. Symmetry, obviously, denies hierarchy or oppression.

Hegel's master–slave dialectic provides a paradigmatic account of this logic of mirroring. It appears to show how the relations of domination and oppression are, at the basic level, symmetrical rela-tions. The motives and desires of the lord and the bondsman are mirror images of each other. The slave wants to be master and the master does not want to be a slave. In this attempt to be a master, the slave is caught in the master's game – a game which is predicated on the desire of the slave to be master … It is this symmetry which enables their reversal. The master becomes the slave and the slave becomes the master. It is this possibility of reversal that continues to justify and legitimatize systems of oppression in the aftermath of the Age of Europe.

In contrast to Hegel's allegory of master–slave, Gilroy (1993) tells a story which provides another reading of lord and bondsman, this time in a black idiom. Gilroy bases his reading on the accounts of Frederick Douglass's personal struggle with Covey (a slave breaker). Douglass's struggle to be free culminates in a two-hour tussle in which Covey is unable to subdue him. As a result Douglass frees himself from Covey and leaves. Gilroy notes the difference between Douglass's account and Hegel's fantasy in which:

> one solipsistic combatant in the elemental struggle prefers his con- queror's version of reality to death and submits. He becomes the slave while the other achieves mastery ... For [Douglass], the slave actively prefers the possibility of death to the continuing condition of in- humanity on which the plantation slavery depends.[22]

Unlike Hegel's bondsman, Douglass does not desire to become a slave breaker; he does not want Covey's position. It is by this refusal that Douglass de-legitimizes slavery, whereas Hegel's allegory endorses slavery by treating it as an elaborate form of saturnalia. In other words, in Hegel's version, the promise of reversal transforms the asymmetry of a relationship of power into symmetrical collusion and compliance. The promise (and fear) of reversal legitimizes the violence of the master at two levels: as a matter of strategic necessity (if the master should relax his grip, the slave will take his place), and as ethical relativism (the slave is no different from the master, if he could he would do the same). The logic of mirroring is based on the assumption that the discourse of the dominant order produces its own resistance. That is, those who resist the hegemonic order can only do so in the terms of that hegemony. It has the effect of transforming any struggle against a particular hegemony as another moment in the expansion of that hegemony. This precisely is the last bastion of eurocentrism: the position that there is nothing outside the Western project.

Eurocentrism and particularities

The argument rejecting the idea that Khomeini's failure to cite western political theory is not significant can be put in the following way. Khomeini does not quote western sources directly, but this does not mean that Khomeini has decentred the West – after all, the provincialization of Europe should depend on something other than an act of plagiarism by an octogenarian religious scholar. One of the dominant themes of the descriptions of Islamism is the irritation in their tone at how Islamists integrate non-Islamic elements while also insisting on the genuine Islamic nature of these elements.[23] The Islamists claim to represent an authentic construction of identity that is not contaminated by any non-Islamic influences, while also being riddled with western influences. Their claims to represent authenticity are based on the discourse of what they deny: their claims of authenticity are based on 'inauthentic' western discourse.

At issue is the question of whether it is possible to escape western discourse. Not surprisingly, many of the guardians of western discourse consider such an eventuality logically impossible. Discussions of cultural authenticity have become the battleground on which the issue of the postmodern encounter with the peripheral 'other' takes place. What I want to do in this section is to investigate the possibility of whether the logic of Islamism can escape being subordinated to the logic of eurocentrism; that is, to discuss the extent to which Islamism is reducible to being an internal moment within the western enterprise. These discussions of cultural authenticity and particularity have a resonance beyond the boundaries of the Muslim world, since they take place in the context of the conflict between eurocentrism and multiculturalism (too often vilified as 'political correctness').

There are a number of steps that have to be taken to establish the position in which the logic of Islamism is consumed by the western enterprise. The first step is clearly to indicate that Islamism is a particularity. This can be done by using Islamist claims for authenticity and difference, as signifiers of 'subaltern nationalism, retrenching nationalism and populist ideologies'.[24] Having established the particularity of Islamism, it is possible to declare, as Aziz Al-Azmeh does:

> The discourse of authenticity has rarely come into its own, outside Islamist circles, without being associated with some universalist discourse. … Resistance to the notion of authenticity in the Arab world has been feeble in the recent past due to a number of manifest political circumstances, not the least of which being that the Arab world has not been immune from the worldwide resurgence of atavism, ethnic and religious bigotry and fundamentalist religiosity.[25]

It would appear that, in the view of Al-Azmeh, Islamists – with their dreams of a global *Ummah* – may be even less universalist and more particular than even Serbian nationalists with their fantasies of an 'ethnically cleansed' Greater Serbia. Can it really be the case that the particularity of a global *Ummah* is even less cosmopolitan than the charms of a Greater Serbia?

The second step, having argued for the link between Islamism and particularity, is to demonstrate the universality of the West. This is often done by proclamation, for example:

> I take it as an accomplished fact that modern history is characterized by the globalization of the Western order. Despite protests of a bewildering variety against this accomplished fact, it remains incontestable especially as, with a few exceptions of an isolated and purely local nature, these protests have taken place either in the name of ideologies of the Western province – such as national independence and popular sovereignty – or substantially in terms of these ideologies, albeit symbolically beholden to a different local or specific repertory such as the Iranian regime of the Ayatollahs. The validation of universalism does not arise from some transcendental or immanent criterion, but simply from affirming the rationality of the real.[26]

What is striking about Al-Azmeh's declaration is not that he sees modern history as the internationalization of the western order, but that he is able to treat this internationalization as being synonymous with universalization. This, of course, is the central thrust of eurocentrism: to put Humpty-Dumpty back together again, to reforge the link between the West and universalism. We saw similar strategies at work in Chapter 1, in the attempt of Sahgal and Yuval-Davis to define fundamentalism.

The expansion of the European project geopolitically comes to denote a set of values and principles that have no particular manifestation. For example, it is this belief that allows someone like Halliday to write: 'I therefore start from a set of universal principles, analytic and normative ... I reject the notion of starting from supposed particularism derived from religion, political virtue, the nation or *anything else*' (my emphasis).[27] In other words, the expansion of Europe leads to a situation in which it is possible to erase all particularities within its universalism; it leads not to Europeanization but to a universalization in which European identity is subsumed under a universal label.[28] This transition from the global to the universal is highlighted by the way in which it is considered that protests against the western order can only be couched successfully in the language inaugurated and enforced by that very same western order.[29] It is the western discourse – of self-determination, popular sovereignty, etc. – which provides the means by which those who are subject to the West have been able to check or disrupt their subordinate status. Even in circumstances in which resistance to the western order is couched in a language different from that sanctioned by the western order, the signifiers are different tokenistically. To put it another way: at the beginning of this book I described the emergence of Islamism as being a product of the shift in Muslim final vocabularies, but for Al-Azmeh this shift is of limited importance. Even though Muslims may use the slogans of 'Islamic revolution' or 'Islam is the solution', what they really mean is the same as the slogans of the Enlightenment.[30] This reduces Islamism (along with other movements which challenge the centrality of western history) to mere 'idioms' or dialects of a universal language – that is, of course, the language of the West.

Having established the particularity of Islam(ism) and the universalism of the West, it is possible to conclude that Islamism is a moment within the discourse of the West. That is, Islamists plagiarize, manipulate, and make use of western resources to further their projects. From Khomeini's reliance on cassettes to deliver his sermons, to the Leninist model of party organization – all the infrastructural devices used are not Islamic. Their use by Islamists refutes the Islamist claim for authenticity[31] and, at the same time, demonstrates the inability of even the most virulent anti-western discourse to escape the West. Thus the rejection of the West is turned into its reaffirmation.

A number of consequences flow from this. First, and most obviously, it reinforces the logic of eurocentrism. By excluding the possibility of a counter-hegemonic project that is external to the West, it is possible to imagine the West as the universal template. This allows the imposition of western history as the destiny of all the planet, and means that all societies and cultures finally reach maturation when their historical developments correspond to the history of the West. For example, an often made argument is that attempts to articulate Islamist positions on issues relating to human rights etc. are doomed to failure, since such positions are possible only through secularization; therefore, the only thing to do is to wait for Muslim societies to secularize.[32] In the case of Islamism, by confining it to the exterior of universalism, it is possible to argue that the Islamist rejection of the West can only be made in the language of the West, therefore, it cannot be a true denial. It is thus suggested that the deceit of the Islamists is to castigate their opponents for Westoxication, while hiding the fact that their own projects are based on the appropriation of western practices.

Secondly, the conflation of the universal with the West, and Islam-(ism) with particularity, also enables the defence of eurocentrism to be couched in terms of the defence of universal principles. So that, for example, it can be argued that one of the reasons behind Islamist advances is the culture of relativism which allows some Muslim groups to be able to reject certain values by appealing to their Islamic heritage.[33]

Thirdly, by linking the West with universalism and Islam with particularism, it is possible to attack Islamism for its incoherence. The argument being that defenders of particularism are caught in a paradoxical position because, at the same time as rejecting universalism, they have to depend on it. As one commentator put it:

> The dilemma of the defenders of extreme particularism is that their political action is anchored in a perpetual incoherence. On the one hand, they defend the right to difference as a universal right, and this defence involves their engagement in struggles for the change of legislation, for the protection of minorities in courts, against the violation of civil rights, etc. That is, they are engaged in a struggle for the internal reform of the present institutional setting. But as they assert, at the same time, this setting is necessarily rooted in the cultural and political values of the traditional dominant sectors of the West, and that as they have nothing to do with that tradition, their demands cannot be articulated into any wider hegemonic operation to reform that system. This condemns them to an ambiguous peripheral relation with the existing institutions which can have only paralysing political effects.[34]

This statement is applicable to Islamist tendencies within Muslim settler groups in the North Atlantic plutocracies as well as those Islamists operating in Muslim countries.

The defence of universalism is often made by painting a picture of what would happen without a universal template. It is suggested that the abandonment of universalism would lead to a world in which 'nothing is true, and everything is permitted'. Universalism takes the place of God in the secularized Enlightenment discourse, preventing the transformation of cosmos into chaos. Without universalism, it is argued that all cultures/societies will no longer have any means to forge unities and agreements. Universalism then has to be defended since the alternative is relativism. This is the view that every belief held by a particular culture is as worthy as every belief held by any other culture.

As Rorty has insisted, however, no one actually holds this view.[35] What he calls relativism is the idea that the ground for choosing between two contending beliefs is not algorithmic.[36] Relativists would argue that the only way in which a particular system of values can be grounded is 'conversationally'.[37] In other words, the abandonment of a 'supercultural' court of appeal that can adjudicate between contending cultural forms does not lead to the abandonment of any possibility of judgement, only to the recognition that any judgement we make can only be made from our perspective of a cultural formation not from some transcendental ground.[38] According to Rorty, there is no 'supercultural platform' from which we interact with other cultures. It is not possible for people to leap outside their culture when they encounter another culture. According to Rorty this kind of ethnocentrism is unavoidable.[39] We have to maintain the constancy of most of our final vocabularies if we are to change other aspects of our vocabularies. For example, when European conquistadors arrived in what for them were new places, they could not help but describe the world they saw in the light of the vocabularies they already had. Rorty's solution to the charge of relativism is that we have our notions of 'good' and 'true' and that these are the only ones which we can rely on when we engage with other cultures; but these notions are merely 'ours' and are not sanctioned by anything other than our 'own' cultural practices. (To be fair to Rorty, he does add that these notions are only opening gambits in transcultural conversations – in other words, they can be transformed as a result of our contact with another culture but they cannot be simply skipped over.)[40] This answer would be unsatisfactory to those who hold that there are intrinsic qualities of being human, and that universalism is an abstraction of these qualities.

If we accept Rorty's argument that there is no 'supercultural platform', how do we understand discourses built around notions – for example, of 'national self-determination' – which seem to be a part of a western culture, but which are used by non-western cultures to oppose western culture? This problem can be set out in the following terms:

> [The] ... possibility of affirming the rights of the people to their self-determination presupposes the legitimacy of the discourses of equality in the international sphere, and these are not natural discourses, but they have conditions of possibility and a specific genesis. That is, why I think it is illegitimate to oppose the universality of Western values to the specificity inherent in the various cultures and national traditions, for asserting the legitimacy of the latter in terms different from those of an unrestricted xenophobia involves accepting the validity of discourses – e.g. the rights of nations to self-determination – which can only be put forward in universalist terms.[41]

Certain kinds of resistance only make sense in relation to the validity of discourses emerging in the West, which makes these discourses universal; that is, the relocation of resistance into the interior of imperialism transforms the imperial into the universal. For example, it is only because of the validity of Wilson's Fourteen Points, and in particular the right of national self-determination, that decolonization movements in the European empires (for example 'Bandung nationalisms') were possible. That is, the use of the vocabulary of 'national self-determination' by the FLN or Indian Congress Party, for example, was simply a result of a pragmatic decision to use whatever means were open and available to them to secure their aims. Such an argument would see in the use of notions bequeathed by the hegemony of the western order the working of an instrumental logic. However, beneath this argument there is a more radical version, in which the use of the signifiers of the western hegemonic discourse is not simply instrumental but actually constitutive. In other words, the meta-narratives associated with the democratic revolution do not just enable resistance, but actually constitute it. It is only when the western imaginary of rights has become hegemonic that those who are subject to that hegemony begin to subvert it by using the very vocabulary of that hegemonic discourse: resistance is internal to the hegemonic order. None of these descriptions avoids the problem of the existence of some meta-language or 'supercultural platform'. In fact, all of them are open to the possibility that what is being described as universal may turn out to be a particular cultural practice. It would be possible for us also to believe that a particular culture (for example the West) may incarnate what we hold to be universal. If we continue to see the universal in the terms outlined above, we will have to conclude that these descriptions legitimize western supremacist discourses – and make it impossible to think beyond eurocentrism. It would seem that, after all these various twists in the argument, surprisingly, the western supremacists were right all along. In other words, their descriptions of the relation between the universal and the particular are correct: there is nothing external to the western project. The West has no limits, since any articulation of its limits has the effect of expanding and deferring the limits of the West once more. Any attempt to draw the boundaries of the West is a mere gesture in the repertory of the West. Said has rightly criticized this position in vigorous terms.[42] I have nothing to add to Said's comments nor do I want to question the empirical grounds of such argumentation; rather I want to consider the theoretical grounds for establishing the universal. What determines whether a discourse is universal or not? Let me isolate three perspectives on universalism, while making no claims as to the extent to which these perspectives are exhaustive.

First, the universal is the common heritage of human beings; it is what unites all of us as a species. That is, the universal is an abstraction of the essence of humankind. The anti-foundationalist criticisms of such an essentialist account are clear and I am convinced by them.[43] Thus we can reject this description of the universal.

Second, the universal refers to the set of procedural agreements that are necessary for any cultural engagement. This position is closely identified with Habermas. The universal would be equivalent to what he calls 'validity claims'. The problem with this approach is that, unless one has a way of constructing a transcultural agreement, there is no neutral language in which to negotiate about procedural matters. Habermas gets around this problem by positing rationality as a neutral language. This attempt to secure reason as a final arbiter is another attempt to claim there is an algorithmic method for deciding between different claims. There is nothing wrong with this, since we all resort to some form of algorithmic reasoning to make decisions. However, algorithmic procedures can only operate under conditions of Kuhnian normal science; they cannot adjudicate in times of paradigmatic shift. By making the universal equivalent to procedural agreement, what is being argued for is the validity of a certain hegemony, rather than uncovering some universal ground.

Third, the universal is what transcends particular discourses. This would be similar to the view suggested by Gramsci. For Gramsci a hegemonic class is one that is able to articulate the interests and desires of other social groups. This can only be done if that class is able to claim that it is not representing its narrow particular interests but the interests of all social groups.[44] This is the moment of political-ideological struggle which is waged on a 'universal not a corporate level'.[45] The problem here is that this approach raises questions about the means by which the various social groups are able to pool their interests together. It would seem to assume that there must be a degree of metaphorical surplus which enables the articulation of various groups around a fundamental class. It would seem that the universal is simply relocated at the level of the metaphorical surplus that acts as an amalgamating point (point of unification) for the various social groups. In Gramsci's account, this would inevitably entail that the universal would be associated with one of the fundamental classes.

Contested genealogies

I want to try out another way of describing universality. I would locate the description of universality that I prefer within a Nietzschean–Foucauldian perspective. That is, I present what we understand to be universal as being the product of a successful hegemony's ability to establish its worldview as the reflection of the natural order. That is, a 'supercultural platform' exists not as a ontological given but as the sedimentation of the political struggle. What is at stake is not the genealogy of western supremacist discourses – how it came to master the world – but rather the status of this mastery. To examine this point in detail, I look at what hegemonic discourses do to become recognized as universal. I start by using metaphors from the field of semantics to make my analysis clear.

In semantics, marking refers to a wide number of phenomena.[46] I will focus on the idea of marking within lexical structures, where marking is based around the differential distribution of morphologically or formally related lexemes within a language. For example, 'lioness' contains a suffix 'ess' which the word 'lion' lacks. This suffix formally marks the presence or absence of some particular element or form. Lexemes that contain such a suffix are considered to be formally marked. The lexemes that are marked tend, on the whole, to be more restricted in the range of contexts in which they can be used than unmarked lexemes. For example, 'bitch' is more specific than 'dog', since the former denotes only female dogs while the latter can be applied in some contexts to refer to both male and female dogs.

It is possible to draw out the implications of this distinction between marked and unmarked lexemes for the political field,[47] especially in relation to the distinction between universality and particularity. A discourse appears universal to the extent that it is able to erase the marks of its particularity. In other words, I would equate an absolute 'supercultural' discourse as being one that was totally constituted by unmarked elements. All hegemonies that are aiming for a 'supercultural' status, however, are confronted by a paradox that prevents their movement towards an absolute universalism, since marking works not only as a restriction on use, but also as a form of identification. Absolute unmarking would remove the identity of the cultural formation, while absolute marking would remove its ability to transcend its cultural boundaries. For a discourse to erase all its marks would mean erasing its cohesion. We can only speak about the West because the West marks a particular historical narrative, without which it would not be possible to identify the West. Particularity is thus necessary for any attempt at universalism. The distinction that Al-Azmeh sets out between the universal and particular, in which the West is universal and the 'Rest' is particular, ignores the particularity of the West itself. It is only by ignoring that particularity that Al-Azmeh can claim that the West is universal. It is the particularity of the West that allows Al-Azmeh to agree with Zubaida that Khomeini remains within the grasp of the western discourse. In other words, the 'specific genesis'[48] of a particular discursive formation allows us to continue to identify the elements that constitute that discursive formation regardless of the use to which the elements are put and the context within which they operate. It is this initial baptism that allows Zubaida to determine the identity of the concepts used by Khomeini.

Unfortunately, while this may be a useful way of continuing to hold on to the idea of western hegemony, there is nothing in what Al-Azmeh says which actually demonstrates this to be the case. How do we know that certain discursive objects are western? For example, as we discussed previously, Zubaida puts forward the argument that Khomeini is indebted to western political thought since his theory assumes a number of categories which are a product of western political thought. At the same time, Zubaida writes that Khomeini fails to cite any western political theories. If Khomeini does not cite the West as a source, how is Zubaida able to conclude that Khomeini is using western concepts?[49]

One answer to this question would be that the term 'western' connotes certain properties which allow us to recognize the West (by recognizing these properties). The problem with this approach is that it is not always clear-cut what the properties that constitute the West are. The West is a discursive object constituted by a variety of narratives. There is no agreement on which narratives of the West we should base our search for those properties which constitute the West. Supposing we may find that certain properties are repeatedly associated with the West. Could we conclude that these are the properties which constitute the core of western identity?

It may be useful to take a slight detour at this point and consider the debate between descriptivism and anti-descriptivism, which may help us to resolve the problem concerning the relationship between properties and identity. I think that the consideration of this issue will help us to appreciate better the way in which Zubaida is able to sustain the western identity of particular concepts, even in a context in which no references are made to western concepts.

Let us state briefly the main area of dispute between the descriptivists and anti-descriptivists. The descriptivists contend that we use a particular word to denote a particular object because the word is descriptive of the properties of that object, and hence of the meaning of that object. For example, we call a chair 'chair' because the word 'chair' refers to a cluster of meanings which identify it as a chair, that is furniture of a particular shape, with a specific number of legs, and so on. Thus words refer to a set of properties and correspond to objects which possess those properties. The word 'tree' is a shorthand expression for all the descriptions that would go together to constitute a tree (something that grows in the ground, has a trunk and a number of branches, that grows in particular climatic zones, etc.). To put it differently, words function as a condensation of descriptions, and the identity of an object corresponds to the descriptive features of that object. As Zizek summarizes: 'Intention has logical priority over extension: extension (a set of objects referred to by a word) is determined by intention (universal properties comprised in its meaning).'[50] Thus a descriptivist solution to the puzzle of Zubaida's identification of certain concepts used by Khomeini as being western would be that those names actually refer to a set of features – including that of being western – that correspond to the properties of that object (which are western). This is the reason why Zubaida has no difficulty in proclaiming the western identity of the concepts used by Khomeini, because these concepts (for example the notion of the people as a political agent) describe features that are western. For the descriptivist, the relation between an object and its name is necessary: names correspond to descriptions of objects. The relation between names and objects is internal and immanent.

In contrast, the anti-descriptivists maintain that the connection between a word and an object (or signifier and signified) is the result of an initial baptism.[51] In other words, the relation between a name and an object is an external link established in the moment of primal baptism. After this initial act, the relation between the word and the object is maintained through transmission and tradition. That is, an initial act of naming sustains itself even when the cluster of descriptions of the object change. Kripke takes an example from John Stuart Mill to illustrate this argument.[52] Originally the town of Dartmouth got its name from being at the mouth of the river Dart; if the river were to change its course so that the town was no longer beside it, we would still call the town Dartmouth. So, according to Kripke, even if the initial baptism can be based on some identifying property, it is this primal act of baptism which functions as a means of fixing the relation between the name and the object. This means that the name given to an object can be used to refer to that object, even in counterfactual circumstances when that object does not have those identifying properties.[53]

According to an anti-descriptivist account, then, the relationship between a western appellation and some political concepts can be explained by primal baptism. These concepts and categories were first inaugurated as being western; since then they have come to be used in many non-western contexts, but this does not mean we have to change their name. For example, Laclau and Mouffe make the point that the democratic revolution began in France, with the French

Revolution, from where it spread all over the world. But it still retained
the name it acquired in the first act of primary baptism – and its link
to the West.[54] A number of consequences follow from this.

First, it is possible to identify any concept as being western
regardless of the situations in which it is used. This means that, even
if we say the meaning of a concept is a product of its use,[55] the use
of a western concept in a 'non-western' discourse cannot call into
question its western identity. Second, the idea that certain political
categories are western would persist even if we were to go along
with recent attempts at 'counter-writing' which try to show the 'non-
westernness' of western identity.[56] The initial baptism ensures the
persistence of the name the West, even if we were to realize that
there was no such thing as a pure western identity.[57]

There are a number of difficulties, however, with the anti-
descriptivist account and these have a bearing on our discussion.
First, as Searle points out, the anti-descriptivists have actually adopted
a descriptivist account of how a name is introduced during the process
of baptism.[58] Second, both descriptivists and anti-descriptivists miss a
crucial point: the act of naming is a radically contingent operation.
To overcome this radical contingency they both have to resort to
myths to limit the contingency and guarantee some kind of necessity.[59]
The descriptivists resort to the myth of the primitive tribe in which
each personal name is unique, dies with the bearer of the name, and
is never repeated. The anti-descriptivists have created a myth of an
omniscient observer of history who is able to recover and trace the
chain of names that leads back to the primal baptism.[60]

Even if we allow for the initial baptism (following Kripke), how
can we recover the causal chain that leads back to the act of baptism?
The answer is that this can only be done by tracing a genealogy, and
to do this means that the invocation of the 'name' must have a mark
which allows us to begin the act of reconstructing the process that
will eventually lead us to the primal baptism. A mark is also a sign
of copyright – it designates a genealogical trace. If we understand
the universal not as some essential category either at the level of
universal itself or its ground, but rather a political operation, the act
of giving particular values a universal identity is itself a hegemonic
operation. This would accord with Zizek's contribution to the debate
between the anti-descriptivists and descriptivists. Zizek's conclusion
can be summarized in two main points: a) the act of naming con-

stitutes the unity of the object, that is the name does not correspond to the object, but the object is a retroactive construction of the act of naming; and b) the act of primal baptism has to be constantly reiterated.[61] What this means is that the denunciation of Islamists for using western categories is actually the reconstruction and main-tenance of particular genealogical traces. It is not that Khomeini uses concepts which are themselves western, but that the description of the concepts as western retroactively constructs them as such. It is not only that Islamists are engaged in an operation of fabrication – that is making up stories about their authentic selves, 'pretending' that the clothes that they wear are 'Islamic' – but also that those who reject Islamist narratives of authenticity do so by making up stories about the West. The need constantly to renew the primal baptism means that the universal must be policed and constantly linked to its particular. This means that the link that is established between universal values and the traces of the West (in opposition to other particularities) is difficult to sustain, since the identity of those values comes from their articulation and not from their historical conditions of emergence. It is not possible to maintain the attachment between a signifier and a particular cultural formation except through a hegemonic operation. In other words, it is not so much that some elements are western and others are not, but rather that eurocentrism operates by laying claim to the copyright on some things and rejecting others. The argument that ethnocentrism is about the rejection of the universal in terms of the rejection of the signifier 'western' does not necessarily imply the rejection of what is being signified, but it is a rejection of that hegemonic operation which attaches a signifier to its signified.

The only way in which the logic of eurocentrism can continue to uncover 'western' elements is by having a notion of the West which is essentialist. That is, we can only identify the western elements in Islamist discourses by claiming the persistence of western identity within the vocabulary of the 'Rest'. In this context, the use of certain political categories by Islamists does not have any effect on the meaning of these categories, since their identity and their link to the West was established in the primal act of baptism.

Zizek's intervention, however, would make this position difficult to sustain, since the use and articulation of categories within a different context reconstitutes those categories and retroactively constructs the objects to which they refer. This would oppose the contention that neither the West nor the categories that were primally baptized as western are not transformed by those who claim to be rejecting the West.

One may ask why some writers wish to maintain the genealogical link between the West and certain values. The possibility of answering this question brings us back to Said and the relationship between power/knowledge and imperialism. One of the points that Said makes throughout his critique of orientalism is the constant refrain in orientalist discourse that the Orient cannot represent itself, but needs the intervention of the (western) expert on the Orient in order to be represented.[62] The ability of the orientalist to discourse about the Orient was founded on the dense network of political-cultural elements, which supported the orientalist. The orientalist could speak for the Orient because he could speak the language of science, rationality, progress, etc. He could use a language by which other languages could be translated and transcribed. The orientalist was part of a 'supercultural' formation reinforced by the facticity of European imperialism. With the breakdown of European imperial systems and the processes of decolonization, the notion of a supercultural formation can no longer be taken for granted. This brings us back to the issue which we touched upon previously, about the relationship between Islamism and the possibility of articulating different sets of cultural canons.

The conflict over the displacement of a western canon is experienced as a loss by those who are most involved in narrating and extending that canon. One strategy employed is to claim that when Islamists articulate their discourse of authenticity, they are still using the language of the West. In this sense, the fate of the universal intellectual is tied to a discourse of universalism.[63] One way of perpetuating this universalism is to relocate all attempts to resist that universalism as mere extensions of such universalism. This is done by making genealogical claims for elements of Islamist discourse. The ability to recuperate discourses like Islamism rests on the ability to 'recover' the culturally copyrighted element in the discourse of Islamism. The battle between eurocentrism and the logic of Islamism is really a conflict about genealogies – a struggle about how to narrate the future of the world.[64] The western discourse is a product of a number of projects which narrate the world in terms of the continuity of the West. The limit of Europe comes when groups of people begin to articulate their position on the basis of the rejection of Europe's claims to copyright. In other words, both the provincialization of Europe and the universalization of Europe are political narratives. What is remarkable about the discourse of European universalization (at least in relation to the Muslim world) is how successful this discourse had been in the period from the 1870s to the 1970s and the 1980s (especially during the period of the unquestioned Kemalist hegemony from the 1920s to the 1970s). The discourse of the universalization of Europe was able to preclude the possibility of any major political order being centred on anything other than the principles provided by eurocentrism. The advent of Islamism challenges eurocentrism. The Islamists' discourse replaces the West not only in terms of geopolitical considerations (there have been many discourses which have rejected western hegemony in the Muslim world) but also as a source of direct emulation. While there is nothing intrinsic about the antagonism between the West and Islam, it is this antagonism which has been produced by a number of discourses, including orientalism and Kemalism, as well as Islamism. As a consequence, the assertion of Islamic identity becomes involved in a zero-sum game, in which every act of assertion of an Islamic identity comes to be read as a rejection of the West.

Conclusion

When Mustafa Kemal came to power, the idea of western cultural superiority was still strong. Mustafa Kemal was a paradigmatic figure in that he was the culmination of many trends (for example Ottoman reformism, westernizing modernization, etc.) and at the same time he extended the logic of these trends into new areas (such as the radical de-Islamization programme). Similarly, it may be useful to see the emergence of Khomeini as marking another paradigmatic shift. Khomeini's success in establishing his regime demonstrated most clearly the possibilities of an Islamic vocabulary to undermine and remove the Kemalist hegemony. Until the establishment of Khomeini's regime, it was always possible to suggest that Islamism was simply a discourse of protest, with no chance of achieving political power. Khomeini's achievement represented the possibility that the way to political power did not necessarily involve an insertion into the discourse of Kemalism. In contrast, by the time Khomeini came to power, the centrality and certainty of western discourse were already being questioned; it is this questioning of the West which has weakened eurocentric discourses. Thus, Khomeini was able to articulate the overthrow of the Shah and establish the Islamic Republic – without having to resort to explaining his political project in terms of western political theory. As a result, he was able to use the antagonistic relationship between Islam and the West constructed by the discourses of Kemalism to articulate Islam as the master signifier of a new political order. Whereas the Kemalists had seen Islam as a metaphor of decay, a sign of the non-western (and, therefore, non-modern) character of their societies, Khomeini saw in Islam a metaphor for resistance both to the Kemalist regimes and to what he considered to be global western power.

In this chapter I have argued that the emergence of Islamism marks an erosion of eurocentrism. It is an erosion that cannot be masked by rearticulating Islamism as another variant of the western project, unless one resorts to an essentialist theorization of the West. An anti-essentialist account of eurocentrism would regard it as a project struggling to maintain political and cultural hegemony. The provincialization of Europe refers to the result of the hegemonic struggle whereby Europe became increasingly less exceptional. It is the normalization of western cultural formations – when the West becomes just another (not exceptional) culture and not the undisputed model for human development – that opens up the possibility of articulating the possibility of something else. As Frantz Fanon declared (perhaps) prematurely, 'the European game has finally ended, we must find something different'; no doubt he would have been surprised to learn that it was Islamists who were most confident of having found 'something different'.[65]

Notes

1. Foucault, 1986, p. 205.
2. Amin, 1989, p. 106.
3. Ibid.
4. Ibid..
5. Ibid., p. 134.
6. Initially, in an article in the *National Interest*, and subsequently in his book (1992). Fukuyama's triumphalism finds its echo in Rorty's complacency regarding the North Atlantic plutocracies, see for example, Rorty, 1991a, pp. 203–10.

7. While Fukuyama's triumphalism has become rather tarnished as a result of the Balkans conflict (where Shabbir Akthar's much scorned prophecy, that the next time they built death camps in Europe it would be for Muslims, has become a chilling reality), the general proposition that there exists no viable alternative to the West still has many supporters.

8. Fukuyama, 1992, p. 347.

9. Wittfogel, 1957, pp. iii and 388–409.

10. See Heller and Feher, 1991, p. 2. See also Young, 1990, pp. 2–3.

11. See Hauner, 1990, for discussion of the significance of Asia in the constitution of an exclusively Russian identity.

12. See, for example, Rorlich, 1986.

13. Khomeini, *BBC Summary of World Broadcasts*, 10 January 1989.

14. In a Borgesian gesture, Carlos Menem retrospectively had Argentina's United Nations voting record changed so that its votes were consistently in favour of the United States. This was a way of establishing Argentina's western credentials.

15. West, in Kruger and Mariani, 1989, p. 87. I prefer to treat West's dates as being illustrative rather than definitive. Questions of when Europe actually achieved supremacy, or when (and if) the age of Europe ends, are far from settled. It is the case that by 1945, all the European empires were on their last legs, but, until 1975 Portugal still controlled large parts of Africa, and it is only since 1989 that we can speak (tentatively) about the decolonization of the Russian empire in Central Asia. Also, there is argument as to whether the United States is actually a culmination of Europe rather than something external, which leaves open the question of whether the Age of Europe is linked to US hegemony as well.

16. West, in Kruger and Mariani, 1989, p. 87.

17. Ibid.

18. Gramsci, 1971, p. 55, note 5. See also Simon (1982, p. 21) for a distinction between hegemony and domination in the work of Gramsci.

19. See Derrida, 1987, for an elaboration of the notion of undecidability.

20. See for example, Halliday, 1996, p. 214; and more generally, Sadiq Al-Azm, 1982.

21. Halliday, 1996, p. 213.

22. Gilroy, 1993, p. 63; for a general discussion see pp. 58–64.

23. See, for example, Hourani, 1983, p. 144.

24. Al-Azmeh, 1993, p. 41.

25. Al-Azmeh, 1991, p. 481.

26. Ibid., p.468.

27. Halliday, 1996, p. 196. It is very difficult to understand what one is to make of such a claim. If we are to take Halliday's claim seriously, his rejection of particularism has implications for the identity of the analyst, in this case Halliday himself. For rejection of particularism also means that there cannot be any identity: the rejection of all particularism means the abandonment of difference. Difference, as we have noted several times before, is constitutive of identity itself. So when Halliday says that one does not start from any particularism, it is the same as saying that he does not have a gender, is not ethnically marked, is not socio-economically located, etc. Under these circumstances it is not clear how we can even speak of 'Halliday' except perhaps as a synonym for some absolute spirit.

28. Compare this with Billig's comment that western nations tend to imagine their nations to be non-nationalist, and speaking for the West becomes equivalent to speaking for the world. Billig, 1993, pp. 77 and 81–2.

29. Lawrence, 1990, pp. 31–2. Lawrence makes a similar point when he argues that Islamists are, in fact, affirming modernity because their opposition to modernity is only possible by using modernity.

30. This position is very similar to Descombes's reading of the Foucault–Derrida debate. Descombes, 1986, pp. 136–9.

31. This is increasingly the strategy of Kemalist regimes, and traditional *ulema* who reject the Islamist description of *asala*.

32. For example, Halliday, 1996, p. 140.

33. An example of this can be found in the argument used by Muslim states against popular political participation – that democracy is western and unsuitable for Muslims. Examples of this can be found in Gosaibi's generally intelligent account: Gosaibi, 1993, p. 74. For criticism of this approach, see Gellner, 1992; Al-Azmeh, 1993, p. 41; Halliday, 1996, p. 141.

34. Laclau, 1996, p. 33.

35. Rorty, 1982, p. 166.

36. Ibid.

37. Ibid., 1982, p. 167.

38. For more details, see Rorty, 1979, pp. 376–9.

39. Rorty, 1991a, p. 212.

40. Ibid., pp. 212–13.

41. Laclau, 1990, p. 188.

42. Said, 1993, p. 251.

43. See Rorty's essay, on 'Contingency of language', in Rorty, 1989.

44. Mouffe in Mouffe, 1979, p. 181.

45. Ibid., p. 180.

46. A clear exposition of markedness can be found in Lyons, 1968, pp. 305–11.

47. For example, see Laclau, 1990, pp. 32–3.

48. Ibid., p. 187.

49. Zubaida, 1989, pp. 1–38.

50. Zizek, 1989, p. 90.

51. Kripke, 1972, p. 302.

52. Kripke, 1980, p. 26.

53. Kripke, 1972, p. 309.

54. Laclau and Mouffe, 1985, pp. 150–51.

55. Wittgenstein, 1958, s. 43.

56. For example, the works of Kuhrt and Sherwin-White, 1987; Bernal, 1987; Springborg, 1992.

57. Kripke, 1972, pp. 315–16. Compare this with the argument Kripke makes about what would happen if we discovered that gold did not actually have the properties we ascribe to it. His conclusion is that we would still continue to call it gold though we may modify our description of its properties. Similarly, that Jesus of Nazareth was born not in AD 1 (there is strictly speaking no year 0) but in 4 BC does not require that the Christian calendar be adjusted by four years – after all, the Americas were supposedly named after the first European man (*sic*) to arrive in the New World.

58. Searle, 1983, pp. 234–5.

59. Zizek, 1989, p. 95.
60. Ibid., pp. 92–5.
61. For a fuller treatment, see Zizek, 1989, Chapter 2.
62. Said, 1985a, pp. 32–6.
63. See Foucault (1980, pp. 126–7) for a definition of universal intellectual.
64. It is remarkable to see the ease with which historians of the 'rise of the West' are able to project eurocentrism into the future. For example, William McNeill concludes his history of humankind by asserting that whatever comes next will be a continuation of the West. See McNeill, 1963, p. 806.
65. Fanon, 1990, p. 252.

Epilogue: Islamism/eurocentrism

The emergence of Islamism is based on the erosion of eurocentrism. There was a time in Muslim majority states when the chanting of the incantation of the West and its cognates was necessary if one was to have any political efficacy. Around the 1970s this situation began to change. Increasingly it became possible to articulate political demands using a vocabulary centred on Islam, without any attempt to associate Islam with the West. The emergence of Islam as a political category highlights the way in which the old order in the Muslim world is increasingly unable to resist calls for the implementation of Islamist projects.

The post-colonial order in the Muslim world was dominated by Kemalist discourses. The rise of Islamism is associated particularly with the crisis of these discourses and with a general crisis arising out of the postmodern condition (or what I prefer to call the 'decentring of the West'). Islamism, by articulating the centrality of Islam, was able to use Islam as a way of rejecting the West. Its success in this venture was founded on two things. First, the Kemalists had used the opposition: 'Islam and the West' as a means of articulating their projects. In their reaction to the rise of Islamism they continued to use this same opposition. Second, the erosion of the idea of the West as a foundation meant that it was no longer as powerful as it had been during the formative years of Kemalism. The entire Kemalist project – like the apologistic reformism of the eighteenth- and nineteenth-century Muslims – was based on the assumption that the West was clearly superior to the 'rest'. After two world wars and decolonization, the notion of western superiority was no longer so straightforward; the balance between the superiority of the West and inferiority of Islam was no longer so heavily weighted against Islam. One effect of this global process of the provincialization of Europe was that the choice between Islam and the West was no longer the choice between the centre and periphery; the playing-field had been levelled out a little.

The Kemalists attempted to re-describe Islam as being aligned with backwardness, superstition, etc. though the success of this description with those subordinated by it is still open to question. As has been indicated in earlier chapters, I am sceptical of the views which see any discourse of resistance as being already within the hegemony. That is, the hegemonic bloc's descriptions of the subaltern are not necessarily reproduced by the subaltern. So what did the future Islamists do while the Kemalists were securely in power? Did they see Islam in the same way as the Kemalists? If they accepted the Kemalist descriptions of Islam, at what time and how did they begin to articulate their own Islamist description of Islamism?[1] This should not be taken to mean that Kemalist descriptions of Islam exhausted all descriptions of Islam. What Kemalism managed to do was to produce an 'Islam' with its obstructionism, its corrupt *ulema*, and its compliance with authorities. This version of Islam was popular among the westernized élites, who formed the bedrock of support for the Kemalist order.[2] There was, however, another Islam: an 'Islam of dreams', a vision of Islam as it 'should be'. As Said writes:

> In the minds and hearts of its adherents, surely Islam has always been resurgent, alive, rich in thought, feeling and human production. And always in the thoughts of the faithful the 'Islamic vision' (in W. Montgomery Watt's useful phrase) has involved them in creative dilemmas. What is justice? What is evil? When are orthodoxy and tradition to be relied upon? When is *ijtihid* (individual interpretation) in order?[3]

This Islam had an iceberg-like existence – it could be seen in the private/ethical domain produced by Kemalism but was generally, at a public level, invisible.[4]

When Kemalism began to unravel, its interpretation of Islam also came under strain. But because Kemalism did not exhaust all subject positions, and its ability to recuperate opposition was limited to the extent that it could recuperate only what it could see, the 'Islam of dreams' was not lost along with Kemalism.[5] Instead this utopian vision of Islam came to occupy an increasingly central place within Muslim communities.

Islamists then were to use this 'Islam of dreams' to articulate a moral universe, in which ethical vocabularies dominate. This is where the understanding of Islam as a religion, as a system of ethical practices, comes to their aid. By articulating their position by using an ethical vocabulary, empowered by the signifier of Islam, they have been able to disarm the discourse of their opponents. The anti-Islamists respond to the ethical vocabulary of Islamists either by resorting to a vocabulary of technology ('the Islamists do not know how to manage the modern world'), or falling back on charges of hypocrisy ('the Islamist leadership is not as ethical as it claims'). Islamists, by using Islam both as an ethical and a political signifier, have managed to transform the terrain upon which the politics of Muslim communities is decided. An appeal to 'western civilization', or 'western' values, is no longer able to legislate political visions against the opposition of Islamist groups.

I described Islamists as those who use Islamic metaphors to narrate their political projects. The implication of what I have been discussing is that Islamism is one of the centres in the polynuclear world. It would be wrong to suggest here that Islamism is a totally cohesive and agreed upon discourse; as countless commentators have pointed out, there are as many variations in Islamism as there are Islamist movements. However, the diversity of Islamist movements does not mean that Islamism lacks coherence, as too many commentators are too quick to conclude.

The decentring of the West has created a space where it is possible for different cultural complexes to find different political vocabularies. In this sense it is more helpful to consider Islamism as (the opening of) a new terrain of ethical, cultural, political and social action, rather than as a name for a group of radical political movements. It is in this sense that various indicators of Islamization have resonance for Islamism, for what these indicators do is point to the emergence of a Muslim subject position.

The emergence of an increasingly visible Muslim subjectivity has brought to the fore the differences between the orientalist and anti-orientalist theorization of Islam and its relation to Islamism. I agreed with Said about the limitations of the orientalist descriptions. However, the anti-orientalist response to Said's critique is not satisfactory, because it replaces the essentialism of the whole with an essentialism of the parts. As an alternative to both these accounts, I suggest that it is more useful to see Islam as a discursive construct. For Muslims, Islam cannot be just an ordinary element of their discourse since it is central to the construction of narratives of Muslimness. Islamists articulate Islam as the master signifier of their political discourse, that is Islam becomes the unifying point of the discursive production of Islamists.

Following the death of the Prophet, Islam became the political signifier that mastered the Muslim *Ummah*. The abolition of the caliphate opened up Islam for re-articulation and reinscription. One attempt to re-describe Islam was made by what I called Kemalists. Kemalism is a metaphor for the regimes that emerged in the Muslim world following decolonization. Kemalists interpreted Islam as antagonistic to the West, and they identified the West with progress, modernization, etc. Thus, Islam in Kemalist discourse became the name for tradition, obscurantism, superstition, and so on. For Kemalists to become modern (and therefore western), it was necessary for them to construct their societies as oriental prior to their intervention, in order to construct their actions as a de-orientalizing drive (excluding and attempting to erase Islam). The logical and historical result of such an operation was to make Islam available for re-articulation.

Central to the success of Islamism is the way it is constructed in opposition to the West. Thus, it benefits from a wider questioning of the conflation between the western enterprise and universalism. The relative success of Islamist projects is based on the combination of the deconstructionist logic of the postmodern critique with a non-western alternative. In other words, the proliferation of groups and movements declaring themselves to be Islamists highlights the inability of the logic of eurocentrism to police as effectively as before the fixity of its articulations.

The central thrust of western supremacist discourses is that the globalization of Europe also involved its universalization and, therefore, all discourses of resistance to the West are always already within the West. In reference to Islamism there are three main contentions. One is that its claims of authenticity are based on either duplicity or stupidity: Islamists are either knowingly fabricating fables of authenticity or they are doing so unwittingly. Second, Islamism is just a reversal of western discourses: it only involves a reversal of hierarchies. Third, Islamists cannot escape the West since they must rely on its language to articulate their project. All these objections hinge upon the possibility of drawing the limits to the western project. If globalization is equivalent to universalization, then there is no such limit. However, the claim of universality both by modern and some postmodern theorists is itself only a hegemonic operation, which retroactively constructs Islamism as a mere reiteration of the western project. The denial of the possibility of rejecting the West is itself a gesture of the West which is intended to recuperate any possible dislocation. Thus, it re-describes its own genealogy. Now, the emergence of Islamism – which points to the erosion of western supremacist discourses – opens up the struggle for the articulation of genealogies. The contest between these attempts is part of the hegemonic struggle to construct the narrative of origins. The conflict between the logic of Islamism and the logic of eurocentrism is the contest about how to write the history of the future.

Recent years have seen a number of publications and interventions which have sought to place the western enterprise as just another civilization. This provincialization of Europe has been associated with postmodernity. It has involved a philosophical critique of the certainties of 'white mythologies', for example the work of Derrida and his critique of western metaphysics and other trends within the field of anti-foundationalism. There have also been historical critiques of the origins of Europe, for example Martin Bernal's *Black Athena* (1987). There is also Springborg's critique of western political theory, which argues that it rests on the construction of a dichotomy between western republicanism and oriental despotism. Many other such instances may be cited. The recent furore over multiculturalism or 'political correctness' is centred around the struggle of European identity.

I have tried to weave a narrative around these two levels: the cultural and the political, since it is at the interface between the cultural critique of Europe and the critique of Europe as a form of politics that Islamism emerges. It is precisely for this reason that many critics of Said point to the way in which his critique of orientalism has been used by Islamists to discredit all forms of western enquiry, be it in the field of journalism or human rights.[6] It is suggested that Said's recklessness has opened doors that cannot be closed. The difficulty in accounting for Islamism is not simply the result of ordinary problems of scholarship, nor is it just the effect of many of the features and practices that Said criticizes in his work. It rests at a most profound level: on the problem of 'strong' orientalism.

When we had only one *episteme* to deal with, the problem of the 'other' was easy to exorcize. We simply carried out an epistemic violence and read the other through our own devices. The picture that Said draws of orientalism has a far greater resonance than simply the scholarship of Muslim societies.[7] Orientalism is about the kind of knowledge that is considered legitimate as knowledge – that is statements produced by western practices. Islamists claim that they reject the West and reject orientalism. Critics of Islamism argue that this rejection is immature and incoherent, since there is no alternative to the West and to orientalism (in the strong sense). The effect of this is to try to domesticate Islamism. This strategy of showing the original 'western' character of any practices used by Islamists works, however, only by maintaining a fixed and hierarchically positioned notion of western identity. What is happening is that Islamists are refusing to recognize statements that perpetuate and position western identity in terms of western discourse about western identity. The effect of this is to make Islamists disruptive, not only of a geopolitical order, but also of an *episteme* which has been dominant for perhaps the last three hundred years. By not accepting claims about western cultural copyright Islamists challenge 'strong orientalism' and western hegemony. This is why recent events have served to perpetuate the image of Islam as the radical other.[8] That is, Islam is the 'other' that we cannot embrace, even when we are at our most tolerant, because this other fails to accept the rules of the game – because it sees the game as a western game.

No doubt the Islamist tide will ebb and flow over the coming years, no doubt Islamists will suffer disappointments, and will advance and retreat. But as long as there are Muslims the promise and fear of Islamism will remain, for in the end, for us Muslims, Islam is another name for the hope of something better ...

Notes

1. It is interesting to note that at this point, Khomeini, while critical of the Shah, did not advocate the end of the monarchy and the establishment of Islamic government. In this he was not unique, since many other Islamist intellectuals were, at least in public utterances, fairly accommodating with the various Kemalist regimes.

2. This can be seen by the way in which Islamist critics lament the current state of Islam. See Shariati, 1979; Maududi, 1992 (especially pp. 18–60).

3. Said, 1981, p. 61.

4. See Scott, 1990, pp. 1–45.

5. One of the most remarkable features of the emergence of Islamism is the extent to which it was ignored by the various Kemalist authorities. It was discounted as a serious contender for political power until the Iranian revolution and the success of Hizbollah in warding off Israeli raids. These two events demonstrated the ability of Islamists to organize politically and to pose a significant challenge to Westernized forces. See Esposito, 1992, pp. 141–50.

6. See, for example, Abaza and Stauth, 1988, pp. 343–5.

7. See Hall's recognition of this, in Hall and Gieben, 1992, pp. 296 and 315.

8. For example, Mouffe declares: 'Hence the problem posed by the integration of a religion like Islam which does not accept these distinctions ... The relegation of religion to the private sphere which we now have to make Muslims accept was only made with great difficulty with the Christian Church and is still not completely accomplished.' Obviously Mouffe's 'we' excludes any Muslim reader and, for an anti-essentialist, she has a very essentialist notion of Muslims and Islam. Mouffe, 1993, p. 132.

Bibliography

Abaza, Mona and Stauth, Georg (1988) 'Occidental reason, orientalism, Islamic fundamentalism: a critique'. *International Sociology*, 3(4): pp. 343–64.

Abdel Malek, Anouar (1963) 'Orientalism in crisis', *Diogenes*, Winter: 103–44.

Abdel Malek, Anouar (ed.) (1983) *Contemporary Arab Political Thought*. London: Zed.

Abdul, Musa (1976) *The Classical Caliphate: Islamic Institutions*. Lagos: Islamic Publications Bureau.

Abercrombie, Nicholas, Hill, Stephen and Turner, Bryan S. (1980) *The Dominant Ideology Thesis*. London: George Allen and Unwin.

Abrahamian, Evrand (1992) 'Khomeini: fundamentalist or populist?', *New Left Review*, 186, March–April.

Abrahamian, Evrand (1993) *Khomeinism*. London: I.B.Tauris.

Abukhalil, As'ad (1991) 'Ideology and the practice of Hizballah in Lebanon: Islamization of Leninist organizational principles', *Middle East Studies*, 27, July: 390–403.

Abu-Lughod, Ibrahim (1982) 'Studies on the Islamic assertation: a review essay', *Arab Studies Quarterly*, 4(1 and 2), Spring: 157–75.

Afshar, Haleh (ed.) (1985) *Iran: A Revolution in Turmoil*. London: Macmillan.

Ahady, Anwar (1992) 'The decline of Islamic fundamentalism', *Journal of Asian and African Studies*, XXVII, No. 3–4.

Ahmad, Feroz (1993) *The Making of Modern Turkey*. London: Routledge.

Ahmad, Jalal Al-i (1984) *Occidentosis*. Berkeley: Mizan.

Ahmed, Akbar S. (1992) *Postmodernism and Islam: Predicament and Promise*. London: Routledge.

Ahmed, Leila (1992) *Women and Gender in Islam*. New Haven: Yale University Press.

Ahsan, M. M. and Kidwai, A. R. (1991) *Sacrilege versus Civility: Muslim Perspectives on The Satanic Verses Affair*. Leicester: Islamic Foundation.

Ajami, Fouad (1978–9) 'The end of Pan-Arabism', *Foreign Affairs*, Winter: 355–73.

Ajami, Fouad (1981) *The Arab Predicament*. Cambridge: Cambridge University Press.

Akhavi, Shahrough (1988) 'Islam, politics and society in the thought of Ayatullah Khomeini, Ayatullah Taliqani, and Ali Shariati', *Middle East Studies*, 24, October: 403–41.

Akhtar, Shabbir (1989) *Be Careful with Muhammad: The Salman Rushdie Affair*. London: Bellew Publishing.

Alavi, Hamza (1973) 'The state in post-colonial societies: Pakistan and Bangladesh', in K. Gough (ed.), *Imperialism and Nationalism in South Asia*. New York: Monthly Review Press.

Al-Azm, Sadiq Jalal (1981) 'Orientalism and orientalism in reverse', *Khamsin*, 8: 5–26.

Al-Azmeh, Aziz (1991) 'The discourse of cultural authenticity: Islamist revivalism and Enlightenment universalism', in Eliot, Deutsch (ed.), *Culture and Modernity: East–West Perspectives*. Honolulu: University of Hawaii Press.

Al-Azmeh, Aziz (1993) *Islams and Modernities*. London: Verso.

Almond, Gabriel and Verba, Sidney (eds) (1980) *The Civic Culture Revisited*. Boston: Little, Brown.

Amin, Samir (1989) *Eurocentrism*. Translated by Russel Moore. London: Zed.

Anderson, Benedict (1990) *Imagined Communities: Reflections on the Origin and the Spread of Nationalism*. London: Verso.

Anderson, Perry (1974) *Lineages of the Absolutist State*. London: NLB.

Appignanesi, Lisa and Maitland, Sara (eds) (1989) *The Rushdie File*. London: Fourth Estate.

Arkoun, Mohammed (1994) *Rethinking Islam*. Translated and edited by Robert D. Lee. Boulder: Westview.

Asad, Talal (1993) *Genealogies of Religion: Disciplines and Reasons of Power in Christianity and Islam*. Baltimore: Johns Hopkins University Press.

Asad, Talal and Owen, Roger (1983) *Sociology of 'Developing Societies': The Middle East*. London: Macmillan.

Ataturk, Mustapha Kemal (1983) *A Speech Delivered by Mustapha Kemal Ataturk, 1927*. Ankara: Basbakanlik Basimevi.

Ayalon, David (1960) 'Studies on the transfer of the Abbasid caliphate from Baghdad to Cairo', *Arabica*, 7: 41–59.

Ayoob, Mohammad M. (1981) *The Politics of Islamic Reassertation*. New York: St. Martin's Press.

Ayubi, Nazih N. (1991) *Political Islam: Religion and Politics in the Arab World*. London: Routledge.

Babeair, Abdulwahab Saleh (1990) 'Contemporary Islamic revivalism: a movement or a moment?', *Journal of Arab Affairs*, 9(2): 122–46.

Baechler, Jean, Hall, John A. and Mann, Michael (eds) (1988) *Europe and the Rise of Capitalism*. Oxford: Basil Blackwell.

Banani, Amin (1961) *The Modernization of Iran 1924–1941*. Stanford: Stanford University Press.

Baram, Amatzia (1991) *Culture, History and Ideology in the Formation of Ba'athist Iraq, 1968–89*. Oxford: Macmillan.

Barthes, Roland (1973) *Mythologies*. Selected and translated from the French by Annette Lavers. London: Paladin.

Barthes, Roland (1990) *S/Z*. Translated by Richard Miller, preface by Richard Howard. Oxford: Blackwell.

Bartlett, Robert (1994) *The Making of Europe: Conquest, Colonization and Cultural Change 950–1350*. London: Penguin.

Bashear, Suliman (1980) *Communism in the Arab East 1918–1928*. London: Ithaca.

Batatu, Hanna (1979) *The Old Social Classes and the Revolutionary Movements of Iraq: A Study of Iraq's Old Landed and Commerical Classes and of Its Communists, Ba'athists and Free Officers*. Princeton: Princeton University Press.

Bayart, Jean-François (1993) *The State in Africa: The Politics of the Belly*. Translated by Mary Harper, Christopher and Elizabeth Harrison. London: Longman.

Bayat, Mangol (1983) 'Secularism and the Islamic goverment in Iran', in Philip

H. Stoddard (ed.), *The Middle East in the 1980s: Problems and Prospects*. Washington DC: Middle East Institute.

Beckwith, Christoper I. (1980) 'Aspects of the history of the Central Asian guard corps in Islam', *Archivum Eurasiae Medii Avei*, 4: 29–43.

Berkes, N. (1965) *The Development of Secularism in Turkey*. Toronto: McGill University Press.

Bernal, Martin (1987) *Black Athena: The Afroasiatic Roots of Classical Civilization*. London: Free Association Books.

Bernard, Cheryl and Khalilzad, Zalmay (1984) *'The Government of God': Iran's Islamic Republic*. New York: Columbia University Press.

Bill, James (1988) *The Eagle and the Lion: The Tragedy of American–Iranian Relations*. New Haven: Yale University Press.

Billig, Michael (1993) 'Nationalism and Richard Rorty: the text as a flag for Pax Americana', *New Left Review*, 202, November/December.

Binder, Leonard (1988) *Islamic Liberalism*. Chicago: University of Chicago Press.

Bloom, Allan (1987) *The Closing of the American Mind*. New York: Simon and Schuster.

Bobbio, Norberto (1989) *Democracy and Dictatorship: The Nature and Limits of State Power*. Translated by Peter Kennedy. Cambridge: Polity.

Borges, Jorge Luis (1985) *Fictions*. Edited with an introduction by Anthony Kerrigan. London: John Calder.

Bowles, Samuel and Gintis, Herbert (1987) *Democracy and Capitalism: Property and Community and the Contradictions of Modern Social Thought*. London: Routledge and Kegan Paul.

Boyne, Roy (1990) *Foucault and Derrida: The Other Side of Reason*. London: Unwin Hyman.

Brennan, Timothy (1989) *Salman Rushdie and the Third World*. London: Macmillan.

Burchell, Graham, Gordon, Colin and Miller, Peter (1991) *The Foucault Effect*. Hemel Hempstead, UK: Harvester Wheatsheaf.

Burke III, Edmund and Lapidus, Ira (eds) (1988) *Islam, Politics and Social Movements*. London: I.B.Tauris.

Butterworth, Charles E. (1980) 'Review of Orientalism', *American Political Science Review*, 74, March: 174–6.

Carrier, James G. (ed.) (1995) *Occidentalism: Images of the West*. Oxford: Clarendon.

Choueiri, Youssef M. (1988) 'Neo-orientalism and Islamic fundamentalism', *Review of Middle East Studies*, 4: 52–68.

Choueiri, Y. M. (1989) *Arab History and the Nation-State: A Study in Modern Arab Historiography 1820–1980*. London: Routledge.

Choueiri, Youssef M. (1990) *Islamic Fundamentalism*. London: Pinter Publishers.

Cizre-Sakalioglu, Umit (1994) 'Kemalism, hyper-nationalism and Islam in Turkey', *History of European Ideas*, 18(2): 255–70.

Cleveland, William L. (1983) 'Ataturk viewed by his Arab contemporaries: the opinions of Sati' al-Husri and Shakib Arslan', *International Journal of Turkish Studies*, 2: 15–23.

Cleveland, William (1985) *Islam Against the West*. London: Al-Saqi Books.

Clifford, James (1980) 'Review of orientalism', *History and Theory*, 19(2): 204–23.

Cole, Juan R. and Keddie, Nikki R. (eds) (1986) *Shi'ism and Social Protest*. New Haven: Yale University Press.

Connolly, William E. (1982) *Appearance and Reality in Politics*. New York: Cambridge University Press.

Connolly, William E. (1991) *Identity/Difference*. Ithaca: Cornell University Press.

Conrad, Joseph (1990) 'Youth: a narrative', in *Heart of Darkness and Other Tales*. Oxford and New York: Oxford University Press.

Crone, Patrica and Cook, Michael (1977) *Hagarism: The Making of the Islamic World*. Cambridge: Cambridge University Press.

Crone, Patricia and Hinds, Martin (1986) *God's Caliph: Religious Authority in the First Centuries of Islam*. Cambridge: Cambridge University Press.

Cudsi, Alexander and Dessouki, Ali E. (eds) (1981) *Islam and Power*. London: Croom Helm.

Davies, Norman (1996) *Europe: A History*. Oxford: Oxford University Press.

Dawisha, Adeed (ed.) (1984) *Islam in Foreign Policy*. New York: Cambridge University Press.

Dekmejian, Hrair R. (1995) *Islam in Revolution* (2nd edn). Syracuse, NY: Syracuse University Press.

Delvin, John (1976) *The Ba'ath Party: A History from Its Origins to 1966*. Stanford: Hoover Institution.

Deringil, S. (1993) 'The origins of Turkish nationalism in Ottoman history', *European History Quarterly*, April.

Derrida, Jacques (1973) *Speech and Phenomena*. Evanston: Northwestern University Press.

De Romilly, Jacqueline (1992) 'Isocrates and Europe', *Greece and Rome*, xxxix(1), April: 2–13.

Derrida, Jacques (1976) *Of Grammatology*. Baltimore: Johns Hopkins University Press.

Derrida, Jacques (1978) *Writing and Difference*. Translation and introduction by Alan Bass. London: Routledge and Kegan Paul.

Derrida, Jacques (1987) *Positions*. London: Athlone.

Derrida, Jacques (1994) *Spectres of Marx: The State of the Debt, the Work of Mourning and the New International*. Translated by Peggy Kamuf. London: Routledge.

Descombes, Vincent (1980/86) *Modern French Philosophy*. Cambridge: Cambridge University Press.

Deutsch, Eliot (ed.) (1991) *Culture and Modernity: East–West Perspectives*. Honolulu: University of Hawaii Press.

Diawara, Manthia (1990) 'Reading Africa through Foucault', *October*, 55, Winter: 79–92.

Djait, Hichem (1985) *Europe and Islam: Cultures and Modernity*. Translated by Peter Heinegg. Berkeley: University of California Press.

Dodd, C. H. (1983) *The Crisis of Turkish Democracy*. Walkington, UK: Eothen.

Dodd, C. H. (1988) 'Political modernization, the state and democracy: approaches to the study of politics in Turkey', in Heper and Evin, 1988.

Donohue, John J. and Esposito, John L. (eds) (1982) *Islam in Transition: Muslim Perspectives*. New York: Oxford University Press.

Dorraj, Manochehr (1990) *From Zarathustra to Khomeini: Populism and Dissent in Iran*. Boulder, Col.: Lynne Rienner.

Dreyfus, Hubert L. and Rabinow, Paul (1986) *Michel Foucault: Beyond Structuralism and Hermeneutics*. With afterword by Michel Foucault. Brighton: Harvester.

Dreyfus, Hubert L. (1991) *Being-in-the-World*. London: MIT Press.

Eckestein, Harry (1988) 'A Culturist theory of political change', *American Political Science Review*, 82(3), September: 789–804.

Eisenstadt, S. N. (1969) *The Political System of Empires*. New York: Free Press.

El-Affendi, Abdelwahab (1991) *Turbani's Revolution: Islam and Power in Sudan*. London: Grey Seal.

El-Awa, Muhammad S. (1980) *On the Political System of the Islamic State*. Indianapolis: American Trust Publications.

Elkins, David J. and Simeon, Richard E. B. (1979) 'A cause in search of its effects, or what does political culture explain?', *Comparative Politics*, 11(2), January: 127–45.

El-Zien, Abdul Hamid (1977) 'Beyond ideology and theology: the search for anthropology of Islam', *Annual Review of Anthropology*, VI: 227–54.

Enyat, Hamid (1982) *Modern Islamic Political Thought*. London: Macmillan.

Esposito, John L. (1980) *Islam and Development: Religion and Social Political Change*. Syracuse: Syracuse University Press.

Esposito, John L. (1983) *Voices of Resurgent Islam*. New York: Oxford University Press.

Esposito, John L. (1990) *The Iranian Revolution: Its Global Impact*. Miami: Florida International University Press.

Esposito, John L. (1991) 'Trail blazers of the Islamic resurgence', in Haddad, Yvonne Yazbeck, Voll, John Obert and Esposito, John L. with Moore, Kathleen and Sawan, David (eds), *The Contemporary Islamic Revival: A Critical Survey and Bibliography*. New York: Greenwood.

Esposito, John L. (1992) *The Islamic Threat: Myth or Reality*. New York: Oxford University Press.

Fanon, Frantz (1990) *The Wretched of the Earth*. Preface by Jean-Paul Sartre, translated by Constance Farrington. London: Penguin.

Faris, Hani A. (1986) 'Heritage and ideologies in contemporary Arab thought', *Journal of Asian and African Studies*, XXI(1–2), January–April: 89–103.

Fatimi, S. Q. (1974) 'The Kemalist revolution and Pakistan freedom movement', *Journal of Regional Cultural Institute*, 1, Winter: 15–29.

Feyziooglu, Turhan (ed.) (1981) *Ataturk's Way*. Istanbul: Otomarasri Publications.

Finkel, Andrew and Sirman, Nukhet (1990) *Turkish State, Turkish Society*. London: Routledge.

Fischer, Michael J. (1980) *From Religious Dispute to Revolution*. Cambridge, Mass.: Harvard University Press.

Fischer, Michael M. J. (1982) 'Islam and the revolt of the petit bourgeoisie', *Daedalus*, III(1), Winter.

Fischer, Michael M. J. (1983) 'Imam Khomeini: four levels of understanding', in J. L. Esposito (ed.), 1983, pp. 150–74.

Fischer, Michael M. J. (1990) *Debating Muslims*. New York: Routledge.

Foster, Hal (ed.) (1983) *Postmodern Culture*. London: Pluto.

Foucault, Michel (1980) *Power/Knowledge*. Edited by Colin Gordon. Brighton: Harvester.

Foucault, Michel (1984) 'What is an author?' Translated by Josue V. Harari, in Paul Rabinow, *The Foucault Reader*. Harmondsworth, UK: Penguin.

Foucault, Michel (1986) *The Archaelogy of Knowledge*. London: Tavistock.

Foucault, Michel (1988) *Politics, Philosophy and Culture: Interview and Other Writings*

1977–1984. Edited with an introduction by Lawrence D. Kritzman. New York: Routledge.

Freud, Sigmund (1976) *The Interpretation of Dreams. Standard Edition.* Harmondsworth: Penguin.

Fukuyama, Francis (1992), *The End of History and the Last Man.* London: Hamish Hamilton.

Fuss, Diana (1989) *Essentially Speaking: Feminism, Nature and Difference.* London: Routledge.

Gamble, Andrew (1988) *The Free Economy and the Strong State: The Politics of Thatcherism.* London: Macmillan.

Gellner, Ernest (1981) *Muslim Society.* Cambridge: Cambridge University Press.

Gellner, Ernest (1992) *Postmodernism, Reason and Religion.* London: Routledge.

Geras, Norman (1987) 'Post-Marxism?', *New Left Review* 163, May–June.

Geras, Norman (1995) 'Language, truth and justice', *New Left Review*, 209, January–February: 110–35.

Ghoussoub, Mai (1988) 'A reply to Hammami and Rieker', *New Left Review*, 170, July/August: 106–9.

Giddens, Anthony (1985) *The Nation-state and Violence.* Cambridge: Polity.

Giddens, Anthony (1990) *The Consequences of Modernity.* Cambridge: Polity.

Gilmartin, Daniel (1988) *Empire and Islam.* London: I.B.Tauris.

Gilroy, Paul (1990/91) 'It ain't where you're from it's where you're at: the dialectics of diasporic identification', *Third Text*, 13, Winter: 3–16.

Gilroy, Paul (1993) *The Black Atlantic.* London: Verso.

Gilroy, Paul (1996) 'Revolutionary conservatism and the tyrannies of unanimism', *New Formations*, 28, Spring.

Gilsenan, Michael (1990) *Recognizing Islam.* London: I.B.Tauris.

Glavanis, Pandeli (1995) 'Orientalism and western feminism'. Paper presented at Middle East Studies Department, University of Manchester.

Glavanis, Pandeli and Ray, Kathryn (forthcoming) *Political Islam, the Stranger within: An Exploration of Feminist Discourse and Postcolonial Identities.*

Goode, James (1991) 'Reforming Iran during the Kennedy years', *Diplomatic History*, 15(1), Winter: 13–31.

Gosaibi, Ghazi A. al- (1993) *The Gulf Crisis: An Attempt to Understand.* New York: Kegan Paul International.

Gowan, Peter (1991) 'The Gulf War, Iraq and Western Liberalism', *New Left Review*, 187, May/June: 39–71.

Gramsci, Antonio (1971) *Selections from Prison Notebooks.* Edited and translated by Quinton Hoare and Geoffrey Nowell Smith. London: Lawrence and Wishart.

Gulalp, Hladun (1992) 'A postmodern reaction to dependant modernization: the social and historical roots of Islamic radicalism', *New Perspectives on Turkey*, 8, Fall.

Gutmann, Mathew C. (1993) 'Rituals of resistance: a critique of the theory of everyday forms of resistance', *Latin American Perspectives*, 20(2), Spring: 74–92.

Habermas, Jurgen (1987) *The Philosophical Discourse of Modernity: Twelve Lectures.* Cambridge, Mass.: MIT Press.

Haddad, William W. and Ochsenwald, W. (1977) *Nationalism in a Non-national State: The Dissolution of the Ottoman Empire.* Columbus: Ohio University Press.

Haddad, Yvonne Y. (1982) *Contemporary Islam: The Challange of History.* Albany: S.U.N.Y. Press.

Haddad, Yvonne Yazbeck (1983) 'The Quranic justification for an Islamic revolution: the view of Sayyid Qutb', *Middle East Journal*, 37(1), Winter: 14–29.

Haddad, Yvonne Y. et al. (eds) (1991) *The Contemporary Islamic Revival: A Critical Survey and Bibilography*. New York: Greenwood.

Hall, John A. (1985) *Powers and Liberties: The Causes and Consequences of the Rise of the West*. Oxford: Basil Blackwell.

Hall, Stuart (1985) 'Authoritarian populism: a reply', *New Left Review*, 151, May/June: 115–24.

Hall, Stuart (1988) *The Hard Road to Renewal*. London: Verso.

Hall, Stuart and Gieben, Bram (eds) (1992) *The Formation of Modernity*. Cambridge: Polity.

Hall, Stuart, Held, David and McGrew, Tony (eds) (1992) *Modernity and Its Futures*. Cambridge: Polity.

Hall, Stuart and Jacques, Martin (1983) *The Politics of Thatcherism*. London: Lawrence and Wishart.

Halliday, Fred (1978) *Iran: Dictatorship and Development*. Harmondsworth, UK: Penguin.

Halliday, Fred (1987) 'The Iranian Revolution and its implications', *New Left Review*, 166, November/December: 29–38.

Halliday, Fred (1996) *Islam and the Myth of Confrontation*. London: I.B.Tauris.

Halliday, Fred and Alavi, H. (1988) *State and Ideology in the Middle East and Pakistan*. London: Macmillan.

Hammami, Reza and Rieker, Martina (1988) 'Feminist Orientalism and Orientalist Marxism', *New Left Review*, 170, July/August: 93–106.

Har-El, Shai (1995) *Struggle for Domination in the Middle East: The Ottoman–Mamluk War 1485–91*. Lieden: E. J. Brill.

Hauner, M. (1990) *What is Asia to Us?* Boston: Unwin Hyman.

Heikal, Mohammad (1983) *Autumn of Fury: The Asassination of Sadat*. London: Andre Deutsch.

Heller, Agnes and Feher, Frenc (1991) *The Postmodern Political Condition*. Cambridge: Polity.

Heper, Martin and Evin, Ahmet (1988) *State, Democracy and the Military in Turkey in the 1980s*. Berlin: Walter de Gruyter.

Herrin, Judith (1989) *The Formation of Christendom*. London: Fontana.

Hesse, Barnor (1996) 'White governmentality: urbanism, nationalism, racism', in Westwood, S. and John Williams (eds), *Imagining Cities*. London: Routledge.

Hippler, Jochen and Lueg, Andrea (eds) (1995) *The Next Threat: Western Perceptions of Islam*. Translated by Lalia Friese. London: Pluto.

Hodgson, Marshal G. S. (1960) 'The unity of later Islamic history', *Journal of World History*, 5: 879–914.

Hodgson, Marshall G. S. (1993) *Rethinking World History*. Edited, with an introduction and conclusion by Edmund Burke III. Cambridge: Cambridge University Press.

Holt, P. M., Lambton, Ann K. S., and Lewis, Bernard (eds) (1970) *The Cambridge History of Islam: The Central Islamic Lands from Pre-Islamic Times to First World War Vol. 1A*. Cambridge: Cambridge University Press.

Hopkins, Keith (1978) *Conquerors and Slaves: Sociological Studies in Roman History Vol. 1*. Cambridge: Cambridge University Press.

Hopwood, Derek (1982) *Egypt: Politics and Society 1945–1981*. London: George Allen and Unwin.

Horn, S. F. (1939) *The Invisble Empire*. Boston: Houghton and Mifflin.

Hosking, Geoffrey A., Aves, Jonathan and Duncan, Peter J. S. (1992) *The Road to Post-Communism 1985–1991*. London: Pinter Publishers.

Hourani, Albert (1983) *Arabic Thought in the Liberal Age 1798–1939*. Cambridge: Cambridge University Press.

Hourani, Albert (1991) *Islam in European Thought*. Cambridge: Cambridge University Press.

Howe, John (1992) 'The crisis of Algerian nationalism and the rise of Islamic integralism', *New Left Review*, 196, November/December: 85–101.

Hulme, Peter (1989) 'Subversive archipelagos: colonial discourse and the break-up of continental theory', *Disposito*, XIV(36–8): 1–3.

Hume, David (1993) *Selected Essays*. Edited with an introduction by Stephen Copley and Andrew Edgar. Oxford: University Press.

Hunter, Shireen (ed.) (1988) *The Politics of Islamic Revivalism*. Bloomington, Ill.: Indiana University Press.

Huntingdon, Samuel P. (1993) 'The clash of civilizations', *Foreign Affairs*, Summer: 22–49.

Hussain, Asaf, Olson, Robert and Qureshi, Jamil (eds) (1984) *Orientalism, Islam and Islamists*. Brattlebro, Vt: Amana Books.

Husserl, E. (1970) *The Crisis of European Sciences and Transcendental Phenomenology: An Introduction to Phenomenological Philosophy*. Translated by D. Carr. Evanston: Northwestern University Press.

Ibrahim, Saad (1980) 'The anatomy of Egypt's Islamic movement', *International Journal of Middle East Studies*, 12(4), December.

Inalcik, Halil (1970) 'The rise of the Ottoman Empire', in Holt, P. M., Lambton, Ann K. S. and Lewis, Bernard (eds) *The Cambridge History of Islam: The Central Islamic Lands from Pre-Islamic Times to the First World War, Vol. 1A*. Cambridge: Cambridge University Press.

Inden, Ronald (1986) 'Orientalist construction of India', *Modern Asian Studies*, 20(3): 401–46.

Inden, Ronald (1990) *Imagining India*. Oxford: Blackwell.

Iqbal, Mohammed (1981) *The Reconstruction of Religious Thought in Islam*. New Delhi: Kitab Bhavan.

Irfani, Suroosh (1983) *Revolutionary Islam in Iran*. London: Zed.

Irwin, Robert (1981) 'Writing about Islam and the Arabs', *Ideology and Consciousness*, 9, Winter: 102–12.

Islamoglu-inan, H. (ed.) (1987) *The Ottoman Empire and the World Economy*. Cambridge: Cambridge University Press.

Ismael, Tareq Y. and Ismael, Jacqueline S. (1985) *Government and Politics in Islam*. New York: St Martin's Press.

Jabari, A. and Olson, R. (eds) (1981) *Iran: Essays on a Revolution in the Making*. Lexington: Mazda Publishers.

Jameson, Fredric (1991) *Postmodernism or the Cultural Logic of Late Capitalism*. London: Verso.

Jansen, G. H. (1978) *Militant Islam*. London: Pan.

Jansen, Johannes J. G. (1986) *The Neglected Duty*. New York: Macmillan.

Jazani, Bihazan (1980) *Capitalism and Revolution in Iran*. London: Zed.

Jessop, Bob (1985) *Nicos Poulantzas: Marxist Theory and Political Strategy*. London: Macmillan.

Jessop, Bob, Bonnet, Kevin, Bromley, Simon and Ling, Tom (1988) *Thatcherism: A Tale of Two Nations*. Cambridge: Polity.

Jones, E. L. (1988) *The European Miracle: Environments, Economies and Geopolitics in the History of Europe and Asia* (2nd edn). Cambridge: Cambridge University Press.

Kabbani, Rana (1983) *Europe's Myths of the Orient: Devise and Rule*. London: Macmillan.

Kadioglu, Ayse (1996) 'The paradox of Turkish nationalism and the construction of official identity', *Middle East Studies*, 32(2), April: 177–93.

Kandiyoti, D. (ed.) (1991) *Women, Islam and the State*. London: Macmillan.

Kazancigil, Ali (1981) *Ataturk: Founder of a Modern State*. London: C. Hurst.

Keddie, Nikki (1963) 'Symbol and sincerity in Islam', *Studia Islamica*, XIX: 27–63.

Keddie, Nikki (1980) *Iran: Politics and Society*. London: Frank Cass.

Keddie, Nikki (1983) *An Islamic Response to Imperialism*. Berkeley: University of California Press.

Kedourie, Elie (ed.) (1980) *Islam in the Modern World*. London: Mansell.

Kennedy, Charles H. (1990) 'Islamization and legal reform in Pakistan, 1979–1989', *Pacific Affairs*, 63(1), Spring.

Kepel, Gilles (1985) *The Prophet and Pharaoh*. Translated by Jon Rothschild. London: Al-Saqi Books.

Kerr, Malcolm (1980) 'Review of Orientalism', *International Journal of Middle East Studies*, 12, December: 544–7.

Keyder, Caglar (1987) *State and Class in Turkey: A Study in Capitalist Development*. London: Verso.

Khalid, Detlev V. (1978) 'The phenomenon of re-Islamization', *Aussenpolitik*, 29, Winter: 433–53.

Khalidi, Rashid, Anderson, Lisa, Muslih, Muhammad and Simon, Reeva S. (eds) (1991) *The Origins of Arab Nationalism*. New York: Columbia University Press.

Khalil , Samir al- (1989) *Republic of Fear: Saddam's Iraq*. London: Hutchinson Radius.

Khomeini, Ruhallah (1981) *Islam and Revolution*. Translated and annotated by Hamid Algar. Berkeley: Mizan.

Khomeini, Ruhallah (1988) 'Text of letter to Khamenei', *BBC Summary of World Broadcasts*, 8 January.

Kili, Suna (1969) *Kemalism*. Istanbul: Mentes Matbaasi.

King, Antony D. (ed.) (1991) *Culture, Globalization, and the World-system*. London: Macmillan Education.

Kinross, Patrick (1993) *Ataturk: The Rebirth of a Nation*. London: Wiedenfeld and Nicolson.

Klausner, Carla L. (1973) *The Seljuk Vezirate: A Study of Civil Administration 1055–1194*. Cambridge, Mass.: Harvard University Press.

Kolb, David (1988) *The Critique of Pure Modernity: Hegel, Heidegger and After*. Chicago: University of Chicago Press.

Kripke, Saul A. (1972) 'Naming and necessity', in Donald Davidson and Gilbert Harman (eds), *Semantics of Natural Language*. Boston: Deriedel, pp. 253–355.

Kripke, Saul A. (1980) *Naming and Necessity*. Oxford: Basil Blackwell.

Kristeva, Julia (1984) *Revolution in Poetic Language*. Translated by Margaret Waller. New York: Columbia University Press.

Kruger, Barbara and Mariani, Phil (eds) (1989) *Remaking History*. Seattle: Bay Press.

Kuhn, Thomas (1970) *The Structure of Scientific Revolution*. Chicago: Chicago University Press.

Kuhrt, Amelie and Sherwin-White, Susan (eds) (1987) *Hellenism in the East: The Interaction of Greek and Non-Greek Civilizations from Syria to Central Asia*. London: Duckworth.

Lacan, Jaques (1977) *Four Fundamentals of Psychoanalysis*. Harmondsworth, UK: Penguin.

Lacan, Jacques (1988) *El Seminario de Jacques Lacan, Libro 3: Las Psicosis (1955–1960)*. Buenos Aires: Paidos.

Laclau, Ernesto (1979) *Politics and Ideology in Marxist Theory*. London: Verso.

Laclau, Ernesto (1990) *New Reflections on the Revolutions of Our Time*. London: Verso.

Laclau, Ernesto (1996) *Emancipation(s)*. London: Verso.

Laclau, Ernesto and Mouffe, Chantal (1985) *Hegemony and Socialist Strategy: Towards a Radical Democratic Politics*. Translated by Winston Moore and Paul Cammack. London: Verso.

Laclau, Ernesto and Mouffe, Chantal (1987) 'Post-Marxism without apologies?', *New Left Review*, 166, November–December: 79–106.

Laclau, Ernesto and Zac, Lilian (1994) 'Minding the gap: the subject of politics', in Ernesto Laclau (ed.), *The Making of Political Identities*. London: Verso, pp. 11–40.

Laffin, John (1979) *The Dagger of Islam*. London: Sphere Books.

Landau, Jacob (1981) *Pan-Turkism in Turkey: A Study in Irredentism*. London: Hurst Publishers.

Landau, Jacob (ed.) (1984) *Ataturk and the Modernization of Turkey*. Leiden: E. J. Brill.

Landau, Jacob M. (1994) *The Politics of Pan-Islam: Ideology and Organization*. London: I.B.Tauris.

Landen, Robert G. (ed.) (1970) *The Emergence of the Modern Middle East*. New York: Van Nostrand Reinhold.

Landi, Oscar (1988) *Reconstrucciones. Las Nuevas Formas de la Cultura Política*. Buenos Aires: Puntosur.

Lapidus, Ira M. (1996) 'State and religion in Islamic Societies', *Past and Present*, 151, May.

Laroui, Abdallah (1976) *The Crisis of the Arab Intellectual: Traditionalism or Historicism?* Translated by Diarmid Cammel. Berkeley: University of California Press.

Lavan, Spenser (1975) 'The Aligarh students', *Modern Asian Studies*, 9(2), April: 227–40.

Lawrence, Bruce B. (1995) *Defenders of God: The Fundamentalist Revolt Against the Modern Age*. London: I.B.Tauris.

Lawson, F. (1982) 'Social bases for the Hamah', *MERIP Reports*, 12(9).

Lay, Shawn (ed.) (1991) *The Invisible Empire in the West: Towards a New Historical Appraisal of the Ku Klux Klan*. Urbana: University of Illinois Press.

Lefort, Claude (1986) *The Political Forms of Modern Society: Bureaucracy, Democracy, Totalitarianism*. Edited and with an introduction by John Thompson. Cambridge: Polity.

Lerner, Daniel (1964) *The Passing of Traditional Society: Modernizing the Middle East*. New York: Free Press.

Lewis, Bernard (1961) *The Emergence of Modern Turkey*. London: Oxford University Press.

Lewis, Bernard (1976) 'The return of Islam', *Commentary*, January.

Lewis, Bernard (1982) 'The question of orientalism', *New York Review of Books*, 24 June 1982: 51.

Lewis, Bernard (1993) *Islam and the West*. Oxford: Oxford University Press.

Lewis, Bernard (1994) *The Muslim Discovery of Europe*. London: Weidenfeld and Nicolson.

Lewis, Reina (1996) *Gendering Orientalism: Race, Femininity and Representation*. London and New York: Routledge.

Liverani, Mario (1993) *Akkad: The First World Empire, Structure, Ideology, Traditions*. Padova (Italy): Sargon.

Lyons, John (1968) *Introduction to Theoretical Linguistics*. Cambridge: Cambridge University Press.

Lyotard, Jean-François (1992) *The Post-modern Condition: A Report on Knowledge*. Translated by Geoff Bennington and Brian Massumi. Oxford: Polity.

Macfie, A. L. (1994) *Ataturk*. London: Longman.

Machiavelli, Niccolo (1979) *The Prince*. Translated, with an introduction by George Bull. Harmondsworth, UK: Penguin.

Mani, Lata and Frankenberg, Ruth (1985) 'The challenge of orientalism', *Economy and Society*, 14(2), May.

Mann, Michael (1986) *The Sources of Social Power: A History of Power from the Beginning to AD 1760*. Cambridge: Cambridge University Press.

Mannheim, Karl (1936) *Ideology and Utopia*. London: Kegan Paul.

Mansfield, Peter (1973) *The Ottoman Empire and Its Successors*. London: Macmillan.

Mardin, Serif (1962) *The Genisis of Young Ottoman Thought*. Princeton: Princeton University Press.

Mardin, Serif (1982) 'Turkey, Islam and westernization', in C. Caldaeola (ed.), *Religion and Societies*. Berlin: Mouton.

Mardin, Serif (1993a) 'Religion and secularism in Turkey', in Albert Hourani, Philip S. Khoury and Mary C. Wilson (eds), *The Modern Middle East*. London: I.B.Tauris.

Mardin, Serif (ed.) (1993b) *Cultural Transitions in the Middle East*. Leiden: E. J. Brill.

Marsot, Afaf Lutfi Al-Sayyid (1984) *Egypt in the Reign of Muhammad Ali*. Cambridge: Cambridge University Press.

Martin, Vanessa (1994) 'Mudrarris, republicanism and the rise to power of Riza Khan', *British Journal of Middle Eastern Studies* 21(2).

Marty, Martin E. and Appleby, Scott R. (1991) *Fundamentalism Observed*. Chicago: University of Chicago Press.

Maududi, Sayyid Abdula (1992) *Islam and the West*. Leicester: Islamic Foundation.

Mazrui, Ali A. (1990) 'Witness for the persecution: a cross-examinaton on The Satanic Verses', *Third Text*, 11, Summer: 31–41.

McNeill, William (1963) *The Rise of the West*. Chicago: Chicago University Press.

Miller, Daniel, Rowlands, Michael and Tilley, Christopher (eds) (1989) *Domination and Resistance*. London: Unwin Hyman.

Minault, Gail (1982) *The Khalifat Movement*. Oxford: Oxford University Press.

Mitchell, Richard P. (1969) *The Society of Muslim Brothers*. London: Oxford University Press.

Moaddel, Mansoor (1993) *Class, Politics, and Ideology in the Iranian Revolution*. New York: Columbia University Press.

Modood, Tariq (1990) 'British Asian Muslims and the Rushdie Affair', *The Political Quarterly*, 61(2), April–June: 143–60.

Moghadam, Val (1987) 'Socialism or anti-imperialism? The left and revolution in Iran', *New Left Review*, 166, November/December: 5–28.

Moore, Barrington Jr. (1966) *Social Origins of Dictatorship and Democracy: Lord and Peasant in the Making of the Muslim World*. Boston: Beacon Press.

Mortimer, Edward (1982) *Faith and Power: The Politics of Islam*. London: Faber and Faber.

Moshiri, Farrokh (1985) *The State and the Social Revolution in Iran*. New York: Peter Lang.

Mouffe, Chantal (ed.) (1979) *Gramsci and Marxist Theory*. London: Routledge and Kegan Paul.

Mouffe, Chantal (1993) *The Return of the Political*. London: Verso.

Mudimbe, V. Y. (1988) *The Invention of Africa: Gnosis, Philosophy and the Order of Knowledge*. Bloomington: Indiana University Press.

Munson, Henry Jr. (1988) *Islam and Revolution in the Middle East*. New Haven: Yale University Press.

Mutman, Mahmut (1992) 'Under the sign of orientalism', *Cultural Critique*, Winter 1992–93.

Naipaul, V. S. (1981) *Among the Believers*. London: Andre Deutsch.

Nash, Manning (1984) 'Fundamentalist Islam: reservoir for turbulence', *Journal of Asian and African Studies*, XIX(1–2), January/April: 73–9.

Nasr, Seyyed Vali Reza (1989) 'Islamic economics: novel perspectives', *Middle Eastern Studies*, 25: 516–30.

Nasr, Seyyed Vali Reza (1992) 'Students, Islam, and politics: Islami Jami'at-i Tuleba in Pakistan', *Middle East Journal*, 46(1), Winter.

Nasr, Seyyed Vali Reza (1993) 'Islamic opposition to the Islamic state: the Jama'at-i Islami, 1977–1988', *International Journal of Middle Eastern Studies*, 25: 261–83.

Nelson, Cary and Grossberg, Lawrence (eds) (1988) *Marxism and the Interpretation of Culture*. London: Macmillan.

Nelson, Brian, Roberts, David and Veit, Walter (eds) (1992) *The Idea of Europe*. New York: Berg.

Niemeijer, A. C. (1972) *The Khalifat Movement in India 1919–1924*. The Hague: Martinus Nijhoff.

Nietzsche, F. (1968) *The Will to Power*. Translated by Walter Kaufman and R. J. Hollingdale. New York: Vintage Books.

Nisbet, Robert (1963) *History of the Idea of Progress*. New York: Basic Books.

Noboari, Ali Reza (1978) *Iran Erupts*. Stanford: Iran–American Documentation Group.

O'Leary, Brendan (1989) *The Asiatic Mode of Production*. London: Basil Blackwell.

Pahlavi, Mohammed Reza (1980) *Answer to History*. New York: Stein and Day Publishers.

Parla, Taha (1985) *The Social and Political Thought of Ziya Gokalp 1876–1924*. Leiden: E. J. Brill.

Petry, Carl F. (1994) *Protectors or Praetorian? The Last Mamluk Sultans and Egypt's Waning as a Great Power*. Albany, NY: S.U.N.Y. Press.

Pieterse, Jan Nederveen (1992) *Emancipation, Modern and Postmodern*. London: Sage.

Pieterse, Jan Nederveen (1994) 'Fundamentalism discourses: enemy images', *Women Against Fundamentalism*, 5(1).

Pipes, Daniel (1983) 'Understanding Islam in politics', *Middle East Review*, 16(2), Winter: 3–15.

Piscatori, James P. (ed.) (1983) *Islam in the Political Process*. New York: Cambridge University Press.

Pitkin, Hanna Fenichel (1984) *Fortune is a Woman: Gender and Politics in the Thought of Niccolo Machiavelli*. Berkeley: University of California Press.

Polybius (1975) *The Histories*. Translated by W. R. Patton. Cambridge, Mass.: Harvard University Press.

Proctor, Harris J. (1965) *Islam and International Relations*. London: Pall Mall.

Pye, Lucian W. (1990) 'Political science and the crisis of authoritaritarism', *American Political Science Review*, 84(1): 3–19.

Qutb, Sayyid (1978) *Milestones*. Kuwait: International Islamic Federation of Student Organizations.

Rabinow, Paul (1986) *The Foucault Reader*. Harmondsworth, UK: Penguin.

Rahnema, Ali and Nomani, Farhad (1990) *The Secular Miracle: Religion, Politics, and Economic Policy in Iran*. London: Zed.

Ramazani, R. K. (1982a) 'Who lost America? the case of Iran', *Middle East Journal*, 36: 5–21.

Ramazani, R. K. (1982b) *The United States and Iran: The Pattern of Influence*. New York: Praeger.

Rattansi, Ali and Westwood, Sallie (eds) (1994) *Racism, Modernity and Identity: On the Western Front*. Cambridge: Polity.

Redhead, Brian (1990) *Plato to NATO: Studies in Political Thought*. London: BBC Books.

Rejali, Darius M. (1994) *Torture and Modernity: Self, Society and State in Modern Iran*. Boulder, Col.: Westview.

Richards, Thomas (1993) *The Imperial Archive: Knowledge and the Fantasy of Empire*. London: Verso.

Roberts, J. M. (1976) *History of the World*. London: Hutchinson.

Robinson, Richard (1963) *The First Turkish Republic*. Cambridge, Mass.: Harvard University Press.

Rodinson, Maxime (1971) *Mohammed*. Translated by A. Carter. Harmondsworth, UK: Penguin.

Rodinson, Maxime (1977) *Islam and Capitalism*. London: Penguin.

Rodinson, Maxime (1979) *Marxism and the Muslim World*. Translated by Michael Pallis. London: Zed.

Roff, William R. (ed.) (1987) *Islam and the Political Economy of Meaning*. London: Croom Helm.

Rorlich, Azade-Ayse (1986) *The Volga Tartars: A Profile in National Resilience*. Stanford: Hoover Institution.

Rorty, Richard (1979) *Philosophy the Mirror of Nature*. Oxford: Basil Blackwell.

Rorty, Richard (1982) *The Consequence of Pragmatism*. Hemel Hempstead: Harvester Wheatsheaf.

Rorty, Richard (1989) *Contingency, Solidarity and Irony*. Cambridge: Cambridge University Press.

Rorty, Richard (1991a) *Objectivity, Relativism and Truth*. Cambridge: Cambridge University Press.

Rorty, Richard (1991b) *Essays on Heidegger and Others*. Cambridge: Cambridge University Press.

Roy, Oliver (1990) *Islam and Resistance in Afghanistan* (2nd edn). Cambridge: Cambridge University Press.

Roy, Oliver (1994) *The Failure of Political Islam*. London: I.B.Tauris.

Rubin, Barry (1980) *Paved with Good Intentions: The American Experience and Iran*. Oxford: Oxford University Press.

Rubin, Barry (1990) *Islamic Fundamentalism in Egyptian Politics*. London: Macmillan.

Rustow, Dankwart A. (1990) 'Democracy: a global revolution?', *Foreign Affairs*, 69(4), Fall: 75–91.

Ryan, Michael (1982) *Marxism and Deconstruction*. Baltimore: Johns Hopkins University Press.

Sabet, Amr G. E. (1994) 'Welayat al-Faqih: an Islamic theory of elite hegemony or, assabiyyat al-khawass', *Orient*, 35(4).

Sahgal, Gita and Yuval-Davis, Nira (eds) (1992) *Refusing Holy Orders*. London: Virago.

Said, Amir A. (1984) *From Nationalism to Revolutionary Islam*. London: Macmillan.

Said, Edward W. (1978) 'The problem of textuality: two exemplary positions', *Critical Inquiry*, Summer: 673–714.

Said, Edward W. (1980) *The Question of Palestine*. London: Routledge and Kegan Paul.

Said, Edward W. (1981) *Covering Islam: How the Media and the Experts Determine How We See the Rest of the World*. London: Routledge and Kegan Paul.

Said, Edward W. (1985a) *Orientalism* (first published 1978). London: Routledge and Kegan Paul.

Said, Edward W. (1985b) 'Orientalism reconsidered', *Race and Class*, XXVII(2), Autumn: 1–16.

Said, Edward W. (1988) 'Identity, negation and violence', *New Left Review*, 171, September/October: 46–62.

Said, Edward W. (1994) *Culture and Imperialism*. London: Vintage.

Salame, Ghassan (ed.) (1994) *Democracy without Democrats? The Renewal of Politics in the Muslim World*. London: I.B.Tauris.

Sardar, Ziauddin (ed.) (1989) *The Revenge of Athena*. London: Mansell.

Sardar, Ziauddin and Davies, Merly Wyn (1990) *Distorted Imaginations: Lessons from the Rushdie Affair*. London: Grey Seal Books.

Sassoon, Anne Showstack (1982) *Approaches to Gramsci*. London: Writers and Readers.

Saussure, F. de (1983) *Course in General Linguistics*. Translated and annotated by Roy Harris. London: Duckworth.

Sayyid, Bobby S. (1987) 'The Iranian Revolution: hegemony and truth regimes', unpublished MA dissertation, University of Essex.

Sayyid, Bobby S. (1994) 'Sign o' times: kaffirs and infidels fighting the ninth crusade', in Ernesto Laclau (ed.), *The Making of Political Identities*. London: Verso, pp. 264–86.

Scammel, G. V. (1989) *The First Imperial Age: European Overseas Expansion c. 1400–1715*. London: HarperCollins Academic.

Scott, James C. (1985) *Weapons of the Weak: Everyday Forms of Peasant Resistance*. New Haven: Yale University Press.

Scott, James C. (1990) *Domination and the Arts of Resistance: Hidden Transcripts*. New Haven: Yale University Press.

Searle, John R. (1983) *Intentionality: An Essay in the Philosophy of the Mind*. Cambridge:

Cambridge University Press.

Shapiro, Michael (ed.) (1984) *Language and Politics*. Oxford: Basil Blackwell.

Sharabi, Hisham (ed.) (1990) *Theory, Politics and the Arab World: Critical Responses*. New York: Routledge.

Shariati, Ali (1979) *On the Sociology of Islam*. Translated from the Persian by Hamid Algar. Berkeley: Mizan.

Shariati, Ali (1980) *Marxism and Other Western Fallacies: An Islamic Critique*. Berkeley: Mizan.

Shaw, S. J. (ed.) (1977) *History of the Ottoman Empire and Modern Turkey*. Vol. II. Cambridge: Cambridge University Press.

Shayegan, Daryush (1992) *Cultural Schizophrenia: Islamic Societies Confronting the West*. Translated from the French by John Howe. London: Saqi Books.

Shepard, W. E. (1987) 'Islam and ideology: towards a typology', *International Journal of Middle East Studies*, 19(4), August: 307–35.

Sherry, Michael S. (1995) *In the Shadow of War*. New Haven and London: Yale University Press.

Sherwin-White, Susan and Kuhrt, Amelie (1993) *From Samarkhand to Sardis: A New Approach to the Seleucid Empire*. London: Duckworth.

Sidahmed, Abdel Salem and Ehteshami, Anoushiravan (eds) (1996) *Islamic Fundamentalism*. Boulder, Col.: Westview.

Sigmund, Paul E. Jr. (1972) *The Ideologies of the Developing Nations*. New York: Praeger.

Silverman, Hugh J. (1989) *Derrida and Deconstruction*. New York: Routledge.

Simon, Roger (1982) *Gramsci's Political Thought: An Introduction*. London: Lawrence and Wishart.

Sivan, Emmanuel (1985) *Radical Islam: Medieval Theology and Modern Politics*. New Haven: Yale University Press.

Skocpol, Theda (1979) *States and Social Revolutions: A Comparative Analysis of France, Russia and China*. Cambridge: Cambridge University Press.

Skocpol, Theda (1982) 'Reniter state and Shi'a Islam in the Iranian revolution', *Theory and Society*, II(2): 265–83.

Slade, Shelley (1981) 'The image of the Arab in America: analysis of a poll on American attitudes', *Middle East Journal*, 35(2), Spring.

Smith, Anthony D. (1995) *The Ethnic Origins of Nations*. Oxford: Blackwell.

Spelman, Elizabeth V. (1990) *Inessential Woman: Problems of Exclusion in Feminist Thought*. London: Women's Press.

Springborg, Patricia (1992) *Western Republicanism and the Oriental Prince*. Cambridge: Polity.

Staten, Henry (1984) *Wittgenstein and Derrida*. Lincoln, Neb.: University of Nebraska Press.

Stavrainos, L. S. (1981) *Global Rift: The Third World Comes of Age*. New York: William Morrow.

Stavrianos, L. S. (1982) *The World Since 1500: A Global History* (4th edn). New Jersey: Prentice-Hall.

Stotodard, Philip H., Cuthell, David and Sullivan, Margaret W. (eds) (1981) *Change and the Muslim World*. New York: Syracuse University Press.

Stowasser, Barbara (ed.) (1987) *The Islamic Impulse*. London: Croom Helm.

Taheri, Amir (1985) *The Spirit of Allah: Khomeini and the Islamic Revolution*. London: Hutchinson.

Talbot, Ian (1982) 'The growth of the Muslim League in the Punjab', *Journal of Commonwealth and Comparative Politics*, XX(1), March.

Taylor, Alan R. (1988) *The Islamic Question in Mid-East Politics*. Boulder, Col.: Westview.

Tibi, Bassam (1983) 'The renewed role of Islam in the political and social development of the Middle East', *Middle East Journal*, 37(1), Winter: 3–13.

Tibi, Bassam (1988) *The Crisis of Modern Islam: A Pre-industrial Culture in the Scientific-technological Age*. Translated by Judith Von Sivers. Salt Lake City: University of Utah Press.

Tilly, Charles (1990) *Coercion, Capital, and European States, AD 990–1990*. London: Basil Blackwell.

Toprak, Binnaz (1981) *Islam and Political Development in Turkey*. Leiden: E. J. Brill.

Toulmin, Stephen (1990) *Cosmopolis*. Chicago: University of Chicago Press.

Treslease, Allen W. (1971) *White Terror: The Ku Klux Klan Conspiracy and Southern Reconstruction*. New York: Harper and Row.

Turbani, Hasan (1983) 'The Islamic state', in John L. Esposito (ed.), *Voices of Resurgent Islam*. New York: Oxford University Press.

Turner, Bryan S. (1974) *Weber and Islam*. London: Routledge and Kegan Paul.

Turner, Bryan S. (1978) *Marx and the End of Orientalism*. London: George Allen and Unwin.

Turner, Bryan S. (1989) 'From orientalism to global sociology', *Sociology*, 23(3), November: 629–38.

Turner, Bryan S. (1993) 'Review of postmodernism and Islam', *Modern Asian Studies*, 27(4): 897–902.

Vaglieri, Laura Vecca (1970) 'The patriarchal and Umayyad caliphates', in Holt, P. M., Lambton, Ann K. S. and Lewis, Bernard (eds), *The Cambridge History of Islam: The Central Islamic Lands from Pre-Islamic Times to the First World War. Vol. 1A*. Cambridge: Cambridge University Press. pp. 57–103.

Vatikiotis, P. J. (1985) *Modern History of Egypt*. London: Weidenfeld and Nicolson.

Vatikiotis, P. J. (1987) *Islam and the State*. London: Croom Helm.

Vattimo, Gianni (1992) *The Transparent Society*. Translated by D. Webb. Oxford: Polity.

Vattimo, Gianni and Rovatti, P. A. (eds) (1990) *El Pensamiento Debil*. Madrid: Catedra.

Voll, John O. (1982) *Continuity and Change in the Modern World*. Boulder, Col.: Westview.

Waldman, Marilyn Robinson (1978) 'Islamic studies: a new orientalism', *Journal of Interdisciplinary History*, III(3), Winter: 542–62.

Wallerstein, Immanuel (1974) *The Modern World System*. New York: Academic Press.

Ward, Robert E. and Rustow, Dankwart A. (eds) (1964) *Political Mobilization in Japan and Turkey*. Princeton, NJ: Princeton University Press.

Warren, Mark (1988) *Nietzsche and Political Thought*. Cambridge, Mass.: MIT Press.

Watt, Montegomery W. (1961) *Islam and the Integration of Society*. London: Routledge and Kegan Paul.

Watt, Montegomery W. (1988) *Fundamentalism and Modernity*. London: Routledge.

Weber, Max (1957) *The Protestant Ethic and the Spirit of Capitalism*. London: George Allen and Unwin.

Weiss, Anita M. (1986) *Islamic Reassertion in Pakistan: The Application of Islamic Laws in a Modern State*. Syracuse: Syracuse University Press.

Wessels, Antonie (1989) 'The so-called renaissance of Islam', *Journal of Asian and African Studies*, XIX(3–4), July–October.

Westwood, S. and Williams, John (eds) (1996) *Imagining Cities*. London: Routledge.

Wickham, Chris (1985) 'The uniqueness of the East', *Journal of Peasant Studies*, 12(2 and 3): 166–96.

Wickham, Chris (1988) 'Historical materialism, historical sociology', *New Left Review*, 171, September/October: 63–80.

Williams, Patrick and Chrisman, Laura (eds) (1993) *Colonial Discourse and Post-colonial Theory: A Reader*. Hemel Hempstead: Harvester Wheatsheaf.

Wittfogel, Karl (1957) *Oriental Despotism: A Comparative Study of Total Power*. New Haven and London: Yale University Press.

Wittgenstein, Ludwig (1958) *Philosophical Investigations*. Translated by G. E. M. Anscombe. Oxford: Basil Blackwell.

Wood, Ellen Meiksins (1986) *The Retreat from Class: A New 'True' Socialism*. London: Verso.

Wright, Robin (1986) *Sacred Rage: The Wrath of Militant Islam*. London: Andre Deutsch.

Yapp, M. E. (1987) *The Making of the Modern Near East 1792–1923*. London: Longman.

Yapp, M. E. (1991) *The Near East Since the First World War*. London: Longman.

Yegen, Mesut (1996) 'The Turkish state discourse and exclusion of Kurdish Identity', *Middle East Studies*, 32(2), April: 216–29.

Young, Robert (1990) *White Mythologies: Writing History and the West*. London: Routledge.

Young, Robert (1994) 'Egypt in America: *Black Athena*, racism and colonial discourse', in Rattansi, Ali and Westwood, Sallie (eds), *Racism, Modernity and Identity: On the Western Front*. Cambridge: Polity.

Zabih, Saphir (1979) *Iran's Revolutionary Upheaval*. San Francisco: Alchemy Books.

Zac, Lilian E. (1995) *Narratives of Order: The Discourse of the Argentinian Military Regime (1976–1983)*. Unpublished PhD thesis, University of Essex, UK.

Zac, Lilian and Sayyid, Bobby (1990) 'The good and the evil: master-signifiers and frontiers', unpublished paper, University of Essex.

Zaman, Waheed-Uz (1985) *Iranian Revolution: A Profile*. Islamabad, Pakistan: Institute of Policy Studies.

Zizek, Slavoj (1989) *The Sublime Object of Ideology*. London: Verso.

Zizek, Slavoj (1990) 'Eastern Europe's Republics of Gilead', *New Left Review*, 183, September–October: 50–62.

Zizek, Slavoj (1991) *For They Know Not What They Do*. London: Verso.

Zizek, Slavoj (1992) *Enjoy Your Symptom! Jacques Lacan in Hollywood and Out*. London: Routledge.

Zubaida, Sami (1989) *Islam, the People and the State*. London: Routledge.

Zubaida, Sami (1995) 'Is there a Muslim society? Ernest Gellner's sociology of Islam', *Economy and Society*, 24(2), May: 151–88.

Zurcher, Erik J. (1993) *Turkey: A Modern History*. London: I.B.Tauris.

Index